VOLUME 596

NOVEMBER 2004

THE ANNALS

of The American Academy of Political
and Social Science

ROBERT W. PEARSON, *Executive Editor*
LAWRENCE W. SHERMAN, *Editor*

Mommies and Daddies on the Fast Track: Success of Parents in Demanding Professions

JERRY A. JACOBS
JANICE FANNING MADDEN
University of Pennsylvania

RADNOR. PA 19087-3699

SAGE Publications Ⓢ Thousand Oaks · London · New Delhi

56749910

H
I
,A4
v. 596

The American Academy of Political and Social Science

3814 Walnut Street, Fels Institute of Government, University of Pennsylvania,
Philadelphia, PA 19104-6197; (215) 746-6500; (215) 898-1202 (fax); www.aapss.org

Board of Directors
LAWRENCE W. SHERMAN, *President*
STEPHEN B. BURBANK, *Chair*

ELIJAH ANDERSON	KLAUS NAUDÉ
HEIDI HARTMANN	NORMAN H. NIE
JERRY LEE	NELL IRVIN PAINTER
JANICE FANNING MADDEN	JAROSLAV PELIKAN
SARA MILLER McCUNE	LOUIS H. POLLAK
MARY ANN MEYERS	ERIC WANNER

Editors, THE ANNALS

ROBERT W. PEARSON, *Executive Editor*   RICHARD D. LAMBERT, *Editor Emeritus*
LAWRENCE W. SHERMAN, *Editor*   JULIE ODLAND, *Managing Editor*

Origin and Purpose. The Academy was organized December 14, 1889, to promote the progress of political and social science, especially through publications and meetings. The Academy does not take sides in controverted questions, but seeks to gather and present reliable information to assist the public in forming an intelligent and accurate judgment.

Meetings. The Academy occasionally holds a meeting in the spring extending over two days.

Publications. THE ANNALS of The American Academy of Political and Social Science is the bimonthly publication of the Academy. Each issue contains articles on some prominent social or political problem, written at the invitation of the editors. Also, monographs are published from time to time, numbers of which are distributed to pertinent professional organizations. These volumes constitute important reference works on the topics with which they deal, and they are extensively cited by authorities throughout the United States and abroad. The papers presented at the meetings of the Academy are included in THE ANNALS.

Membership. Each member of the Academy receives THE ANNALS and may attend the meetings of the Academy. Membership is open only to individuals. Annual dues: $75.00 for the regular paperbound edition (clothbound, $113.00). For members outside the U.S.A., add $24.00 for shipping of your subscription. Members may also purchase single issues of THE ANNALS for $23.00 each (clothbound, $31.00). Student memberships are available for $49.00.

Subscriptions. THE ANNALS of The American Academy of Political and Social Science (ISSN 0002-7162) (J295) is published six times annually—in January, March, May, July, September, and November— by Sage Publications, 2455 Teller Road, Thousand Oaks, CA 91320. Telephone: (800) 818-SAGE (7243) and (805) 499-9774; FAX/Order line: (805) 499-0871; E-mail: journals@sagepub.com. Copyright © 2004 by The American Academy of Political and Social Science. Institutions may subscribe to THE ANNALS at the annual rate: $490.00 (clothbound, $554.00). Add $24.00 per year for subscriptions outside the U.S.A. Institutional rates for single issues: $95.00 each (clothbound, $106.00).

Periodicals postage paid at Thousand Oaks, California, and at additional mailing offices.

Single issues of THE ANNALS may be obtained by individuals who are not members of the Academy for $33.00 each (clothbound, $46.00). Single issues of THE ANNALS have proven to be excellent supplementary texts for classroom use. Direct inquiries regarding adoptions to THE ANNALS c/o Sage Publications (address below).

All correspondence concerning membership in the Academy, dues renewals, inquiries about membership status, and/or purchase of single issues of THE ANNALS should be sent to THE ANNALS c/o Sage Publications, 2455 Teller Road, Thousand Oaks, CA 91320. Telephone: (800) 818-SAGE (7243) and (805) 499-9774; FAX/Order line: (805) 499-0871. E-mail: journals@sagepub.com. *Please note that orders under $30 must be prepaid.* Sage affiliates in London and India will assist institutional subscribers abroad with regard to orders, claims, and inquiries for both subscriptions and single issues.

Printed on recycled, acid-free paper

THE ANNALS

© 2004 by The American Academy of Political and Social Science

All rights reserved. No part of this volume may be reproduced or utilized in any form or by any means, electronic or mechanical, including photocopying, recording, or by any information storage and retrieval system, without permission in writing from the publisher. All inquiries for reproduction or permission should be sent to Sage Publications, 2455 Teller Road, Thousand Oaks, CA 91320.

Editorial Office: 3814 Walnut Street, Fels Institute for Government, University of Pennsylvania, Philadelphia, PA 19104-6197.

For information about membership° (individuals only) and subscriptions (institutions), address:
Sage Publications
2455 Teller Road
Thousand Oaks, CA 91320

Sage Production Staff: Joseph Riser and Esmeralda Hernandez

From India and South Asia, write to:
SAGE PUBLICATIONS INDIA Pvt Ltd
B-42 Panchsheel Enclave, P.O. Box 4109
New Delhi 110 017
INDIA

From Europe, the Middle East, and Africa, write to:
SAGE PUBLICATIONS LTD
1 Oliver's Yard, 55 City Road
London EC1Y 1SP
UNITED KINGDOM

°Please note that members of the Academy receive THE ANNALS with their membership.
International Standard Serial Number ISSN 0002-7162
International Standard Book Number ISBN 1-4129-1566-X (Vol. 596, 2004 paper)
International Standard Book Number ISBN 1-4129-1565-1 (Vol. 596, 2004 cloth)
Manufactured in the United States of America. First printing, November 2004.

The articles appearing in *The Annals* are abstracted or indexed in Academic Abstracts, Academic Search, America: History and Life, Asia Pacific Database, Book Review Index, CAB Abstracts Database, Central Asia: Abstracts & Index, Communication Abstracts, Corporate ResourceNET, Criminal Justice Abstracts, Current Citations Express, Current Contents: Social & Behavioral Sciences, Documentation in Public Administration, e-JEL, EconLit, Expanded Academic Index, Guide to Social Science & Religion in Periodical Literature, Health Business FullTEXT, HealthSTAR FullTEXT, Historical Abstracts, International Bibliography of the Social Sciences, International Political Science Abstracts, ISI Basic Social Sciences Index, Journal of Economic Literature on CD, LEXIS-NEXIS, MasterFILE FullTEXT, Middle East: Abstracts & Index, North Africa: Abstracts & Index, PAIS International, Periodical Abstracts, Political Science Abstracts, Psychological Abstracts, PsycINFO, Sage Public Administration Abstracts, Social Science Source, Social Sciences Citation Index, Social Sciences Index Full Text, Social Services Abstracts, Social Work Abstracts, Sociological Abstracts, Southeast Asia: Abstracts & Index, Standard Periodical Directory (SPD), TOPICsearch, Wilson OmniFile V, and Wilson Social Sciences Index/Abstracts, and are available on microfilm from ProQuest, Ann Arbor, Michigan.

Information about membership rates, institutional subscriptions, and back issue prices may be found on the facing page.

Advertising. Current rates and specifications may be obtained by writing to *The Annals* Advertising and Promotion Manager at the Thousand Oaks office (address above).

Claims. Claims for undelivered copies must be made no later than six months following month of publication. The publisher will supply missing copies when losses have been sustained in transit and when the reserve stock will permit.

Change of Address. Six weeks' advance notice must be given when notifying of change of address to ensure proper identification. Please specify name of journal. POSTMASTER: Send address changes to: *The Annals* of The American Academy of Political and Social Science, c/o Sage Publications, 2455 Teller Road, Thousand Oaks, CA 91320.

Volume 596 November 2004

IN THIS ISSUE:

Mommies and Daddies on the Fast Track:
Success of Parents in Demanding Professions

Special Editors: JERRY A. JACOBS
JANICE FANNING MADDEN

FORTHCOMING

Cultural Production in a Digital Age
Special Editor: ERIC KLINENBERG
Volume 597, January 2005

The Rise of Regulatory Capitalism:
The Global Diffusion of a New Order
Special Editors: DAVID LEVI-FAUR
and JACINT JORDANA
Volume 598, March 2005

Preface

By
JANICE
FANNING MADDEN

The past thirty years have seen dramatic increases in the numbers of women being prepared for professions in which few women had previously been employed, including law, medicine, academe, corporate management, engineering, and financial management. For example, women earned 2.8 percent of the MBAs awarded in 1971 but 40.7 percent by 2001 and, similarly, 0.6 percent of the Ph.D.s in engineering in 1971 but 16.5 percent by 2001. The female percentages for Ph.D.s in other subjects for these years, respectively, are 16.3 and 44.1 percent in the life sciences, 28.8 and 60.3 percent in English, and 24.0 and 68.3 percent in psychology.[1] Women earned 5.4 percent of law degrees in 1970 but 47.3 percent by 2001 and 8.4 percent of medical degrees in 1970 but 43.3 percent by 2001.[2]

Women's dramatic increases in professional educational attainment are the culmination of longer-term trends in women's participation in the paid labor force. Over the past century, the proportion of women in the labor force grew steadily (Goldin 1990). While these trends have been accompanied by increases in the proportions of women who are not married and by decreases in the number of children born to the average woman, the employment patterns have also changed dramatically for mothers. Over the past thirty years, the most rapid growth in labor force participation has been among married

Janice Fanning Madden is a professor of sociology, real estate, and regional science at the University of Pennsylvania and a former director of the Alice Paul Center for Research on Women and Gender. She came to Penn in 1972 after completing a Ph.D. in economics at Duke University. Her research concentrates on the effects of race, gender, and urban location on labor market outcomes. She has written numerous articles in professional journals and four books: The Economics of Sex Discrimination *(1972, reprinted 1975);* Post-Industrial Philadelphia *(1990);* Work, Wages, and Poverty *(1991); and* Changes in Income and Inequality within U.S. Metropolitan Areas *(2000).*

DOI: 10.1177/0002716204268886

mothers with children younger than six. Only 30 percent of married mothers of children younger than six were in the labor force in 1970, but the proportion has doubled, with 60.8 percent of such women in the labor force in 2002. The participation rate is even greater for mothers of older children, 75.3 percent for those with children aged six to thirteen and 80.5 percent for those with children aged fourteen to seventeen. Data from the past few years, however, show that these labor force participation rates have reached a plateau, or even decreased, since 1998.[3] It is not clear whether this change is only a cyclical effect of the overall decrease in jobs in the U.S. economy (and the decrease in labor force participation over the same time period for men)[4] or a signal of a change in the pattern of increasing labor force attachment for mothers, in particular.

Stories about the workplace-family issues faced by highly educated women who have also been highly successful in the workplace, that is, "fast trackers," have been appearing with increasing frequency in the popular media, although many incorrectly imply that fast-track women are increasingly choosing family over work. The Sunday *New York Times Magazine* featured a cover story titled "The Opt-Out Revolution."[5] Although the title and the opening discussion suggested that the story was about women who had decided that spending time with their families was better than spending time at work, the story actually describes the circumstances of mothers who were offered no flexibility in their jobs to allow them to accommodate both their work and their families. And most of the mothers interviewed for the article were still employed, just in a different way than in their previous fast-track jobs. *Time* magazine ran a cover with a picture of a young boy clinging to his mother with the caption, "The case for staying home: Why more [*sic*] young moms are opting out of the rat race."[6] Once again, the articles actually dealt with the inflexibility of fast-track jobs, not with the desires of mothers to be home rather than to pursue their careers. The articles also provided no evidence of an increase in the proportions of mothers opting out of fast-track jobs. Recognizing that job inflexibility is the issue, *The Wall Street Journal* wrote about male and female executives who successfully challenged their employers to accommodate the flexibility that their families required.[7] Most recently, *Business Week* has written about the enduring compensation and status differences between men and women over their careers, including the lifetime costs paid by women who spend more time with family at some stage of their careers.[8]

While a substantial proportion of the educational preparation for the most demanding professional jobs has been allocated to women over the past few decades, the career paths (that is, the structured norms for success and progress by stage in the life cycle) in those jobs have changed little. These norms, which set the age at which specific achievements or milestones should be met if a worker is to remain on track for promotion to the most prestigious jobs, were developed earlier in the twentieth century when men, whose wives were full-time homemakers with the responsibility to care for their families, occupied the jobs. Because higher-ability workers produce more per hour than lower-ability workers, the volume of work produced became an easily identified and therefore important criterion for judging promotion potential for high-level jobs. Knowing that the amount of output produced mattered for promotion, fast-track workers responded by working longer hours to further increase their production. The competition among workers that leads to very long hours is commonly referred to as "the rat race."[9] The norms about the timing of achievement for fast-track jobs, which were historically designed around productivity expectations that were reasonable for men with few family responsibilities, will inevitably disadvantage mothers (or fathers) of equal ability whose partners are also employed full-time in demanding jobs. Other things being equal, employees who devote more hours to their jobs are expected to produce more for the firm and, to the extent that earnings reflect value to the firm, to be paid more when they do so. The career-family balance challenge for fast-trackers is not about the understandably relatively lower pay for parents during periods of more intense family obligations and fewer work hours. Rather, the issues arise around whether and how fast-track workers become parents. Are women and men in fast-track jobs being inappropriately (that is, in a socially suboptimal way) forced into delayed (and for many, ultimately no) parenthood? Do workers who reduce their hours to accommodate their family obligations stay on track, or do they become ineligible for the most competitive jobs in the future? Should employers be allowed to structure a job in a manner that only long-hours workers can qualify? Is the "mommy track" a temporary way station on the fast track, or must it be a total derailment?

The work-family issues for parents in fast-track jobs are fundamentally different from those faced by employed parents in other jobs. While many employed parents struggle to meet the costs, or even to find, quality care for their children, this is not the problem for fast-track parents. The compensation paid to fast-track parents is generally sufficient to cover the costs of quality care for children and for other components of home care. For them, the issue is a shortage of time rather than of money or quality child care.

Recently, scholars from a variety of disciplines have been studying how current organizational structures, legacies of the times when highly talented workers were men married to full-time housewives, affect (1) the career success rates of comparably talented women workers, or men, who devote more time to their families for a period of their lives; and (2) the ability of women who succeed in these jobs to also have families. Some have investigated alternative organizational structures and career designs that would allow women to succeed at the highest levels of their professions without forgoing families. Other researchers have been concerned with restructuring social and personal expectations about family life and mothering to make high-level jobs more attractive to talented women. Several of the most prominent researchers in the field came together for a conference hosted by the Alice Paul Center for Research on Women and Gender at the University of Pennsylvania to present new research focused on the highest levels of the professions and on the structure of career milestones from the perspectives (or needs) of firms as well as workers. I am grateful to the Alfred P. Sloan Foundation and Penn alumna Andrea Roberts, who provided financial support for the conference. This volume includes the research papers presented at the conference, followed by an essay review that assesses the contribution of several recent books in this area.

Within the Professions

Studies of academe, law, finance, and medicine are included in this volume as particular examples of fast-track jobs for which the conditions of employment may have complicated the family lives or aspirations of workers.[10] These studies yield some results that are common across the professions. Not surprisingly, long hours are typical for workers pursuing these careers. There is also evidence that workers with longer hours are more productive. In academe, Jerry Jacobs and Sarah Winslow find that longer hours lead to greater research productivity. Mary Blair-Loy and Amy Wharton find that longer hours lead to higher pay, presumably reflecting greater productivity among financial professionals and managers. Nonetheless, Amy Wax, Jacobs and Winslow, and Blair-Loy and Wharton also find that workers are dissatisfied with their long hours. Wax reports that her surveys of University of Pennsylvania and University of Virginia law students taking first jobs indicate that they preferred to receive lower wages in order not to work such long hours.

Although each of these professions involves long hours for those on the fast track, some important differences in the structures of their career paths may make them more or less feasible for parents who are primary caregivers. While performance early in one's career is important to succeeding on the fast track in virtually all professions, the rate of progression appears to be less rigidly set in (non-academic) medicine and finance than in academe or law. The tenure track in academe probably poses the greatest challenge for workers who start families while in a pretenure appointment, followed by the associate track to partnership in private law firms.[11] The tenure-track system in academe and the associate system preceding partnership in law firms are systems of five- to ten-year initial appointments followed by an "up-or-out" decision with respect to promotion to a tenured professorship or partner. The tight time period for performance typical of these systems, which also overlap with peak childbearing years, make it difficult for parents who have no partner available to care for young children, or who desire to spend time with their children themselves, also to work sufficient hours to be competitive with those who have no family responsibilities. These parents are likely to find the high performance demands during the initial appointment in tenure-track or associate positions difficult to meet, regardless of their innate abilities or future potential to excel as academics or lawyers. Because the tenure track and the associates track require that those who are not promoted leave their employer, there may be greater impediments in law and academe than in other professions to getting back on the fast track at a later date. Different structures for career paths of fast-trackers may contribute to differences across academe, law, finance, and medicine in the career success of primary caregivers and in the ability of those who are successful to also be primary caregivers.

There are two reasons why the effects of career path structures may differ by gender, that is, differ for mothers and fathers. First, fathers are less likely to have the same family demands to provide care. They are more likely to have a spouse who is either not employed or, if employed, working shorter hours in a less demanding job. And even in those less frequent situations when spouses are also in fast-track positions, Scott Coltrane and Heidi Hartmann point out there is less social pressure on fathers to take responsibility for care of children than there is on mothers. Second, the biological differences in fertility by sex mean that women have a shorter time horizon than men over which they can have children of their own. Women are less able than men to postpone having children until they have passed inflexibly set milestones for continuing on the fast track.[12]

For [parents in fast-track jobs], the issue is a shortage of time rather than of money or quality child care.

One way to resolve these work-family time conflicts in such positions is to forego family. Mary Ann Mason and Marc Goulden find this to be a common response for women in academe. Women who successfully pursue tenure-track jobs are quite different in their patterns of family formation from comparably situated men and from women who receive a Ph.D. but do not take tenure-track positions. Tenure-track faculty women are less likely to marry and have children and are more likely to divorce. To the extent that successful completion of a tenure-track appointment (i.e., getting tenure) requires most women to forgo motherhood, the proportion of women among the senior faculty of our most competitive colleges and universities will inevitably remain low. If women must give up motherhood to be professors, then a substantial share of the most talented women will inevitably choose motherhood and relinquish fast-track academic careers. If our universities and colleges are to attain the highest quality possible, we must design a selection system for faculty that also allows women academics to be mothers.

While Mary Noonan and Mary Corcoran also report that female University of Michigan Law School graduates are less likely to be married and to have children than their male counterparts, they do not find the association between success on the associate track and family outcomes for women in law firms that Mason and Goulden found for tenure-track women in academe. Noonan and Corcoran find that parenting has no adverse effect on the likelihood of a law graduate becoming a partner in a private firm. They actually find slightly higher marriage and childbirth rates for women who become partners than for those who do not. They find that women are strongly disadvantaged relative to comparably qualified men, however, in terms of salary and of the likelihood of making partner, regardless of their family status. Noonan and Corcoran find no evidence that family status is associated with higher rates of leaving firms or with negative partnership outcomes for men or women. They do find, however, that lawyers who stop practicing for a time for child rearing are less likely to become a partner, even after considering their family and job characteristics.

[W]ithin these fast-track jobs, mothers feel greater stress than fathers in balancing their careers with their families.

Further research is necessary to confirm that the differences in work-family results for tenure tracks in academe and associate-partner tracks in law firms found in the studies included here are general, rather than related to the specific groups/ time periods studied. There are, however, reasons why academic tenure tracks might be expected to have different effects than law firm associate tracks. Because tenure is substantially harder to revoke than partnership, the decision to award tenure may be a more cautious one. Simply, law firms can be more flexible than universities and colleges because positive mistakes in the partnership decision are more easily corrected. The length of the academic tenure track is formally set within each institution and is lengthened only by other equally formal policies, such as an additional year being allowed for a primary caregiver or a woman giving birth. Duration of time as an associate in a law firm, however, is usually flexible and is not formally cut off at an arbitrary number of years for all associates. Law firms, then, can more easily allow valued mothers (or fathers) who are working fewer hours to spend more time with their children to have longer-duration appointments as associates before being considered for promotion to partner. Also, law degrees take less time to earn than the Ph.D.[13] Female recipients of law degrees may become a partner and still be young enough to bear children. As female Ph.D. recipients are likely to be older when they achieve tenure, both because their degrees take longer to attain and because tenure tracks are typically of longer duration than associate tracks, they typically achieve tenure at ages when they are not likely to be able to bear children. Jacobs and Winslow note that the average age of faculty still on the tenure track is over forty.

Mary Blair-Loy and Amy Wharton's study of managers and professionals in a financial investment services firm and Ann Boulis's study of physicians include fast-track professions whose career paths are not as rigidly structured around an up-or-out decision after an initial appointment, as in academe and law. Workers who leave the fast track do not necessarily have to change employers, potentially making reentry to the fast track and a future promotion more possible. Both finance and medicine, however, offer less flexibility with respect to the scheduling of hours than does academe. Nonetheless, many results for finance and medicine are similar to those for academe and law. As Jacobs and Winslow find for academics, Blair-Loy and Wharton find that financial professionals and managers who work longer hours are more successful but have higher levels of stress with respect to work-family issues. As Noonan and Corcoran find for lawyers, Blair-Loy and Wharton find that mothers in finance do as well as nonmothers, and Boulis finds no penalty for mother physicians, but there is evidence of a continuing gender gap in pay for both physicians and financial managers/professionals: women, regardless of their family status, earn less than men of equivalent qualifications. As Mason and Goulden report for academics, female physicians and financial managers/professionals are less likely to marry and have children than are comparable men. Blair-Loy and Wharton find that mothers report more stress over meeting the needs of their families than do fathers with similar job demands, reflecting the gender differences in parenting expectations discussed by Hartmann and Coltrane. On a more positive note, Blair-Loy and Wharton find that there are options for firms to lower the stress of family-work balance for those in high-level positions. Specifically, they find that flexibility in schedules and corporate policies supporting families help to lower reported feelings of stress.

Ann Boulis finds that overall there are fewer gender differences in 2000, relative to 1990, in the likelihood of physicians having children in their households and that, among employed physicians, gender differences in earnings and work hours have also decreased. Boulis notes large increases in the proportion of women combining medicine and family but also an increase in the number of female physicians who are not working.

A comparative reading of the studies of academe, law, medicine, and finance included in this volume illustrates the effects of organizational norms on the ability of workers to balance primary responsibility for the care of children with their own fast-track jobs. When the milestones for success are more rigid and formal, as in academe, women who succeed are more likely to forgo families than either men or women who are not on the fast track. When the milestones are more flexible, as in medicine and finance (or in politics, as discussed by Gwen Moore), there is less evidence that women forgo families to succeed, but there is evidence that women regardless of family status are disadvantaged relative to men in their likelihood of success. And within these fast-track jobs, mothers feel greater stress than fathers in balancing their careers with their families.

The General Context

Three articles provide a larger context for these studies of academe, law, medicine, and finance. Claudia Goldin places the discussion of combining family with demanding jobs in historical perspective. She tracks the extent to which college-educated women have combined career and family over the twentieth century, starting with the first generation for whom the choice was either career (teaching) or family, moving on to generations that achieved family or job (as distinct from career) sequentially (rather than together), to the more recent generations who have tried to combine family and career. The early baby boomers (born between 1944 and 1957) sequentially combined career then family with between 13 and 18 percent succeeding at doing both. The late baby boomers (born between 1958 and 1968) were the first to achieve family and career at the same time, with between 21 and 27 percent succeeding at both, compared to 45 to 55 percent for their male counterparts. While women in colleges today indicate strong preferences for having both a family and a career at the same time, only very recently have women been able to do both. Still, Goldin finds that only a minority of college-educated women have been successful in combining family and career.

Clearly, the policy solution to poorer employment outcomes for women, in general, is for government to effectively enforce antidiscrimination legislation.

While studies of careers in academe, law, medicine, or finance inevitably concentrate on employed mothers, mothers who have left fast-track jobs also can help in understanding how work hours, scheduling flexibility, and parenting norms affect job participation. Pamela Stone and Meg Lovejoy study forty-three highly educated women who have decided to stay home for a few years or more to raise their children, most after having had successful careers. These women withdrew from their jobs because they were severely constrained by some combination of inflexible workplaces, their husbands' preferences and behavior, and their own high standards of parenting. Because of these constraints, the alternative they seem to have most wanted to pursue—having successful careers and being good parents—was unavailable to them. These mothers appear not to have opted out of the fast track but rather were "squeezed off."

If highly talented women (and men) desire jobs that allow them more time with their families, why have employers not responded by providing jobs with fewer hours and more flexibility? (Note that if shorter hour/more flexible jobs are more attractive to workers, employers have an incentive to provide such jobs because they could pay lower wages and/or attract more workers.) Amy Wax examines why employers may not be able to respond to the increasing interest in fast-track jobs that are structured to allow for a fuller family life. Using game theoretic analyses, she shows that the imbedded incentives for individual fast-track workers lead to rat race conditions of very long hours, even when these same workers would prefer an alternative work organization that allows for more family time, and even though such an organization would be more socially desirable. An external control on work hours is necessary if these workers are to be saved from their own perverse behavior on work hours. The problem is that it is very hard effectively to design such an hours control for workers in fast-track jobs. Government regulation of the length of the workweek will obviously have no effect because these workers cannot be monitored when they are outside the office to make sure they are not "working." Fast-track workers understand that their likelihood of promotion will be increased if they have produced more. For that reason, they work longer hours than they desire to improve their total production. Quality-based performance criteria, rather than quantity-based criteria, for promotion decisions might be effective, but quality criteria are more difficult, and maybe impossible, to develop. In the end, it is easier to count the amount of output produced by a worker than to evaluate the quality of the output produced per unit of effort. To achieve the socially optimal family-work balance, new mechanisms or systems for judging performance may be necessary.

Panel: Where We Are Now and Future Possibilities

While changes in the workplace may reduce work-family conflict or stress for parents on the fast track, changes in work demands at home may also reduce stress or at least increase the gender equity of stress. Scott Coltrane argues that the continued symbolic significance of intensive mothers and breadwinner fathers serves to reproduce unequal gender relations at a time when gender equality is gaining acceptance in education and in the workplace. In other words, mothers will be less likely than fathers (or nonparents) to succeed on the fast track as long as they are expected to bear more responsibility for the functioning of the family. Coltrane points to a redefinition of gender roles in the home as key to gender equality in the workplace. Starting from the premise that the talent of women who could succeed on the fast track but do not because they stay home to take care of their families represents a waste of valuable talent, Heidi Hartmann echoes Scott Coltrane's concerns about the need to reformulate notions of successful mothering and fathering and to develop policies that allow fast-trackers to spend time with their families.

Joyce Jacobsen provides a cautionary note on the research results reported here and elsewhere. She gives a reminder that the correlations between family outcomes and workplace success for women, or men, do not demonstrate causation. When mothers are less successful than nonmothers, it may be because they performed more work in the home and had less energy to achieve on the job, or it may be that as a result of disappointment on the job, they have decided that time at home is more desirable, leading to the birth of more children and/or to spending more time with their families.[14] Similarly, family men may earn more because employers feel the need to pay them more, because wives and children provide incentives for them to work harder, or because women select higher-earning men to be their husbands and to father their children. The appropriate response to any correlation between lack of career success and family status depends critically on the underlying causation.

Gwen Moore examines how family and work are combined for male and female political leaders in developed countries throughout the world. These men and women mirror the results reported in the studies of academe, law, finance, and medicine in the United States. While most leaders and politicians have families, women are less likely than men to have them. The family status differences around the world are largest in the business sector and smallest in the political sector. They are smaller in the political sector because politics is more open than private business to entry at later ages. Female political leaders do not work part-time; nor do they withdraw from their work for any time period for their families. Yet women consistently report taking more responsibility than men for the care of their families in addition to their workload outside the home. While the Nordic countries have fewer gender differences in family status and duties than elsewhere, it is still the case that Nordic women do more household tasks than men.

The Policy Challenge

The articles included here provide evidence that fast-track jobs that require long work hours at the point in the life cycle when workers bear and rear children make those jobs less accessible to mothers and to fathers who devote time to their families. In the jobs studied here, successful women were less likely than other women to be mothers, suggesting that some women who pursue the fast track forgo family to do so. There is no evidence that men in fast-track jobs have in any numbers decided between families and their jobs. Successful men are not less likely to be fathers than other men and in many cases are more likely to be fathers (although this is likely a result of mothers' selection of men as fathers rather than of employers favoring fathers).

In some jobs (finance and law), mothers were as successful as women who had no children, but women—regardless of motherhood status—fared worse than comparable men.[15] The articles included in this volume suggest that the similar outcomes for mothers and nonmothers may be due to the exceptional (and unmeasured) talent of the women who currently pursue both motherhood and the fast track. Clearly, the policy solution to poorer employment outcomes for women, in general, is for government to effectively enforce antidiscrimination legislation.

If fast-track jobs were to be as open to parents who have family care responsibilities as they are to those who spend few hours with family, then the rules of the competition for those jobs must change so that they do not disadvantage highly talented workers who spend time with their children. For fast-track jobs, it is not likely that governmental programs subsidizing day care or after-school care will matter because fast-track jobs offer sufficient wages for workers to obtain these services in the private marketplace. Regulations lowering the length of the workweek by requiring overtime pay beyond a set number of daily or weekly hours will also have no effect because fast-track workers are not paid by the hour, although Jacobs and Gerson (2004, 184) have pointed out that overtime pay could easily be mandated for salaried workers. It is more problematic, however, that a regulation setting a maximum number of hours per day or week that salaried workers may work, or even that workplaces may be open, would have no effect when the work can be performed in other locations and at home (and for no direct pay because the hours are "not reported"). Rat race hours are frequently "chosen" by workers as a strategy to obtain prestigious jobs; the employer does not directly impose the hours.

The only way for change to occur in fast-track jobs is for the workplace norms about hours to change and/or for norms about the amount of contact that young children need with their own mothers to change. Employers, employees, and governmental regulations create workplace norms. Parents and their social contacts create parenting norms. Policies to change norms among fast-track workers must succeed within those venues. The policies that work in one firm in one location may not work in another industry or community, both because the people are different and also because the needs of the consumers differ across firms, industries, and locations.

Policies may create incentives for employers to take actions that change the norms within their workplaces. For example, if lower success rates for mothers in fast-track jobs or lower rates of family formation for women in fast-track jobs were taken as evidence of unlawful workplace discrimination for which the firm was liable, employers would have an incentive to find ways to change norms in the same way that they have changed workplace norms about sexual harassment behaviors and even the very acceptability of women in fast-track jobs. Joan Williams (2000, 103-7) has suggested that promotion tracks that screen out mothers have a disparate impact on women and could be found unlawful under Title VII of the Civil Rights Act of 1964.

It is harder to think about how governmental actions might change norms about child care and the amounts performed by mothers versus fathers. Certainly, the past thirty years have seen large changes in the social acceptability of employed mothers. These changes have occurred as the large majority of mothers became employed. If employers are successful at changing rat race norms in fast-track jobs to allow for more parenting time, then the changes in work norms will surely affect norms about fatherhood and motherhood.

Jobs with up-or-out decisions, such as in law and academe, can develop policies that allow for longer periods of time before such decisions are forced for parents who have devoted substantial time to family care. While as Amy Wax reminds us here, such changes in policies are not without costs if rat race hours have been an effective screen for selecting the most talented heretofore, they are essential if women in these jobs are to have the same opportunities as men to have families. Any job that demands that women forgo families is never likely to attract large numbers of the most talented women.

Notes

1. Table no. 302, *2003 Statistical Abstract of the United States* (Census 2003).

2. Table no. 303, *2003 Statistical Abstract of the United States* (Census 2003).

3. In 1998, 63.7 percent of mothers with children younger than six, 76.1 percent with children aged six to thirteen, and 78.4 percent with children aged fourteen to seventeen were in the labor force. See Table no. 597, *2003 Statistical Abstract of the United States* (Census 2003); Table no. 572, *2001 Statistical Abstract of the United States* (Census 2001); Table no. 578, *2000 Statistical Abstract of the United States* (Census 2000); Table no. 654, *1999 Statistical Abstract of the United States* (Census 1999); and Table no. 660, *1998 Statistical Abstract of the United States* (Census 1998).

4. The male labor force participation rate was 75 percent in 1997 but also declined to 73.5 percent in 2003. See U.S. Bureau of Labor Statistics, *Employment and Earnings*, ftp://ftp.bls.gov/pub/suppl/empsit. cpseea2.txt/.

5. Lisa Belkin, "The Opt-Out Revolution," *New York Times Magazine*, October 26, 2003.

6. *Time*, March 22, 2004.

7. Carol Hymowitz, "In the Lead," *The Wall Street Journal*, March 30, 2004.

8. "Women's Pay: Why the Gap Remains a Chasm," *Business Week*, June 14, 2004.

9. See Landers, Rebitzer, and Taylor (1996), for example.

10. The studies of specific professions—law, medicine, academe, and finance—inevitably deal mostly with data on women and mothers in these professions. While men who take primary responsibility for the rearing of their children face the same problems, their numbers are far fewer than is the case for women. Fathers employed in these demanding professions are more likely than their female counterparts to have a spouse who either does not have a career making similar demands or who makes her career secondary to family concerns. Because fathers in these professions are less likely than mothers to be the primary caregivers for their children, relatively few researchers have focused on career progress among professional fathers who cut back on their work schedules.

11. Jacobs and Winslow identify some other important differences between academe and other professions that potentially affect the relative ability of parents to compete. On one hand, greater flexibility with respect to when long hours are worked may be an advantage for parents in academe relative to law, medicine, and finance. On the other hand, lower wages in academe lead to greater employment commitments for spouses, leaving less adult time in the home.

12. Jacobs and Winslow show that time demands are not easily circumvented because they are also an enduring feature of many fast-track jobs. For example, the survey data indicate that academics do not substantially cut back their working time after receiving tenure.

13. The law degree takes three years; the average time for completing a Ph.D. varies by field, but the median years after the baccalaureate award to receipt of the Ph.D. is 11.8 in the humanities, 10.3 in the social sciences, 9.6 in the life sciences, and 8.3 in the physical sciences (National Research Council 1998, Table A-3).

14. In their article in this volume, Stone and Lovejoy report that many of the mothers who "dropped off" the fast track had school-age or teenage children. Heidi Hartmann suggests in her comment in this volume that these mothers may be responding to disappointment at work more than to the needs of their children.

15. There is a larger research literature that has found similar results for college-educated women. See, for example, Anderson, Binder, and Krause (2003).

References

Anderson, D. J., M. Binder, and K. Krause. 2003. The motherhood wage penalty revisited: Experience, heterogeneity, work effort, and work-schedule flexibility. *Industrial and Labor Relations Review* 56 (2): 273-94.

Goldin, Claudia. 1990. *Understanding the gender gap: An economic history of American women*. New York: Oxford University Press.

Jacobs, Jerry A., and Kathleen Gerson. 2004. *The time divide: Work, family, and gender inequality*. Cambridge, MA: Harvard University Press.

Landers, Renee M., James B. Rebitzer, and Lowell J. Taylor. 1996. Rat race redux: Adverse selection in the determination of work hours in law firms. *American Economic Review* 86 (3): 329-48.

National Research Council. 1998. *Summary report 1995: Doctorate recipients from United States universities*. Washington, DC: National Academy Press.

U.S. Bureau of the Census. 1998. Statistical Abstract of the United States: 1998 (118 edition). Washington, DC: Author.

———. 1999. Statistical Abstract of the United States: 1999 (119 edition). Washington, DC: Author.

———. 2000. Statistical Abstract of the United States: 2000 (120 edition). Washington, DC: Author.

———. 2001. Statistical Abstract of the United States: 2001 (121 edition). Washington, DC: Author.

———. 2003. Statistical Abstract of the United States: 2003 (123 edition). Washington, DC: Author.

Williams, Joan. 2000. *Unbending gender*. New York: Oxford University Press.

SECTION ONE

Overviews

The Long Road to the Fast Track: Career and Family

By

CLAUDIA GOLDIN

The career and family outcomes of college graduate women suggest that the twentieth century contained five distinct cohorts. The first cohort, graduating college from 1900 to 1920, had either "family or career." The second, graduating from 1920 to 1945, had "job then family." The third cohort, the college graduate mothers of the baby boom, graduated from 1946 to the mid-1960s and had "family then job." Among the fourth cohort, graduating college from the late 1960s to 1980 and whose stated goal was "career then family," 13 to 18 percent achieved both by age forty. The objective of the fifth cohort, graduating from around 1980 to 1990, has been "career and family," and 21 to 28 percent have realized that goal by age forty. The author traces the demographic and labor force experiences of these five cohorts of college graduates and discusses why "career and family" outcomes changed over time.

Keywords: college graduate women; career; family

Women who graduated college at the dawn of the twentieth century were of a generation that contained two groups, equal in size yet highly dissimilar. One married and had children but had few jobs and even fewer careers. The other had no children and married at much lower rates.[1] Many in that group had jobs at some point in their postcollege lives. Some even had careers. Thus, half of this generation of college graduate women had "family." Some in the other half had "career." Few had both.

Claudia Goldin is Henry Lee Professor of Economics at Harvard University and director of the Development of the American Economy program of the National Bureau of Economic Research (NBER). She has been on the faculties of the University of Pennsylvania, Princeton University, and the University of Wisconsin. Goldin was president of the Economic History Association in 2000 and vice president of the American Economic Association in 1991. From 1984 to 1988, she was editor of the Journal of Economic History. Goldin received her B.A. from Cornell University and her Ph.D. from the University of Chicago.

NOTE: This article draws on a public lecture presented at "Mommies and Daddies on the Fast Track," October 30, 2003. It relies heavily on Goldin (1992, 1997).

DOI: 10.1177/0002716204267959

Long after this generation, college women began a struggle to "have it all," to have both "career and family." It would not be one *or* the other. Nor would it be one *then* the other. It would be *both*.

My article is about the "long and winding road" from the cohort who had "family or career" to the latest generation of college graduate women who define their goal as "career and family." They are women who want to be "mothers on the fast track."

It was about fifteen to twenty years ago that I first began to realize that college women as a group were talking about their futures in ways that would have been unimaginable to me when I was in college. They spoke, candidly and honestly, of desiring "CAREERANDFAMILY" or "FAMILYANDCAREER," as if the words were not three but one and as if the timing of the two goals would not be an issue. They were aware that only atypical and extraordinary college woman had been able to accomplish both career and family in the past. But in defense of their optimism, they noted that their generation was different. Barriers had fallen. They were as well trained and as able as their male friends, the majority of whom would achieve these two goals.

I became curious about the evolution of this change in "attitude," and over the years I have compiled evidence concerning the labor force and demographic histories of college women from the late nineteenth century to the present.[2] The sources range widely and include census materials; Current Population Surveys; U.S. Women's Bureau surveys; alumni records; and for the most recent cohorts, the National Longitudinal Survey (NLS) of Young Women (1968) and the NLS of Youth (1979) (http://www.bls.gov/nls/home.htm). As I looked at the data, I realized that college women across the past century had widely different attainments concerning family and job and career. I want to share these data with you.

Five Cohorts of
College Graduate Women

The experiences of the cohorts of college women across the past century suggested to me that the full one hundred years contained five distinct cohorts—not necessarily of equal length by birth year. The cohort boundaries emerged from the data. They are not arbitrary and imposed. Each of these cohorts was faced with a different set of constraints, and each made its choices concerning family and career subject to these constraints. Table 1 will serve to introduce the five cohorts.

To summarize, the first cohort that I am able to track graduated college from the beginning of the twentieth century to the close of World War I and had either "family or career."[3] The second cohort graduated college from around 1920 to the end of World War II and had "job then family." This cohort was, as will soon be made clear, a transitional generation linking one of low marriage and low fertility rates to one of high marriage and high fertility rates. The third cohort graduated college from around 1946 to the mid-1960s and had "family then job." These women were the college graduate mothers of the "baby boom." The fourth cohort graduated

TABLE 1
FIVE COHORTS OF COLLEGE GRADUATE WOMEN

Cohort	Interval When Graduated from Four-Year College	Approximate Birth Interval (Assuming College Graduation at Twenty-Two Years Old)	Characterization of Desired (or Achieved) Family and Career Path
1	1900-19	1878-97	Family or career
2	1920-45	1898-1923	Job then family
3	1946-65	1924-43	Family then job
4	1966-79	1944-57	Career then family (13 to 18 percent attained)
5	1980-90	1958-68	Career and family (21 to 27 percent attained)

college from the late 1960s to the late 1970s and aspired to have "career then family." The fifth cohort graduated from around 1980 to 1990 and is the most recent one that can be studied. Its goal has been "career *and* family." These are five distinct cohorts. Yet each one's achievements and ability to attain its goals built on both the accomplishments and frustrations of the previous cohorts.

I should note at the outset that I must truncate the groups studied with the fifth cohort. The reason is that I can categorize and assess the achievements of these women only if they are now old enough to have been given a chance to have "family and career." I have used a cutoff of about forty years old, and for that reason, the last cohort I can study—cohort 5—is that born in the 1960s.

Cohort 5, whose members proclaimed that they would achieve *both* family and career (and not career first and then family), is now old enough for the researcher to observe if its members have broken through to the "fast track" in substantial numbers. Researchers can also assess how this cohort differed from (or was similar to) previous generations of college women in its ability to achieve career and to combine it with family. And for this particular cohort, researchers can compare the "family and career" success of college graduate women with that of comparable men. The NLS Youth (1979) data set, which I will use to assess the success of cohort 5, has a large sample of *both* females and males traced over time, something absent in data sets for previous cohorts. The NLS Young Women (1968) data, used to evaluate the career and family accomplishments of cohort 4, began with a large group of male respondents, but attrition led to the discontinuation of that portion of the survey.

I will trace the demographic and labor force experiences of these five cohorts of college graduates and discuss some of the constraints they faced, the trade-offs they made, and their "career and family" outcomes. I will first give the "broad-brush" details for each of the cohorts separately (given in tabular form in Table 2) and then link the cohorts together in a more continuous fashion, using graphs.

TABLE 2
DEMOGRAPHIC AND ECONOMIC CHARACTERISTICS
OF THE FIVE COHORTS

College Graduation Years	Nonmarriage (by age fifty)	No Children (by age forty)	Work at Age Thirty (if married)	Work at Age Forty-Five (if married)	Dominant Occupation
Cohort 1, 1900-19	>30%	>50%	Low	20%	Teaching, office work
Cohort 2, 1920-45	15%-20%	30%-35%	25%	50%	Teaching, office work
Cohort 3, 1946-65	8%	17%	25%-30%	75%	Teaching
Cohort 4, 1966-79	12% (but deferral)	28%	65%	80%	Varied professions
Cohort 5, 1980-90	(too young)	26%	80%	(too young)	Varied professions

SOURCE: Goldin (1997); Current Population Survey data (http://www.bls.census.gov/cps/cpsmain.htm).

NOTE: Labor force participation rates, nonmarriage rates, and childlessness rates are approximations based on the decennial censuses.

Cohort 1

Recall that this cohort graduated college during the first two decades of the twentieth century and was born during the last two decades of the nineteenth century. More than 30 percent of this cohort never married by age fifty, a rate that was four times that for their female counterparts who attended no college at all. College graduate men in this cohort, furthermore, had about the same marriage rates as did noncollege men. Among the women who married, about 30 percent had no children. Putting these two facts together (that is, weighting the numbers by their relative proportions in the relevant population) reveals that more than 50 percent of the group did not have children. This rather high rate of childlessness led some contemporaries, in an era of rampant nativism, to ruminate about "race suicide," for a substantial number of these college women were from upper-class families. Many questioned the appropriateness of college for women.

Despite their low rate of family formation, these women also had surprisingly low rates of labor force participation when young and married. Even when they were around age forty-five, their participation rate was around 20 percent, on average, for those who had married. Among those who had jobs, teaching was, by far, the main occupation.

These women had made a clear choice between family and career. Given the constraints of their day, they could *not* easily have had both. Many of this generation wrote and spoke of their careers—as teachers, librarians, social workers, and nurses, among other professions—as *higher callings*. Their careers liberated them from the constraints of marriage and household duties.

Cohort 2

Cohort 2 graduated college mainly during the interwar years of the twentieth century. The generation was transitional in yet another sense. The fraction of the cohort who never married by fifty years old was about 15 to 20 percent, a decrease from cohort 1, and the fraction who never had a first birth was about 30 to 35 percent, also a decrease from that experienced by cohort 1. Although the rate of family formation was higher than that for cohort 1, it was much smaller than that for cohort 3.

It was about fifteen to twenty years ago that I first began to realize that college women as a group were talking about their futures in ways that would have been unimaginable to me when I was in college.

The fraction of cohort 2 who worked when young and married was much higher than that for cohort 1. About 25 percent of the group was in the labor force when they were about age thirty (conditional on being married). This cohort was the first whose members did not exit the labor force at the precise moment of marriage but, in general, waited until they were pregnant with their first child. As a group, therefore, they had "job then family." Among those with occupations, teaching was, once again, the most customary.

Mary McCarthy's semiautobiographical novel *The Group* (1954) best epitomizes this cohort. In its description of the "group's" mothers, it also characterizes the previous cohort of college graduate women (cohort 1). The novel depicts a group of eight Vassar women, graduates of the class of 1933, who resolve to be different from their conventional parents. Each embarks on a career ranging from journalist, to veterinarian, to airplane pilot, although most marry and eventually exit the labor force. Their mothers achieve some vicarious satisfaction that their daughters occupied exciting positions, if only for a while. That is, cohort 2 built on the frustrations of cohort 1.

Cohort 3

Cohort 3 graduated from college during the era of the "baby boom"—from the end of World War II to the turbulent and socially transformative era of the mid-

1960s. The cohort married and had children at exceptionally high rates. Just 8 percent never married—a rate that was almost as low as it was for women who attended no college at all. Just 10 percent of those who married did not have a first birth in their lifetime. Once again, this is an extremely low rate. Therefore, putting together these numbers, correctly weighted by the proportions in the population, yields just 17 percent of the entire group who were childless in their lifetime.

Not only was their rate of marriage high, but their age at first marriage was extremely low by historical standards for college graduate women. The median age at first marriage was less than twenty-three years old. Of those who ever married, a substantial fraction—57.2 percent—married within one year of graduating college or during college (the drop-out rate because of marriage and often pregnancy was also substantial). Given the timing of marriage relative to college graduation, a considerable portion of these women must have met their future husbands while in college, raising interesting issues regarding the role of college as a "marriage market."

The fraction of this cohort that was in the labor force when young and married was 25 to 30 percent, or almost the same level as for cohort 2. But the fraction in the labor force at age forty-five was 75 percent, considerably higher than for the previous cohort. These college graduate women had "family then job." Family came *first* both in terms of priority and timing.

College women had gained considerably in "family" but had not advanced much in terms of "career." Cohort 3 became the frustrated group described by Betty Friedan in her influential volume *The Feminine Mystique* (1963). As a group, its members became increasingly discontent with a labor market that offered college women little in the way of career advancement and with employment officers who often asked them just one question: "Can you type?"

Cohort 4

The women of cohort 4, the "baby boom generation," graduated college during the heady days of the late 1960s and early 1970s. A substantial fraction put off getting married for several years after college. In consequence, the age at first marriage rose by more than two years—from twenty-three years old for the cohort born in 1950 to more than twenty-five years old for that born in 1957.[4] But even though this generation married late, its members deferred marriage rather than avoiding it altogether, and just a small fraction—12 percent—remained single by their midforties.

Even though a substantial fraction married at some point in their lives, the delay in marriage, together with several other factors, led 19 percent of the ever-married group to have no births by age forty. Together with the group that never married and had no children, about 28 percent of the entire group remained childless by age forty.

The labor force participation rate of the group when it was young and married soared relative to that of the previous cohort. About 65 percent of its members were in the labor force at age thirty (conditional on being married). About 80 percent were in the labor force at age forty-five (again, conditional on being married). The dominant occupation for college graduate women in this cohort shifted from teaching to a variety of professions, including those at the very top of any occupational prestige scale.

The dominant occupation for college graduate women in [cohort 4, the baby boom generation] shifted from teaching to a variety of professions, including those at the very top of any occupational prestige scale.

College women gained in careers but lost in family. As a group, I will show that about 13 to 18 percent of this cohort achieved "career and family" by age forty. Among those who placed their careers first, children were put "on hold," sometimes forever.

Cohort 5

This cohort, graduating from college in the 1980s—the "decade of greed"—and the last one that can be tracked to around age forty, looked to previous generations for direction. Putting career first and then trying for a family, as was attempted by cohort 4, had led to substantial "childlessness." Putting family first and then getting a job, as cohort 3 did, would not be the route either. Cohort 5 would try for both together. But did it succeed?

College graduate women in cohort 5 deferred marriage, just as did those in cohort 4. They achieved a slight decline in the fraction with no births—26 percent by around age forty rather than 28 percent for the previous cohort. Their labor force participation when young and married was extremely high—around 80 percent—and their dominant occupation was a group of diverse professions, as was the case for cohort 4. A larger fraction of this cohort managed to achieve career and family by around age forty. The range is about 21 to 27 percent for cohort 5, as opposed to 13 to 18 percent for cohort 4. The answer, then, is that cohort 5 did succeed to a greater extent than did its predecessors in large part because those with children did better at attaining a career.

Cohort Summary

In sum, cohort 1 had either family or career, rarely both. Cohort 2 was a transition cohort who married and had children to a greater degree but who also had a greater variety of jobs when young. By cohort 3, college women had discovered family to an almost equal degree as noncollege women. But these women eventually became deeply frustrated by their treatment in the labor market and by potential employers who did not take them seriously. Cohort 4 delayed marriage and childbirth and aimed to have career first and then family. Cohort 5, recognizing the problems with the biological clock, claimed it could balance the two together. It has achieved more success in managing family and career than cohort 4 and probably has had the greatest achievement in this regard among all cohorts of college graduate women in U.S. history.

Whether the fraction of cohort 5 that has attained family and career is large is a question I will address in a moment. Before I do that, I would like to confront an important issue concerning the selectivity of women into the group of college graduates in each of the cohorts and how that might influence my findings. I would also like to give the more continuous details of marriage and childbearing using all years of college graduates to show how I demarcated the cohorts.

College Graduation Rates by Cohorts

The rate of college graduation (from four-year institutions) increased over time for both men and women, as can be seen in Figure 1, but at different moments for much of the century. Graduation rates were not much different by sex for those born early in the twentieth century, such as cohort 1. In fact, the rate of college going (not shown here), rather than graduation from a four-year institution, was about the same for men and women until the birth cohorts of the 1920s. The cohorts of men who fought in World War II and Korea (those born from around the early 1920s to the early 1930s) had vastly increased college going and graduation rates. By the cohorts born in the 1930s, and thus who graduated from college in the 1950s (such as cohort 3), the ratio of men to women in college was two to one or more. But the rate of graduation for young women also began to rise for cohort 3. Although the rates for women rose, college graduation rates for the men of cohort 4 increased precipitously with the draft deferments of the Vietnam War. But by the close of cohort 4, graduation rates were on par by sex and have remained so for cohort 5.[5]

Thus, the earliest cohorts of college graduates studied here must have been from a highly select group of families by income and social standing. By midcentury, however, the middle class had found its way to college, and by the end of the period, college graduation included individuals from most types of families. The selection of young people into college and the families from which they came could affect the conclusions I have made about marriage, family, and career goals.

FIGURE 1
GRADUATION RATES FROM FOUR-YEAR COLLEGES AND UNIVERSITIES FOR
MEN AND WOMEN, BY BIRTH COHORT (AS OF THIRTY-FIVE YEARS OLD)

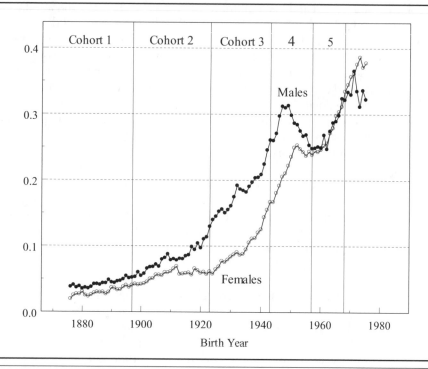

SOURCE: De Long, Goldin, and Katz (2003).
NOTE: Data for cohorts born after 1970 are based on extrapolations.

Although selectivity might affect many issues of importance concerning college graduate women, the characterizations of each of the cohorts I have offered remain robust to selectivity concerns. When the group is limited to a particular college, such as a private women's college like Wellesley and Radcliffe, or a co-educational, public institution such as the University of Michigan, the portrayals of each of the cohorts with respect to marriage, family, occupation, and career remain the same. That is, women from particular colleges, and even those from elite colleges, conformed to the trends described.

Marriage and Childbearing for College Graduate Women during the Past One Hundred Years

To connect the various cohorts I have delineated and to give more information about the demarcations selected, I have constructed continuous series for mar-

FIGURE 2
PERCENTAGE NEVER MARRIED,
COLLEGE GRADUATE WOMEN (WHITE)

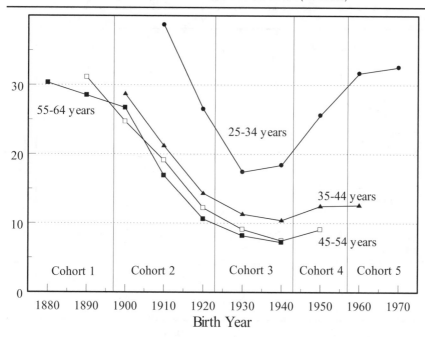

SOURCE: Goldin (1992, 1997).

riage rates and childbearing that encompass as many of the cohorts as the data
would allow. The data on marriage rates, given in Figure 2, show the very high rate
of nonmarriage—about 30 percent for even the oldest age group—for cohort 1.[6] In
sharp contrast, the extremely low rates of nonmarriage for cohort 3 reveal why
cohort 2 was a transitional cohort. The rate of nonmarriage among the members of
cohort 3 bottomed out around the 1940 birth cohort when the rate dropped to
about 7 percent for women forty-five to fifty-four years old. Note as well that
although the rate of marriage for cohort 4 by the time it was thirty-five to forty-four
years old was almost as high as for cohort 3, it deferred getting married until it was
considerably older. By the start of cohort 5, more than 30 percent of the twenty-
five- to thirty-four-year-old group was not yet married, whereas that figure was 17
percent for cohort 3.

For the birth data, which are measured when the cohort reached thirty-five to
forty-four years, only three of the cohorts can be precisely studied. Cohort 1 was
born too early to be tracked with the 1940 population census, and cohort 5 is too
young to be studied with any surveys.[7] But related data suggest what the childlessness rates of these cohorts were or will be.

FIGURE 3
PERCENTAGE OF WOMEN (WHITE) OF ALL MARITAL STATUSES WITH NO
BIRTHS BY AGE THIRTY-FIVE TO FORTY-FOUR

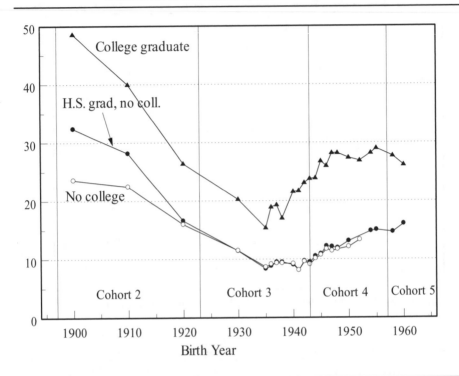

SOURCE: Goldin (1992, 1997).

Figure 3 gives the fraction of women by cohort (and educational attainment) who had not yet had a first birth by ages thirty-five to forty-four. Although the trend for college graduate women mimics that for the two other educational groups, it has a more extreme dip and later rise.[8] Note that the fraction without children for the youngest in cohort 1 was around 50 percent. Alumni records for various colleges suggest that the fraction may have been higher for all of cohort 1. Also note that by the midpoint of cohort 3, about 15 percent of college graduate women did not have a first birth by ages thirty-five to forty-four, the lowest figure on record here.

Career and Family among Cohorts 4 and 5

I can now return to the more recent cohorts and assess the extent to which they have achieved family and career. First of all, I have to define "family" and "career." No single definition will satisfy everyone, and thus I have employed several.

I define "family" as ever having a first birth (adoptive children can easily be added, but they do not change the results by much). Note that having a "family" does not necessarily mean that the individual in question is currently married or that the individual was ever married.

"Career" is a more difficult concept. The word comes from the French for "race-course" and means a person's progress through life. In common parlance, it means a success that is not ephemeral but that exists over some period of time. To assess "career," one needs longitudinal data, and these are, luckily, available for both cohorts 4 and 5 in two of the NLSs.

I define "career" as reaching an annual income (or hourly wage) level greater than that achieved by a comparable college graduate man who was at the 25th percentile of the male annual income (or hourly wage) distribution. This accomplishment, moreover, must exist for two or three years running when the woman in question was in her late thirties or early forties. Thus, the definition of "career" entails earning more than a college graduate man whose income is well below that of the median man (but about equal to the median of the female earnings distribution) for several consecutive years.

Many of [the women in cohort 1] wrote and spoke of their careers—as teachers, librarians, social workers, and nurses, among other professions—as higher callings.

To assess both career and family for cohort 4, I use the NLS of Young Women. When the survey began in 1968, these women were fourteen to twenty-four years old. That is, the women interviewed were born from 1944 to 1954 and were thirty-four to forty-four years old in 1988, around the year when I assess career. I restrict the sample to (white) college graduate women and employ four definitions of career. Two use hourly earnings and two use annual earnings. The latter definition of income will include more individuals, such as the self-employed and those who did not list usual weekly hours. For each income measure, I require that the individual earn at least the cutoff amount for either two years or three years. Because the NLS Young Women skipped some years, these are not all consecutive.

The results given in Table 3 show, first of all, that about 29 percent of the group did not have a first birth, consistent with the aggregate data, and that about 25 to 28 percent attained career. The numbers in boldface give the fraction that had both family and career, which ranges from about 13 to 18 percent, depending on the def-

TABLE 3

CAREER AND FAMILY FOR THE COLLEGE GRADUATE
WOMEN OF COHORT 4 (IN PERCENTAGES)

Career	Family		Family	
	Kids	No Kids	Kids	No Kids
	Hourly Wage: Three Years[a]		Annual Income: Three Years[b]	
No	55.3	16.7	58.9	15.8
Yes	**14.0**	14.0	**12.9**	12.4
	Hourly Wage: Two Years[c]		Annual Income: Two Years[d]	
No	51.8	13.8	53.5	11.5
Yes	**17.8**	16.6	**18.4**	16.7

SOURCE: National Longitudinal Survey of Young Women (1968) (http://www.bls.gov/nls/home.htm).
NOTE: The "hourly wage" columns use only observations that give annual earnings and usual hours. The income measure uses annual earnings and includes the self-employed. "Kids" are biological and exclude adoptive children and stepchildren. The inclusion of adoptive children does not change the results much. Some of these results differ slightly from those in Goldin (1997) and correct minor errors in them. See text and Goldin (1997) for the definition of "career." The numbers in boldface give the fraction that had both family and career.
a. Uses hourly wage measure for 1985, 1987, 1988 ($N = 443$).
b. Uses income measure for 1985, 1987, 1988 ($N = 550$).
c. Uses hourly wage measure for 1987, 1988 ($N = 477$).
d. Uses income measure for 1987, 1988 ($N = 550$).

inition of career used. Whether one judges this to be high or low will depend on a reference group, and there is none in this survey. But there is one in a subsequent survey.

Luckily, the NLS 1979 has followed both men and women who were fourteen to twenty-one years old in 1979. These individuals, born from 1957 to 1964, are members of cohort 5. I employ the same definitions of career and family, except that career is now calculated with respect to the college graduate man at the 25th percentile in a later year. Also, the NLS 1979 was performed biennially, so the years chosen could not be consecutive. Table 4 gives the results for the women, and Table 5 gives them for the men.

The results for the women show, first of all, that the fraction with children rose ever so slightly, consistent with the aggregate data. The real change is that the fraction with careers rose to around 35 to 40 percent, up by about 10 percentage points from the previous cohort. Thus, the fraction with both family and career (in boldface) increased to around 21 to 27 percent. Whether this is considered large or small can be judged relative to the men in the sample.

The fraction of the men who claimed never to have fathered a child is a bit higher than the fraction of the women who stated they never had a birth—from 30

TABLE 4

**CAREER AND FAMILY FOR THE COLLEGE GRADUATE
WOMEN OF COHORT 5 (IN PERCENTAGES)**

Career	Family		Family	
	Kids	No Kids	Kids	No Kids
	Hourly Wage: Three Years[a]		Annual Income: Three Years[b]	
No	47.8	17.9	50.4	14.9
Yes	**23.7**	10.6	**21.4**	13.3
	Hourly Wage: Two Years[c]		Annual Income: Two Years[d]	
No	44.9	15.4	48.9	13.6
Yes	**26.7**	13.0	**22.9**	14.6

SOURCE: National Longitudinal Survey of Youth (1979) (http://www.bls.gov/nls/home.htm).
NOTE: The "hourly wage" columns use only observations that give annual earnings and usual hours. The income measure uses annual earnings and includes the self-employed. "Kids" are biological and exclude adoptive children and stepchildren. The inclusion of adoptive children does not change the results much. See text and Goldin (1997) for the definition of "career." The fraction with both family and career is given in boldface.
a. Uses hourly wage measure for 1996, 1998, 2000 ($N = 536$).
b. Uses income measure for 1996, 1998, 2000 ($N = 611$).
c. Uses hourly wage measure for 1998, 2000 ($N = 570$).
d. Uses income measure for 1998, 2000 ($N = 611$).

to 34 percent. But the fraction of men that had a career was much higher than that of women, ranging from 61 to 74 percent.[9] In consequence, the fraction with career and family for the male sample ranged from 45 to 55 percent or about double that for the women. But even though men managed to achieve career and family about two times as often as women, this is probably the lowest that figure has been in U.S. history.

Why Did Change Occur?

What were the main factors that led college graduate women to take the long and winding road to the fast track? The transitions occurred, by and large, because constraints were loosened on women's ability to work in fulfilling careers, first after marriage and later after childbearing.

Some of these changes were rooted in the labor market—such as the growth of a wide variety of white collar jobs (as was the case in the 1920s and again in the 1950s) and the greater ability of women in various periods to hold certain professional jobs. These changes were also rooted in schools—such as the increase in labor-market-relevant college majors for women beginning in the 1970s and the related increase in the enrollment of women in professional schools.

TABLE 5

CAREER AND FAMILY FOR THE COLLEGE GRADUATE
MEN OF COHORT 5 (IN PERCENTAGES)

Career	Family		Family	
	Kids	No Kids	Kids	No Kids
	Hourly Wage: Three Years[a]		Annual Income: Three Years[b]	
No	25.2	14.1	17.9	13.8
Yes	**44.6**	16.2	**51.4**	17.0
	Hourly Wage: Two Years[c]		Annual Income: Two Years[d]	
No	17.7	12.5	14.3	11.3
Yes	**48.0**	21.8	**55.0**	19.4

SOURCE: National Longitudinal Survey of Youth (1979) (http://www.bls.gov/nls/home.htm).
NOTE: The "hourly wage" columns use only observations that give annual earnings and usual hours. The income measure uses annual earnings and includes the self-employed. "Kids" are biological and exclude adoptive children and stepchildren. The inclusion of adoptive children does not change the results much. See text and Goldin (1997) for the definition of "career." The definition for men is the same as for women. The fraction with both family and career is given in boldface.
a. Uses hourly wage measure for 1996, 1998, 2000 (N = 505).
b. Uses income measure for 1996, 1998, 2000 (N = 582).
c. Uses hourly wage measure for 1998, 2000 (N = 527).
d. Uses income measure for 1998, 2000 (N = 582).

But many of these changes occurred in the personal lives of college women. For example, cohort 2 was able to be married *and* have a job, at least for a short while. Cohort 4 achieved a later age at marriage and delay of childbirth because of better contraceptive methods, such as "the pill," that enabled them to control their fertility and thus plan for "career then family."

Conclusion

I have described the path to the fast track that college graduate women have taken starting with cohort 1, which graduated in the first two decades of the twentieth century and had "family or career," to the latest group, cohort 5, which has achieved a modicum of success in combining career and family. Each generation built on the successes and frustrations of the previous ones. Each stepped into a society and a labor market with loosened constraints and shifting barriers. The road was not only long, but it has also been winding. Some cohorts of college graduate women gained "family," whereas others gained "career." Only recently has a substantial group been able to grasp both at the same time.

Notes

1. Throughout this article, having no children and the term "childless" will mean having no *biological* children. In the analysis of more recent cohorts, the fraction adopting can also be included, but it is small.

2. The data I use here are primarily for white college graduate women because the numbers of African American college graduate women in the early years of this study are too small. I hope that a future project will tap into the alumni records of historically black colleges to get a larger sample of black female college graduates.

3. Historians often call this group the "second cohort" of female college graduates to distinguish it from the "first cohort" that attended college just after the establishment of many of the fine women's colleges in the 1870s and 1880s. The fraction of women in cohort 1 that graduated from women's colleges was only about 20 percent, far lower than most presume. In 1897, it was 18 percent, and in 1924, it was 23 percent (these calculations use the data sources given in Goldin and Katz [1999, e.g., Table 1]).

4. The age at first marriage among college graduate women remained fairly constant from the cohort born in 1930 to that born in 1950 (see Goldin and Katz 2002). The age at first marriage continued to rise after the cohort born in 1957, although more slowly.

5. The more recent increase in college enrollments for women relative to men is reflected in the extrapolations in Figure 1 for college graduation rates achieved by thirty-five years old.

6. It should be noted that nonmarriage means that the woman was never married by the age given.

7. The 1940 federal population census was the first to include information on educational attainment.

8. The other two educational groups are no college and no college but a high school graduate. The latter group is given for the earlier years when college graduation was less common and high school graduation was not yet the norm.

9. The income levels for the man at the 25th percentile come from the Current Population Survey (http://www.bls.census.gov/cps/cpsmain.htm) and are a bit lower than those from the NLS. Thus, the fraction of men with income exceeding this mark for two years can even exceed 75 percent. Since the same cutoff is used for both men and women, this should not affect the comparisons for cohort 5.

References

De Long, J. Bradford, Claudia Goldin, and Lawrence F. Katz. 2003. Sustaining U.S. economic growth. In *Agenda for the nation*, edited by H. Aaron, J. Lindsay, and P. Nivola. Washington, DC: Brookings Institution.

Friedan, Betty. 1963. *The feminine mystique*. New York: Norton.

Goldin, Claudia. 1992. The meaning of college in the lives of American women: The past hundred years. NBER Working Paper no. 4099, National Bureau of Economic Research, Cambridge, MA.

———. 1997. Career and family: College women look to the past. In *Gender and family issues in the workplace*, edited by Francine Blau and Ronald Ehrenberg. New York: Russell Sage Foundation.

Goldin, Claudia, and Lawrence F. Katz. 1999. The shaping of higher education: The formative years in the United States, 1890 to 1940. *Journal of Economic Perspectives* 13 (Winter): 37-62.

———. 2002. The Power of the pill: Oral contraceptives and women's career and marriage decisions. *Journal of Political Economy* 110 (August): 730-70.

McCarthy, Mary. 1954. *The group*. New York: Harcourt, Brace, Jovanovich.

Family-Friendly Workplace Reform: Prospects for Change

By
AMY L. WAX

The recent surge of women and mothers into the workforce has generated a call for changes that make it easier to combine employment with family life. Because neoclassical economic theory assumes that existing workplace structures are efficient, suggestions for reform have encountered resistance on the grounds that family-friendly reforms will prove costly for firms and society as a whole. In particular, so-called "accommodation mandates," which require employers to extend benefits like paid leave and job protection to parents, have been attacked as potentially inefficient and as harmful to those they are designed to help. This article challenges the suggestion that existing arrangements maximize social welfare and that family-friendly reforms will undermine efficiency. Using dynamic game-theoretic models, it explains how management-worker interactions can get stuck in equilibria that generate less well-being overall than more family-friendly alternatives, and it shows how family-friendly arrangements may be difficult to maintain despite their potential for making everyone better off. The article speculates on measures that might foster the adoption and stability of family-friendly workplace forms.

Keywords: game theory; family-friendly workplace; accommodation mandates; work-family balance

One of the most dramatic demographic changes of the past thirty years has been the surge of women, including mothers, into the workforce. This social revolution has given rise to a feminist critique of existing workplace structures geared to an "ideal worker" who is able and willing to devote himself single-mindedly to paid employment (Williams 2000). Calling for reforms that make it easier to combine employment with family life, critics seek to create a workplace that is more welcoming to employees with family responsibilities (Williams 2000; Hochschild 1989, 1997). The "wish list" of features for the new family-friendly workplace includes, among other things, shorter, more predictable, and more flexible working hours; new part-time and job-sharing options; time off for

DOI: 10.1177/0002716204269189

ANNALS, *AAPSS*, 596, November 2004

emergencies and child care; guaranteed leave with job security for childbearing and child rearing; child care subsidies and tax breaks; and on-sight day care options (Alstott 2004; Jacobs and Gerson 2004). In addition, proponents of reform advocate deep-seated structural changes in conventions for allocating compensation and rewards and for assigning positions of power and responsibility within the workplace. They push for the abolition of the so-called "mommy track," which relegates to a second-class status workers who adopt patterns of work more amenable to family life.

The debate triggered by the influx of employees with familial responsibilities has spawned two principal approaches to easing the lot of working families. One stresses the importance of action from within, with emphasis on private, internal, local initiatives within firms and organizations to alter workplace norms, conventions, and practices (Williams 2000). The other approach calls for government interventions designed to facilitate proper care for children with less sacrifice of parents' job opportunities, advancement, and compensation (Fineman 2004; Crittenden 2001; Burggraf 1997; Wax 1999a, 1999b; Folbre 2001). Proposals for government intervention are grounded in the argument that society as a whole has a special responsibility to support families (Alstott 2004; Folbre 2001). This approach stresses subsidies; legal protections for caretakers; and so-called "accommodation mandates," which require employers to extend protective benefits and employment terms (such as paid leave and parental job protection) to workers (Jolls 2000; Margalioth 2003).

The calls for reform have created dilemmas for private actors and for governments alike. Corporations in their function as employers must confront the issue of whether and how to ease the difficulties employees experience in discharging their duties on the job and at home. Governments must decide how to intervene. They must determine whether and when to enact regulations forcing private actors to accommodate family needs.

Private actors and governments must also grapple with how and to what extent to mitigate the disadvantages that commonly accrue to individuals who fall short of the traditional "ideal worker" model. One particularly nettlesome issue is how proposed reforms should affect compensation and prospects for promotion and advancement. Although there is widespread acceptance that pay should reflect hours worked, it is unclear how work rewards and career trajectories should be adjusted to reflect differential use of family-friendly policies. As noted, feminists envision a workplace in which family-friendly patterns of work are no longer associated with career suicide, relegation to a second-class status, or higher hurdles to advancement, authority, or prestige. As Joan Williams (2002, 812, 817) stated, "The key is to replace the marginalized mommy tracks available today with a variety of possibilities that offer flexibility *without marginalization*." This suggestion raises the question of whether "flexibility without marginalization" is economically viable, feasible, or fair. Is it possible to devise a workable reward system that attaches no special penalties to the constraints inherent in discharging family responsibilities? Can the government establish this system, or is it best accomplished by spontaneous change from within? What sorts of rules are most likely to bring about results that are fair to caretakers and noncaretakers alike? Is family-friendly reform compatible with a diversity of preferences or patterns of work, or must it lead inexorably to a new, uniform pattern of "one track for all?"

Answering these questions requires developing models of labor market and workplace dynamics that incorporate mechanisms for tying performance to reward. The challenge is confounded by the wide variation in workplace organization, conventions, and compensation structures. Critics focus on professional workplaces—including, for example, private law firms—as particularly incompatible with family responsibilities (Williams 2000; Epstein et al. 1999). The "up-or-out" advancement structure of law firms relegates those who seek family-friendly accommodations to a "second tier" that virtually rules out career advancement and, in some cases, continued employment with a particular firm. What leads to the adoption of these structures? What alternative principles of organization and reward are feasible? Although the real-world workplace is very complex, certain simplifying assumptions make it possible to explore these issues with an eye toward assessing costs and benefits and investigating routes to constructive reform.

This article makes use of economic analyses of workplace dynamics to address the question of why the family-friendly workplace is in short supply. It builds on models from neoclassical economics and game theory to investigate possibilities for influencing workplace structures in a more family-friendly direction and to examine the consequences of various reforms and interventions for workplace actors and society as a whole.

Economic Approaches: Neoclassical Models of Family-Friendly Interventions

In developing approaches that could show the way to family-friendly reform, one important consideration is whether proposed workplace changes are efficient or more efficient than existing arrangements. If the answer to this question is positive, it follows that proposed reforms will increase net social welfare, which will make society better off overall. Although discussions of efficiency mask complex distributional issues and raise questions about how well-being is to be measured, the claim is that efficiency is important because the extra resources generated through the most efficient arrangements are available, at least in theory, to compensate those who lose out from the change (Jolls 1998). Even if reforms do not directly benefit everyone or all equally, there is at least the potential to make everyone somewhat better off through adjustments in work compensation or through reallocation of the resulting surplus using tax and transfer schemes. If the answer to the efficiency question is negative, however—that is, if family-friendly workplace reforms reduce net social welfare compared to existing arrangements—then someone must pay the costs. Proponents will then face an uphill battle in persuading governments and private actors that proposed reforms should be adopted.

Neoclassical economic theory carries a heavy presumption that existing work-place structures are efficient. Because arrangements that maximize net social wel-fare will generally emerge on their own under the pressure of free, competitive markets (including markets for labor), it follows that firms can be expected to adopt the most cost-effective arrangements on their own (Malloy 2002). This presump-tion leads to the conclusion that family-friendly reform—whether by private action or through government intervention—will move society away from the efficient ideal, which will impose costs on firms and society as a whole. This conclusion has both positive and normative implications. The notion that existing practices repre-sent the most efficient and "best of all possible worlds" bodes ill for any positive prediction that firms will spontaneously adopt family-friendly policies, as firms will avoid arrangements that will place them at a disadvantage relative to competitors. The prospect that easing burdens on families will cut into corporate profits also undermines the normative case in their favor by creating a potential conflict between firms' desire to help workers and the obligation to maximize profits for shareholders. For these reasons and others, the question of whether family-friendly reforms will prove socially efficient is of great consequence.

Given the valorization of efficiency within neoclassical economics, it is not sur-prising that law and economics scholars have generally been skeptical of family-friendly changes in workplace practices. Most critiques have focused attention on legal mandates such as family leave legislation. The thrust of the commentary so far has been that, although such mandates do not inevitably undermine efficiency, they will often do so, and they may also harm some groups they are designed to help (Jolls 2000; Alstott 2004; Ruhm 1998). Even economists who are willing to enter-tain the possibility that markets sometimes fail, or that the status quo can deviate from a perfectly efficient equilibrium, stress caution in implementing seemingly desirable programs. Because mandates are designed from the top down, there is no guarantee that a particular benefit will be efficient. And although family-friendly interventions might enhance overall well-being in some circumstances, regulatory measures generally impose out-of-pocket expenditures or losses on firms for which "someone must pay" (Sunstein 2001, 205, 237). Very often, it is the worker who pays: if labor markets operate on straightforward principles of supply and demand, expensive mandates will not result in a simple transfer of resources from firms (capital) to workers (labor). All or most of the out-of-pocket costs of accommodation will be passed on to the workers themselves in the form of lower wages or fewer jobs or both. If the mandates are efficient, some workers will come out ahead. If they are not efficient, many or all workers will lose.

This picture emerges from the work of Lawrence Summers (1989), who has analyzed the effects of legislated benefits, such as health insurance or a minimum wage, that go to workers as a whole (see also Jolls 2000). Summers showed that these types of mandates cause shifts in the supply and demand curves for labor. The magnitude and overall effect of the shifts on employment levels and pay de-pend on the relative value and costs of the mandated benefit. Although workers may end up being paid less, their net welfare will increase if the subjective value they place on the benefits exceeds the cost to the employer of providing them.

Christine Jolls (1998, 2000) has extended the Summers paradigm to the case where mandated benefits are directed to a discrete subcategory of workers. Unlike the "universal" benefits Summers (1989) analyzed, family-friendly mandates are available to or used mostly by women or mothers. The analysis is complicated by the fact that partial mandates will affect targeted employees differently from others. Jolls concluded that the effect of selective mandates on the beneficiary group depends not only on the relative cost and value of the mandate (as in the Summers model) but also on the extent to which employers are free to pass program costs selectively onto targeted workers by lowering their wages or by hiring fewer workers from that group. The "pass-through" potential will in turn be a function of the effectiveness of laws designed to protect targeted workers from this kind of treatment.

The concern is that businesses will respond by avoiding hiring workers from protected categories (such as women or mothers), by lowering those workers' compensation, by cutting back on other job benefits, or by shunting women into segregated job categories to avoid equal pay requirements.

In the case of family-friendly mandates, the pertinent protective rules are of two types: equal pay legislation and laws prohibiting sex discrimination in employment. If equal pay legislation is enforced effectively but antidiscrimination laws are not, employers seeking to offload the costs of selective mandates will tend to employ fewer targeted workers. If equal pay rules are actually avoidable (which occurs when the workforce is segregated by sex) but antidiscrimination legislation is effectively enforced, firms will tend to reduce the wages of the benefited group. When wage equality rules and prohibitions on group discrimination are both fully binding, then employers will be barred from reducing the wages or employment of the benefited group selectively. In that case, any pass-through costs will be spread among all employees and not just those who enjoy the mandate. Sometimes this will result in a net shift of resources from employees as a whole to the targeted group, which will produce a net gain for the latter group regardless of whether the mandate is efficient overall. (If it is not efficient, other workers may lose more than targeted workers gain.) Finally, if neither equal pay laws nor antidiscrimination laws are effectively enforced, then the Summers analysis allows for both wage and employment adjustments for the targeted group. Once again, whether that group is better off with the mandate will depend on the value of the mandate to the targeted group relative to its cost.

The Sommers/Jolls analysis is "partial equilibrium": both authors suspended the strong "best of all possible worlds" assumption that there can be no efficiency-enhancing role for government intervention in labor markets because an efficient state will already have been achieved through the force of competition. The analysis does not assume that all mutually beneficial deals will be struck or that any benefits with net positive value will already have been incorporated into the bargain between firms and workers through adjustments in pay. The possibility that regulation in the form of mandated benefits might enhance efficiency is left open, but not guaranteed. The analysis thus stresses the dangers as well as benefits. The concern is that businesses will respond by avoiding hiring workers from protected categories (such as women or mothers), by lowering those workers' compensation, by cutting back on other job benefits, or by shunting women into segregated job categories to avoid equal pay requirements. The results might well prove counterproductive: attempts to displace the costs of mandates, and the distributional shifts that result, may end up hurting the very persons the regulations are designed to help.

In the end, however, whether protected workers come out ahead depends critically on whether the total value of the mandated benefits to workers exceeds the cost to the employer. Unfortunately, there is no a priori guarantee that this pattern will prevail for mandated employment benefits. The Summers/Jolls framework offers no reason to assume that any particular benefit scheme will leave targeted employees better off. There is no reliable way to determine whether the value of any given family-friendly intervention will exceed its cost or whether costs and benefits will end up being distributed in a way that enhances beneficiaries' well-being. In sum, although the best-developed analysis proceeding from a neoclassical economics framework is not entirely dismissive of the case for accommodation mandates, it provides little cause for optimism about either the overall efficiency effects of such interventions or positive impact on the workers they seek to help.

This article argues that the Sommers/Jolls framework, although valid up to a point, is incomplete. Recent work in labor economics, sociology, and management, which is informed by empirical observation and insights of cognitive psychology, suggests that labor markets deviate in important ways from the neoclassical ideal and that participants in those markets do not always behave like ideal rational actors (Sunstein 2001; Bewley 1999; Jolls 1998). The market for employees is not like the market for widgets, and employers and employees do not always behave like simple price takers. The workplace is a realm of unique assets, sunk costs, ongoing relationships, and quasi-monopolistic bargaining. Above all, it is a sphere of complex, nuanced, and strategic interactions between workers and management and among workers themselves. All of these realities must be taken into account in analyzing the effects of family-friendly reforms.

Three principal features of workplace structures cause them to deviate from the neoclassical ideal. First, the workplace is a highly interactive setting. Workers and manager do not operate in isolation. Each participant's behavior affects the well-being of others who work in the same firm or even the same industry. Payoffs or rewards to workers depend on what other workers do and on the range of choices that firms offer. Any particular move will tend to set off responses in other workplace actors (Estlund 2003), and workers can choose to cooperate or compete with their fellows, with differential results for all.

---

*[M]ost [law] students would vote
to work fewer hours for less pay.*

Second, there are entrenched elements of *comparative* assessment in most workplace structures that neoclassical models fail to take into account. Workplace actors find it hard to resist making decisions about others based on relative position as opposed to absolute measures of quality and quantity (Frank 1999; Sunstein 2001). Managers tend to set expectations, develop assessments, and rank-order workers' performance based on how others perform, with pay and promotions fixed accordingly. Workers therefore come to see themselves as engaged in a competition with coemployees and to assign great importance to outperforming their peers. This tendency is exacerbated by the hierarchical structure of most workplaces, in which well-paid positions carrying authority and prestige are in short supply, and only a few can be promoted. The importance of relative position and relative productivity to employer decisions and worker strategy significantly complicates labor market dynamics in ways that bear importantly on the proper analysis of the effects of mandated benefits and of family-friendly reforms as a whole.

Finally, firms need to assess and monitor employee performance. If employers find it difficult and expensive to evaluate productivity and quality, they cannot effectively make decisions about hiring, firing, promotion, or discipline. Management also seeks to prevent workers from shirking and to motivate them to work harder or better. Where the information costs associated with direct supervision and evaluation are especially high—as with upper-level workers with complex and sophisticated outputs—firms tend to favor reward structures that spur worker performance despite imperfect supervision. Such structures include above-market "incentive" wages, whereby firms hire fewer employees but pay them more than their marginal product (Charny and Gulati 1998). This strategy is believed to reduce shirking by enhancing the worker's fear of losing a scarce, well-paid job. Firms may also adopt tournament-type work rules and structures, which can exaggerate the hierarchies already endemic to employment settings (Galanter and Palay 1991). Workers compete over a probationary period for scarce bonuses or prizes—such as promotion to partnership—that are based chiefly on easily measured outputs such as longer hours or greater volume of work. The steeply pyramidal reward structure means that all but a few winners are marginalized or fired (Wilkins and Gulati 1998; Sunstein 2001; Bognanno 2001; O'Keeffe et al. 1984).

These features create a workplace in which rewards or payoffs to employees and firms are the product of complex interactions among individuals jockeying for personal advantage. Rewards are not determined independently of how others perform. Rather, they are sensitive to group effects and to what others in the workplace choose to do. The same individual performance may yield very different outcomes, depending on the strategies pursued by fellow workers. Newer models of workplace dynamics—including schema drawn from game theory—capture these workplace realities better than the conventional neoclassical view. Game theoretic models are especially useful in helping to show how the payoffs employees can expect, and the choices they will make in light of those, vary with the strategies other workplace actors adopt.

Perhaps the most important contribution of game-theoretic analysis, however, is that it explains how management-worker interactions can get stuck in stable equilibria that fail to maximize overall social welfare. Unlike neoclassical economic analysis, game theory does not indulge the assumption that all economic arrangements, including the real-world workplace, exemplify the "best of all possible worlds." Game-theoretic models of economic interaction do not assume that ordinary competitive forces will always produce an efficient outcome in the long run or that efficiency will arise spontaneously. Rather, unlike the neoclassical model, game-theoretic approaches are centrally concerned with what neoclassicists would term market failure. By showing how perverse interactive effects might drive the workplace toward suboptimal equilibria, these paradigms provide a basis for challenging the assumption that existing workplace practices—especially those that are hostile to reconciling work with family responsibilities—are invariably optimal and efficient. This approach offers the best hope for developing an analytically rigorous explanation for why beneficial time/money trade-offs and other family-friendly workplace adjustments might not occur despite many workers' desire for them and willingness to pay for them. This explanation can help make the case for interventions that foster family-friendly change.

Interactive Models of Workplace Dynamics: The Rat Race

As already noted, many lawyers work in large group settings, or firms, in which problems of monitoring and quality control loom large. It is not surprising, then, that law firms tend to be run as "up-or-out" tournaments in which a few winners garner the top prize of a lucrative partnership, and many losers remain at the firm with lower pay and responsibility or are forced out altogether. This tournament structure notoriously gives rise to intense competitive pressures that lead lawyers to put in long hours on the job, with those at prestigious firms logging the longest workweeks. These pressures have increased over time: lawyers, like managerial and professional workers generally, have been logging more hours at work in recent years. There is evidence to suggest that lawyers, like some other professional workers, put in more hours than they would prefer (Landers, Rebitzer, and Taylor 1996; Reynolds 2003).

An informal poll the author has conducted at the University of Virginia and University of Pennsylvania Law Schools each year suggests that most students would vote to work fewer hours for less pay. But fledgling attorneys are not getting the deals they want. Students with some experience on the job market insist that the opportunity to make the desired trade-off simply is not available. Rather, a narrowly defined pattern is prescribed for all. The prestigious or "high-quality" law firms that make jobs available to graduates from elite law schools hire virtually all new associates at the same extremely high rate of pay. In exchange, firms expect associates to work hard and long.

Why can no one get what almost all these young lawyers say they want? The first impulse is to point to the increased costs for the firm required to change workplace practices. These increases potentially stem from many sources. A decision by the firm to discard tournament-type personnel systems for selecting workers (Landers, Rebitzer, and Taylor 1996) or to ignore surrogate signals for productivity such as long hours or "face time" (Spence 1973, 1974; Weiss 1995) adds to the expense of monitoring, motivating, and evaluating employees. Additional costs include the expense of hiring new workers to make up for work time lost (which includes legally mandated benefits of all kinds), the task of coordinating flexible and part-time work schedules, the tensions inherent in client adjustment to new routines, and the inefficiencies of a workforce consisting of less experienced employees. Although some of these dislocations can be expected to diminish over time with the establishment of new workplace conventions and practices, their costs still must be absorbed initially by companies choosing to innovate. As a practical matter, reforms will initially produce gains to employees at the firm's expense.

Nonetheless, conventional market theory suggests that firms could price in and recoup any increased costs from changing workplace practices by adjusting pay. Neoclassical economists must then explain why the full range of deals permitting fewer hours of work at lower pay is not offered. Indeed, neoclassical theory has difficulty explaining systematically why part-time work and other diverse options are not available more generally to all sectors of the workforce, as market forces should enable firms to price in, and then "claw back," extra operating costs by adjusting worker compensation accordingly (McCaffery 1993).

Why are there "missing markets" for job terms and schedules? Why might observed patterns of work get stuck in a few narrowly defined options that fail to satisfy expressed preferences and thus appear to reduce social welfare overall? One explanation makes use of Robert Frank's "rat race" paradigm (Frank and Cook 1995; Frank 1999). John Stuart Mill first described the forces that tend to generate a perverse pattern of increasing hours and intensity of work, and the point has been noted since by others (Folbre 2001; Sunstein 2001). On this scenario, employees may genuinely wish to limit hours at work to spend more time with their families, even at the sacrifice of some monetary compensation. But that goal may prove elusive. The problem is that individuals often feel impelled to work very long hours to avoid being placed at a competitive disadvantage relative to coworkers—a disadvantage that can have excessively costly, and even devastating, consequences. Signaling a willingness to work harder and longer helps a worker gain a competitive edge over others within the same workplace setting. The difficulties employers face in directly monitoring the quality of output in the modern workplace lead to dependence on signals and surrogates for quality, which enhances the importance of "face time" and reinforces workers' incentives to display dedication by putting in long uninterrupted hours on the job. Employers may encourage this response by limiting part-time and flexible options, by penalizing the use of those options, and by handsomely rewarding workers who "win the race."

As Frank (1999) has argued, however, this process is not necessarily efficient. It can be "good for one but bad for all." Although the rat race rewards the few workers who outflank their fellows, those benefits may be outweighed by the sum total of harm to most employees who work harder than they would if they could agree among themselves to "stop the race" and work more reasonable hours. The difficulties of coordinating individuals' interests impedes this process.

The dynamic of the resulting collective action problem stems from the independent pursuit of self-interest by discrete workplace actors. The rat race paradigm shows how all workers might be better off, and total social welfare enhanced, if self-interested action could somehow be suppressed and cooperation enforced. Some type of outside intervention, or the development of a stable and robust internal norm, would be necessary to force individual employees to relinquish their independent, self-serving strategies in favor of coordinated conduct that is collectively superior. Only then can the rat race be stopped and the surplus gains in well-being be realized and allocated.

To be sure, there is no a priori assurance that gains to employees from shutting down the rat race will exceed costs to firms (or to some employees who benefit excessively from the rat race). Even if the rat race immiserates most employees, halting it may sometimes detract from firm profits even more. The family-friendly workplace may not represent a more efficient result in every case because conditions may be such that workers are unwilling or unable to pay for the ideal workplace they desire. But this article proceeds from the assumption that this will not always happen and often will not be the case. By offering models that demonstrate how the family-friendly workplace might be efficient, it shows how firms may potentially benefit from revamping workplace practices to allow family-friendly routines to thrive.

Interactive Models of Workplace Dynamics: The Prisoner's Dilemma (PD)

The well-known PD game offers a way to model the dynamic that reduces the availability of benefits such as family leave and prestigious part-time work despite workers' avowed desire for them and willingness to accept lower compensation in exchange. The array of payoffs for strategies within the PD game are well known. As applied to the workplace, the PD can be played as a two-party game between workers (W1 and W2) with identical preferences to produce payoffs as follows:

W1, W2	Long	Short
Long	1, 1	5, 0
Short	0, 5	3, 3

If all workers cooperate in demanding from their firm some package of family-friendly benefits (including, perhaps, shorter hours as denominated by the "short" option), and all uniformly take advantage of those benefits, workers as a whole would be better off, enjoying a total of 6 units of payoff or well-being (3 + 3). Unfortunately, that cooperation is unlikely to occur spontaneously. The choice to cooperate in this context (by demanding and following a more reasonable short schedule) is not a rational strategy for *individual* employees. Assuming that firms will reward long hours and that workers cannot control or predict what coworkers will do, the overall expected payoff to W1 (or W2) is greater for working long hours: if W1 works long hours, his or her payoff is 1 when fellow worker W2 works long and 5 if W2 works short. If W1 works short hours, his or her payoffs are 0 and 3, respectively. Long hours are W1's dominant strategy (with highest expected payoff, assuming there is an equal chance that coworkers will choose long or short, and no gain from switching strategies). The same would be the case for W2. Because long is dominant for all players, universal cooperation (short) is not a "stable equilibrium." That is, it is not a state in which individual players do best to stick with their chosen strategy (Dixit and Skeath 1999). In the absence of some mechanism for coordinating choices and controlling what other workers will do, each individual does best overall by "defecting"—that is, by working longer hours—rather than by cooperating in trying to bring about a more family-friendly workplace. Long—which corresponds to the family-unfriendly option—is the sole equilibrium strategy in this game.

If the PD game accurately models payoffs for employees, the potential for the spontaneous emergence of a cooperative family-friendly equilibrium as the dominant workplace norm seems remote. Nonetheless, halting the race generates more units of well-being overall, so it would be in workers' collective interest to break out of the long/long equilibrium and work in a family-friendly setting.

Left out of this discussion so far, however, is a "third player" in the form of the employer firm itself. As already noted, family-friendly policies, whether efficient or not, often impose new out-of-pocket costs on firms. If costs exceed potential benefits to workers, companies can be expected to resist more flexible practices. But just because some family-friendly dislocations reduce firms' profits and make some employees worse off does not mean those policies are inefficient. The costs generated could well be less than the *total*, aggregate utility gains to employees who benefit from halting the rat race. If the reform scenario initially entails some expenditure of resources by employers, there is at least theoretically the potential for a net beneficial reallocation between firms and workers. If permitting a different trade-off of compensation for shorter hours and/or greater flexibility would produce a net gain overall, the expectation is that companies would assign enough costs to workers and arrogate enough benefits to themselves to make the adjustment worthwhile. In other words, companies would be expected to take measures to solve the PD and then reallocate the resulting surplus to compensate themselves for the costs of shifting to family-friendly policies. Employees should also be willing to negotiate a deal to allocate costs and benefits so everyone comes out ahead.

Even if family-friendly arrangements are efficient, however, firms may still resist innovating if they cannot find a way to share in the surplus generated by increased employee well-being. Why might the optimal reallocation not be realized? To illustrate the problem, assume that a firm shifts to a family-friendly work schedule that includes many features to facilitate better work-family balance. Worker compensation is at first adjusted straightforwardly to reflect reduced hours worked by employees who take time off to care for their families. There is no change in effective hourly rate. The "before" and "after" payoffs to firms (F) and workers (W), as represented by the shift from a conventional (long/long) to a family-friendly (short/short) workplace produces a set of payoff possibilities something like this:

F, W	Long	Short
Long	4, 2	0, 0
Short	0, 0	3, 5

For these payoffs, the change from long to short is efficient: a total of 8 units (3 + 5) is generated when employers play the short workplace strategy and workers follow suit, whereas everyone working on a long schedule generates a total of 6 units (4 + 2). (If the players mismatch so that the firm offers long and the workers offer short, it is assumed that no deal is struck: workers refuse to work on the terms offered or the firm refuses to offer the terms desired.) But on the short/short scenario in this array, workers gain (a payoff of 5 is more than 2) and the firm loses (3 is less than 4). The firm will then resist the shift from long/long to short/short, since it stands to lose 1 unit. It will resist, that is, *unless* it can change the game's payoff array by bargaining further with employees to capture more of the net gain for itself. A deal that allowed the firm to recoup more of the costs of family-friendly adjustments would require workers to agree to a pay cut that would effectively reduce their hourly rate. The result might be as follows:

F, W	Long	Short
Long	4, 2	0, 0
Short	0, 0	5, 3

This time, the short/short option is Pareto-superior to long/long: everyone gains. The pattern is now one of a simple coordination game. Assuming this picture is at least potentially valid, what are the implications? If transaction costs are negligible, this deal should be struck and parties should end up in the right lower box—that is, the workplace should move to shorter hours.

This analysis suggests that, even if workers are initially playing a PD game among themselves, management ought to step in and "solve" the dilemma by halting the self-seeking race for advantage. If halting the arms race among workers could realize surplus to be divided between workers and firms, employers should take steps to reduce the dysfunctional competition among workers that detracts from overall well-being. That step would appear to be within the firm's power: after all, the PD payoff structure, although reflective in part of workers' intrinsic preferences, is ultimately determined by the external rewards allocated by firm management. These would appear to be within the firms' effective control. Why do firms not effect a solution by changing those rewards? Why is an optimal deal struck so seldom?

The answer must look to why those in authority within firms feel impelled to set up and maintain the rat race. Understanding the obstacles to family-friendly reform will require understanding the structural forces that lead firms to create and maintain the competitive structures and compensation schemes that reward family-unfriendly behavior. As already suggested, the benefits of relying on surrogate signals for productivity, incentive wage structures, and tournament reward systems provide a powerful impetus for sticking with current arrangements. Eliminating these structures will introduce disruption and uncertainty and will impose large initial costs on firms. Those costs will be more immediate and salient than the remote, speculative prospect of future gains that could be realized by adopting a new regime.

Additional, and formidable, factors impede changes in the way firms do business. These include the problem of valuing nonmonetary benefits and pricing them accordingly, legal obstacles to reallocation of costs and benefits of workplace reform through compensation adjustments that are tailored to individual need (Wax 2003), the difficulties (cognitive and otherwise) of making a transition to new workplace structures, the conflicts of interest among employees with different desires for family-friendly accommodations, the inherent intransigence of customary workplace expectations (Wax 2003), and the existence of coordination problems among firms that create the potential for adverse selection. These factors undermine the employer's willingness or ability to achieve an optimal result.

The difficulty of assigning value to benefits is a particularly thorny impediment to bargaining over the reallocation of costs and resources in the face of new workplace routines. The costs of nonmonetary benefits or flexible working conditions are very difficult to measure, and their value to workers is hard to assess. The problem is exacerbated by diverse preferences. Not all workers attach the same value to particular workplace features. Because employees vary in their preferences, employers will have a hard time coming up with offers that satisfy everyone. Employee diversity creates a collective action problem. Because workers will have trouble agreeing among themselves on the principles and practice of fair allocation, it will be difficult for them to present a united front in bargaining. Employers will be tempted to assign the costs of change to those who take advantage of family-friendly features, and workers who are less interested in flexibility will resist paying for them. Workers who benefit from flexible conditions will seek to offload the costs to other workers, both from self-interest and on the grounds that cost spreading will avoid the development of a "mommy track" and that subsidies for caretakers are right and fair. A self-serving bias will lead all workers to underestimate the value they place on family-friendly reforms. A lack of reliable information about firm costs and employee preferences will impede agreement by generating mistrust and second-guessing.

Several factors may lead workers to resist employer efforts accurately to "price in" the costs of change through reductions in pay. As noted, even if family-friendly reforms end up generating enough gains to increase total well-being overall, firms might still need to recoup the increased out-of-pocket expenditures from implementing reforms by asking workers to accept an effective reduction in the hourly rate that prevailed under the old-model workplace regime. The front-loading of firm expenditures, coupled with the stickiness of compensation schedules, may cause workers to fear they will be undercompensated in the long run. Workers may also seek assurances of opportunities for advancement and other nonmonetary benefits usually associated with winning the rat race. It is an open question whether these assurances could be made in many cases. In the absence of binding guarantees, workers who seek reform may balk at their reduced pay, even if their compensation is fairly priced. Moreover, if employees tend to "anchor" in preexisting compensation schedules, this may cause resistance to pay adjustments that actually reflect the costs of reform. Faced with a significant decline in rate of pay, even employees who set great store by family-friendly features may conclude that reform is undesirable. All these difficulties of valuation, coordination, and allocation may lead to an overemphasis on monetary compensation to the exclusion of other valued benefits. The outcome is less family-friendly reform than is optimal.

Legal mandates such as equal pay and nondiscrimination requirements complicate the situation even further. As noted by Jolls (2000), equal pay laws may make it difficult for some employers (and especially those who compensate using an hourly rate) selectively to reduce pay for some groups (such as women) to reflect the costs of incorporating more flexible structures. Employers must either spread the costs among all workers by reducing pay or decreasing hiring—with an effective subsidy to those who most benefit from flexibility or reduced hours—or absorb some of the costs through reduced profits, or pass them on through higher consumer prices. By impeding employers' freedom to recoup surplus shares or allocate costs of family-friendly changes, laws that prevent employers from selectively passing the costs of workplace reform onto protected groups through lower pay sap firms' willingness to move toward efficient arrangements. Moreover, if legal mandates require employers to extract surplus from the entire group (with equal pay requirements in effect serving as a coordinating device to enforce a uniform deal for everyone), employees with weaker preferences for family-friendly benefits will be less enthusiastic about change. In the absence of a consensus about whether making it easier for people—and especially mothers—to combine work and family should be "everyone's problem," this may undermine political support for reform.

Firms may resist offering a choice of family-friendly benefits because these create the potential for an adverse selection of workers.

Even if all these obstacles could be addressed, other puzzles of implementation would need to be solved. It is unclear how companies could handle all the practical issues raised by trying to reduce dysfunctional competition among employees. Family-friendly proponents attack structures of authority and advancement that reward the few employees who work hardest and longest. As already noted, the "up-or-out" convention that prevails at elite law firms, which bars part-time lawyers or those taking time off to raise children from the partnership track altogether (Noonan and Corcoran 2004 [this volume]), is the exemplar of this structure. But critiques will not go very far without a well-developed picture of what the workplace would look like if the offending features were removed. One possibility is to abolish the partnership track altogether and decree equality of status for all workers. Egalitarian workplaces, however, raise many practical and motivational difficulties and are rare. Alternatively, the "winner-take-all" or tournament reward structure could be replaced with a hierarchy that gears advancement to a uniform yardstick. What is needed is something like a measure of quality of output per unit of time worked. Work experience could also be factored, perhaps by looking at total duration of work experience without regard to interruptions. An assessment of workers on the basis of quality of output normalized to actual time spent working, regardless of how that time was scheduled, would come close to realizing the goal of a system that would not penalize persons who work at a reduced pace or intensity to attend to family matters. Part-time or flex-time workers would at least remain in the running for all potential bonuses, promotions, and positions of authority and responsibility. Employees would no longer be required to neglect their families as the absolute price of success.

How realistic is this vision? The reformist picture implicitly rests on the assumption that the structures that contribute so decisively to the marginalization of people with family responsibilities are imposed from above. Management deliberately sets terms that force employees to run an arms race or at least suffers that race to persist. It follows that these workplace structures are optional, and—ultimately— dispensable at the firm's discretion.

On closer scrutiny, however, it is not clear that management can control destructive competition so easily. Structures and practices that cause dysfunctional equilibria to emerge, such as the existence of a pyramidal hierarchy of authority, promotion, and escalating rewards, may be inherent in the modern workplace itself and thus difficult to extirpate. It is not obvious which rules of employee assessment, evaluation, and reward are best suited to minimizing objectionable patterns and whether the rules are feasible in the long run. Feminist critics suggest that undesirable marginalization could be minimized if workers were not penalized for working short, interrupted, irregular schedules rather than long, regular, continuous periods. As already suggested, this would require moving toward a pro-rata system that assesses workers based on quality or output per unit time and that discounts cumulative or experiential measures like continuous time on the job, sum total output, or overall output compared to others. But this shift may be very hard to accomplish. Measuring or comparing productivity is not easy where work patterns vary even modestly and work output is more complex than producing simple, divisible, identical units. Today, all but a tiny fraction of unskilled jobs entail complex tasks and discretion. Necessarily, then, assessing quality of work normalized to time spent working is administratively complicated and often infeasible. Even on the same job, employees working longer hours without interruption are not easily compared to those working fewer hours with interruptions. The comparison is even harder across jobs.

The limitations inherent in comparing incommensurable elements of performance suggest that firms interested in improving family-friendliness may be forced to employ crude mechanisms for constraining workers from advancing their own self-interest at group expense. These mechanisms may include moving all employees to one uniform set of expectations for duration and pace of work, limiting work hours, or affirmatively penalizing failure to take advantage of family-friendly policies. These possibilities have drawbacks. By forcing workers with diverse preferences into uniform rules, they undermine the very flexibility and accommodation that family-friendly change seeks to achieve. Yet there may be no other practical way to solve the collective action problem that leads to dysfunctional workplace practices.

Finally, a key impediment to potentially efficient family-friendly reform can be traced to competitive interactions among firms. Even if halting the rat race by moving to more family-friendly policies would be more efficient, interfirm competition may make firms reluctant to introduce such reforms. Indeed, competition among firms can explain how a dysfunctional equilibrium might arise even if firms benefit *directly*—that is, without extracting bargaining concessions from employees—from the shift to more reasonable and family-friendly terms of employment. The discussion so far has emphasized the costs to firms of introducing family-friendly reforms—costs that must be recouped through lower pay for employees. But there are also potential benefits. These include reducing adverse employee turnover, minimizing worker burnout, fostering worker loyalty to the firm, and generating a competitive advantage in recruiting among a larger pool of potential workers. Where such innovations serve corporate interests and profitability relative to more rigid workplace conditions, the expectation is that firms would adopt them spontaneously. But rat-race or game-theoretic type approaches help explain why, even under this "best-case" scenario, change might not occur.

Firms may resist offering a choice of family-friendly benefits because these create the potential for an adverse selection of workers. That potential threatens to place some companies at a competitive disadvantage by saddling them with a disproportionate number of more costly employees. As already suggested, the payoff arrays listed above are too simple in assuming that employees are similar in their desire to trade money for better working conditions. Even if most full-time employees would prefer a more family-friendly mix, workers still differ significantly in the strength of their desire for family-friendliness at work. Although, by hypothesis, firms can come out ahead by adopting family-friendly structures and bargaining with employees to share benefits and costs, the availability and size of the benefits to bargain over depend critically on how much employees value family-friendly terms, how much firms must spend to implement the desired changes, and whether firms can fully price in the costs. Some firms may attempt to reduce their short-term transaction costs—and enhance their profits—by catering to workers who do not seek or require expensive family-friendly features, are more willing than most to work long hours with single-minded devotion, and prefer to be rewarded with higher pay. In the absence of some mechanism for forcing all firms to offer the same family-friendly package, workers with a greater need or desire for family-friendly benefits will gravitate toward firms that offer more generous terms, potentially driving up those companies' out-of-pocket costs relative to others firms. If the segmentation is sufficiently pronounced, the costs to companies that become magnets for those seeking family-friendly features might become great enough to overwhelm even the direct benefits that accrue from offering the family-friendly option. The competitive disadvantage could be eliminated if companies could perfectly recoup costs from workers. But for the reasons already suggested, that scenario is unlikely. This means that family-friendly companies will be less profitable than more conventional competitors, leading them to shun most family-friendly innovations. The ultimate equilibrium outcome that results may be worse for everyone than the cooperative alternative. But there is no obvious way to enforce cooperation.

A variation on the theme of interfirm competition is presented when firms compete with others to signal their superiority and desirability to potential employees. Corporate employers vie with each other for good workers. As noted, an employee's willingness to compete with other job holders for advantage may function as an important indicator of quality and seriousness. Firms may therefore feel impelled to demand long hours not only as a way to elicit that valuable signal from workers but also to reassure all job candidates about the quality of the workplace and their coworkers. That is, traditional practices may serve as a way for firms to advertise the quality of their workforce to current and prospective workers. That does not mean that demanding long hours will necessarily optimize profits for the firm. Employees may function more effectively, and firms may experience less turnover, when work schedules are more flexible and working hours are more reasonable. But even if all firms might benefit by adopting more humane working conditions, none will do so for fear of losing a competitive edge in the scramble for prestige and well-qualified personnel. Breaking out of this equilibrium will require coordination across firms. In the absence of effective mechanisms for such coordination, companies may persist in suboptimal behavior, including making excessive demands on workers, to maintain the firm's position as compared with competitors.

Alternative Models of Workplace Practices: Employee Interaction as a "Stag Hunt" or Coordination Game

The PD game presents only one possible framework for understanding modern workplace dynamics. Another variation on the theme, involving somewhat different payoffs for workers, is modeled on the so-called "stag hunt" (SH) game (Dixit and Skeath 1999; Rasmusen 1989). The SH model arguably has several advantages over the PD game as a basis for game-theoretic analysis of the problem of family-friendly workplace reform: it potentially provides a more nuanced and more realistic picture of the payoffs to employees from choosing "ideal worker" as opposed to family-friendly worker options. As an added advantage, it has less pessimistic and more interesting implications for spontaneous order in developing and stabilizing a family-friendly workplace equilibrium. The possibility that a stable, self-sustaining, family-friendly norm could emerge in this game potentially lends itself to exploration through dynamic computer simulations. Those simulations may help identify workplace conditions that are most conducive to achieving efficient results.

A payoff array modeled on a simplified SH as played between two workers (W1 and W2) with identical preferences is represented as follows:

W1, W2	Long	Short
Long	2, 2	3, 0
Short	0, 3	4, 4

In the SH array, the individual's payoff is greatest (4) when both players cooperate to produce the family-friendly arrangement (short/short). That arrangement is also the most efficient, with the highest total payoff (8) overall. This pattern stands in contrast to the PD game discussed above, in which the individual maximizes his or her utility by "besting" another player in a mismatch (long/short or short/long). In the PD game, however, the individually optimal strategy is *not* the one that produces the highest utility payoff overall. As with the PD game, a mismatch of strategies in the SH situation is also less efficient, with the total social utility lower than when workers cooperate.

The SH payoff pattern—in which the individually optimal strategy is also the most efficient overall—may better reflect the real-world priorities of most ordinary workers. The payoffs to individual players in the SH array represent the vectoral sum of several components of utility, including (positive) external rewards conferred by the firm (pay, benefits, opportunities for promotion), intrinsic consumption value of work, and (negative) opportunity or substitution costs that reflect the worker's loss from time away from family members and family life. Although employees who outcompete others by working longer or harder than their fellows—a position corresponding to the "topside" or "long" position in an hours mismatch—may garner large rewards in the workplace, the personal costs incurred to attain such a position will significantly undermine the net payoffs enjoyed. That is, the disutility of working long hours under rigid conditions—and the positive utility from working shorter hours under more family-friendly conditions—will be large enough to overwhelm the positive payoff from gaining a competitive advantage over others. Workers concerned with caring for their families can be expected to enjoy higher net utility from working reasonable hours (as long as others do also) than from working longer hours than coworkers. Despite the large external advantages gained in the latter situation, intrinsic and family-centered costs of working unreasonably hard seriously detract from the net benefits workers enjoy under those conditions. In other words, for many workers, outcompeting fellow workers just is not as rewarding overall as being part of a coordinated, family-centered workplace. The SH array—but not the PD array—reflects that preference profile. (The PD payoffs, in contrast to those under the SH array, assume that outcompeting fellow workers provides larger rewards for individuals overall than enjoying the benefits of a cooperative, family-friendly setting.)

Predicting the equilibrium strategies that emerge from repeated rounds of the SH game is a more complex exercise than for the PD game. Unlike in the PD game, no one strategy dominates for all players. Assuming others' moves cannot be predicted or controlled, there is no single "best" strategy that will maximize each SH player's average expected payoffs overall. In game theory, this means that there are two Nash equilibria in the two-person SH game. Even though one combination is Pareto-superior (short/short), the move that is best for an individual player depends on what the other player chooses. If both players work short, no player can improve his or her situation by working long. If both play long, neither can do better by switching unilaterally to short. When the game is generalized to include many players exposed to repeated rounds of interaction, either of two possible norms or equilibrium patterns—short/short and long/long—might emerge over time.

In a recent article, Mahoney and Sanchirico (2001) have analyzed the dynamics of the SH game in situations that match many players through multiple rounds of play. The authors demonstrate that the population will quickly converge on one or another equilibrium: short/short or long/long. The dominant equilibrium depends on the initial mix of strategies (that is, how many players in the population start out playing long or short), and on how often and under what conditions workers change their strategies. If a small number of workers is chosen to "reoptimize" or "mutate" on each round by reassessing their strategy, either norm may be "tipped" to the other.

The most important insight of the authors' analysis is that, paradoxically, the more efficient short/short norm is easier to "tip" through low-level mutations than the less rewarding long/long equilibrium. Relatively fewer long-hours workers must be introduced into a population stabilized to the short/short equilibrium to effect a transition to long/long. In contrast, considerably more short-hours workers are needed to cause a group stabilized to long/long to shift over to short/short. This disparity is traceable to the differential "downside risk" that players suffer from a mismatch. This point can be seen by considering the consequences for players if the population has stabilized to one or the other cooperative norm. In the iterated game protocol, a player confronting some random number of players with the opposite strategy (the mismatch situation), periodically faces a choice: whether to continue the current strategy or switch course. If the population has stabilized to the efficient short/short norm, a player who encounters a renegade long-hours worker stands to lose utility by continuing to play short. That loss can be mitigated by abandoning that strategy and switching to long. (A short worker playing against a long worker obtains a payoff of 0. That payoff can be increased to 2 units if that worker switches to long, for a net gain of 2 units.) In contrast, if the population has stabilized at long/long, a long player who suddenly encounters a renegade short player will obtain a payoff of 3 (which is higher than his previous payoff of 2), but can increase his payoff to 4 if he abandons his long strategy and switches to short, for a net gain of 1 unit. This calculation shows that short players who encounter long players suffer a greater net loss from staying with their current, mismatched strategy than long players who encounter short players. The larger "mismatch risk" suffered by short players operating within a dominant short/short norm drives them to abandon their previous strategy—and the dominant norm—more readily than long players will abandon a dominant long/long norm. Although the precise "tipping point" depends on the actual size of payoffs in the array, the threshold is lower for the efficient short/short norm than for the less efficient long/long equilibrium.

This result has interesting implications for the problem of workplace reform. The dynamics of the multiround SH model, as opposed to a multiround PD game, offer some initial reason for optimism: the family-friendly, or short/short, combination at least represents one potential equilibrium outcome for the SH model, whereas the PD game lacks such an equilibrium altogether. Mahoney and Sanchirico's (2001) analysis suggests, however, that a suboptimal long/long norm will predominate in most venues where the game is played.

The analysis implies that family-friendly conditions are best achieved when firms consist of like-minded employees who place a similar value on workplace accommodation.

The SH payoff array provides the model for an important workplace reality: despite the potential for everyone being better off under a uniformly family-friendly regime, the efficient equilibrium is hard to achieve and maintain. That is because the risk of being "mismatched" to those who work longer carries great costs, and besting others in the workplace by acting more like an ideal worker still confers some advantages. As Mahoney and Sanchirico (2001, 2048) explain, "The possibility that evolutionary processes will select for the inefficient norm is driven in part by the risk to the efficient actor of encountering others not similarly disposed." Uncertainty about fellow workers' choices, preferences, and intentions, and lack of control over what workers and managers will do, all contribute to a pattern that leaves everyone less well off than if more information could be obtained or choices could be effectively coordinated.

The Mahoney and Sanchirico (2001) analysis provides a stark illustration of how individual workers' independent pursuit of their own self-interest does not always produce the most efficient workplace arrangements. Where payoffs are interdependent, suboptimal patterns may dominate and resist change or reform from within. Moreover—and most significantly for the purposes here—this result is not inconsistent with most workers' genuinely valuing a more family-friendly work-family balance than currently prevails.

Assuming that the SH model is basically valid, might it be possible to "manage" the lack of predictability and information, or to minimize the mismatch risk, to enhance the emergence and persistence of a family-friendly equilibrium? Recent work in evolutionary game theory points the way to some conditions in which, in the words of Mahoney and Sanchirico (2001, 2049), "Evolution will select for the efficient strategy even when the strategy's mismatch risk outweighs its efficiency advantage." The authors' analysis suggests that the stability of the fragile but efficient norm in a coordination game modeled on SH depends on players' ability to associate almost exclusively with those willing to conform to the efficient norm. This in turn depends on similar players being able to find and identify one another, isolate themselves from those who reject the dominant convention, or flee at low cost to more congenial workplace settings. In effect, the group must somehow protect itself from "mutations" from within and from nonconforming interlopers from without. Populations of persistent cooperators must be able to come together, discourage or quell nonconformist "workaholics," expel renegades, and screen out untrustworthy intruders. That is most likely to happen when the costs of group separation are low, there are no significant size effects, and individuals can know what strategies will be adopted by players "at all locations." (Mahoney and Sanchirico 2001, 2049).

The analysis implies that family-friendly conditions are best achieved when firms consist of like-minded employees who place a similar value on workplace accommodation. At the very least, the possession of reliable information about fellow workers' preferences and plans may be essential to the stability of family-friendly work practices. These requirements are exacting and unlikely to be perfectly achieved in any real-world setting. It is difficult to determine which workers are likely to cooperate with shorter hours and which ones are most likely to defect to longer hours. Even if that information problem could be solved, excluding competitive players from the workplace under current conditions and conventions may not be feasible. Refusing to hire workers because they have the "wrong" preference set or express willingness to work hard might render a firm vulnerable to charges of discrimination. And even if workers who profess similar preferences initially join forces to establish a family-friendly firm, the agreement to cooperate in adhering to the desired norm is always vulnerable to breakdown and subversion. A firm that needs to expand must constantly introduce fresh players. This impedes quality control because it is more difficult to detect and block the entry of unfamiliar applicants with preferences and intentions not matching the group. Even if the firm does not grow, normal attrition and turnover require the hiring of new employees, who must be assessed for their reliability and commitment to group conventions. Existing employees also may pose a threat over time as their tastes and preferences evolve. Or they may be tempted by the short-term rewards of competing with, and gaining an advantage over, fellow workers. Moreover, the firm may be vulnerable to invasion by an undesirable "third type" of player—workers who believe that a more relaxed family-friendly setting offers the best "cover" for shirking on quality and productivity.

An employment contract that fixes family-friendly terms of employment and punishes deviation offers, at best, an imperfect solution to the coordination problem. Such a contract would either be too general to anticipate all circumstances, resolve all disputes, and suppress all potentially destructive variations or too rigid to respond to changing conditions and meet the very needs for flexibility that family-oriented workers desire. Moreover, the contract does not enforce itself. Rather, workers must be willing to impose the norm against potential violators. But enforcement is costly and creates a public good that is ripe for free-riding by those who want to enjoy the benefits of the convention without bearing the costs. The costs of enforcing cooperative norms in such situations—whether through contract or otherwise—creates a fresh coordination problem that is not easily resolved (Kameda, Masanori, and Hastie 2003; Sanchirico and Mahoney 2003).

These considerations make it difficult to achieve conditions that maintain the efficient short-hours regime. Indeed, the situation may be more constrained than the model above suggests because workers who desire more work-family balance are not identical in their preferences. Even if most workers would on average prefer to move closer to the family-friendly model, and even if most tastes are more consistent with the SH than the PD payoff values, some will have a stronger interest than others in monetary rewards and less interest in sacrificing earnings for time or flexibility. The array below illustrates the possible payoff structure in a two-person SH game between a person with a weaker preference for family-friendly features ("marathon worker" [MW]) and one with a stronger preference ("balanced worker" [BW]):

MW, BW	Long	Short
Long	3, 2	4, 0
Short	–1, 3	5, 6

Differential tastes produce asymmetric payoffs and disparate "mismatch risks" for row and column players in the game (Peyton-Young 1998). As is characteristic of the SH game, the short/short norm provides the highest absolute payoff for each individual player as well as the most utility overall. However, the payoffs of each strategic combination differ for each player. Because MW places less value on working shorter hours at the cost of foregone earnings than BW, MW enjoys less utility (5) than BW (6) from efficient cooperation. The mismatch payoffs and risks will also differ, with the mismatch risk higher for MW than BW. Because MW minds working longer hours less and values monetary rewards more, and because BW suffers more from working longer hours despite higher earnings, MW will enjoy a relatively higher payoff (4) than BW (3) from "besting" fellow workers in a mismatch. Morever, MW stands to gain more than BW from abandoning the efficient norm if caught on the downside of a mismatch. An MW worker playing short who encounters a BW worker who has adopted the long strategy earns –1, which increases to 3 if MW switches to long, for a net gain of 4. In contrast, a BW worker playing short who is matched to a MW worker playing long earns 0, which increases to 2 if BW abandons the short position and switches to long. This pattern should make MW more likely than BW to abandon the efficient short/short norm in the face of fellow worker defections or "mutations." The analysis suggests that the ease of tipping away from the efficient short/short norm will be a complex function of the proportion of MW and BW workers in the mix as well as the payoff array values for each. In general, more MW workers in the population will cause faster tipping to the family-unfriendly norm. Beyond that, understanding of the workings of firms populated by workers with diverse preferences and the dynamics that will emerge from worker interactions in these settings can only be gained by conducting computer simulations of rounds of repeated play. Precedent exists for such computer simulations as applied to other dynamic social conditions (Epstein and

Axtell 1996). That method offers promise for a more systematic approach to the problem of stabilizing family-friendly conditions in diverse workplace settings.

Conclusion

The massive influx of women into the workplace in recent years has generated a call for workplace reform and governmental regulations designed to make jobs easier to combine with family responsibilities. Economists and law and economics scholars have criticized proposed and existing legislated mandates, such as family leave and job protection for parents, as inefficient and counterproductive. Critics of these innovations predict that businesses will respond by avoiding hiring mothers, by lowering women's compensation, by cutting back on other job benefits, and by shunting women into segregated job categories to avoid equal pay requirements. The results will be perverse: mandates will end up hurting the very persons the regulations are designed to help.

The prediction that the benefits of family-friendly accommodations will be wiped out by costs imposed on intended beneficiaries rests on a key assumption: that family-friendly reforms will prove costly and inefficient for firms and, by implication, for society as a whole. This article uses game-theoretic models to challenge the assumption that existing workplace practices—especially those that make it hard to combine work with family responsibilities—are invariably optimal and efficient. These models are useful in shedding light on how management-employee interactions can get stuck in stable equilibria that fail to maximize social welfare compared to possible alternative arrangements. Because existing workplace practices may not always represent the "best" result that can be achieved for some or all parties, disturbing or modifying dominant practices may sometimes be desirable. Some firms could be made better off if they gave employees more of what they claim to want. The challenge is to figure out how to accomplish that goal in ways that can be sustained.

The organizational status quo can be disturbed from the outside by governmental regulation or intervention. Change can come from within organizations through directives from management or via the evolution of spontaneous order. If the payoffs to workers from cooperating to produce a more family-friendly workplace resemble the SH array, not only will family-friendly workplace reforms advance overall efficiency, but they would potentially be self-sustaining. There are weighty impediments, however, to the spontaneous emergence and persistence of such an equilibrium. Game-theoretic modeling suggests that, without either firm direction by management or self-selection by workers with similar preferences, family-friendly norms will quickly erode. Turnover inevitably exposes firms to new employees with diverse preferences, which tends to destabilize family-friendly norms. Although more work needs to be done to determine which conditions might be most conducive to family-friendly workplace reforms, showing how family-friendly changes need not inevitably operate to undermine efficiency or compromise corporate interests is an important first step in making the case for change.

References

Alstott, Anne L. 2004. *No exit: What parents owe their children and what society owes parents*. New York: Oxford University Press.

Bewley, Truman. 1999. *Why wages don't fall during a recession*. Cambridge, MA: Harvard University Press.

Bognanno, Michael. 2001. Corporate tournaments. *Journal of Labor Economics* 19:290-315.

Burggraf, Shirley. 1997. *The feminine economy and economic man: Reviving the role of family in the post-industrial age*. Reading, MA: Addison-Wesley.

Charny, David, and G. Mitu Gulati. 1998. Efficiency wages, tournaments and discrimination: A theory of employment discrimination law for "high-level" jobs. *Harvard Civil Rights and Civil Liberties Law Review* 33:68-72.

Crittenden, Anne. 2001. *The price of motherhood: Why the most important job in the world is still the least valued*. New York: Metropolitan Books.

Dixit, Avinash K., and Susan Skeath. 1999. *Games of strategy*. New York: Norton.

Epstein, Cynthia Fuchs, Carroll Seon, Bonnie Oglensky, and Robert Saute. 1999. *The part-time paradox: Time norms, professional lives, family, and gender*. New York: Routledge.

Epstein, Joshua, and Robert Axtell. 1996. *Growing artificial societies: Social science from the bottom up*. Washington, DC: Brookings Institution.

Estlund, Cynthia. 2003. *Working together: How workplace bonds strengthen a diverse democracy*. Oxford: Oxford University Press.

Fineman, Martha Albertson. 2004. *The autonomy myth: A theory of dependency*. New York: New Press.

Folbre, Nancy. 2001. *The invisible heart: Economics and family values*. New York: New Press.

Frank, Robert. 1999. *Luxury fever: Why money fails to satisfy in an era of excess*. New York: Free Press.

Frank, Robert, and Philip Cook. 1995. *The winner-take-all society: How more and more Americans compete for ever fewer and bigger prizes, encouraging economic waste, income inequality, and an impoverished cultural life*. New York: Free Press.

Galanter, Marc, and Thomas Palay. 1991. *Tournaments of lawyers: The transformation of the big law firm*. Chicago: University of Chicago Press.

Hochschild, Arlie. 1989. *The second shift: Working parents and the revolution at home*. New York: Viking.

———. 1997. *The time bind: When work becomes home and home becomes work*. New York: Metropolitan Books.

Jacobs, Jerry A., and Kathleen Gerson. 2004. *The time divide: Work, family, and gender inequality*. Cambridge, MA: Harvard University Press.

Jolls, Christine. 1998. Behavioral economics analysis of redistributive legal rules. *Vanderbilt Law Review* 51:1653-77.

———. 2000. Accommodation mandates. *Stanford Law Review* 53:223-306.

Kameda, R., T. Masanori, and R. Hastie. 2003. The logic of social sharing: An evolutionary game analysis of adaptive norm development. *Personality and Social Psychology Review* 7:2-19.

Landers, Renee M., James Rebitzer, and Lowell Taylor. 1996. Rat race redux: Adverse selection in the determination of work hours in law firms. *American Economic Review* 86:329-48.

Mahoney, Paul, and Chris Sanchirico. 2001. Competing norms and social evolution: Is the fittest norm efficient? *University of Pennsylvania Law Review* 149:2027-62.

Malloy, Thomas. 2002. Regulating by incentives: Myths, models, and micromarkets. *Texas Law Review* 80:531-605.

Margalioth, Yoram. 2003. The many faces of mandates: Beyond traditional accommodation mandates and other classic cases. *San Diego Law Review* 40:645-700.

McCaffery, Edward. 1993. Slouching towards equality: Gender discrimination, market efficiency, and social change. *Yale Law Journal* 103:595-675.

Noonan, Mary C., and Mary E. Corcoran. 2004. The mommy track and law firm partnership: Temporary delay or dead end? *Annals of the American Society of Political and Social Science* 596:130-150.

O'Keeffe, Mary, W. Kip Viscusi, and Richard Zeckhauser. 1984. Economic contests: Comparative reward schemes. *Journal of Labor Economics* 2:27-56.

Peyton-Young, H. 1998. *Individual strategy and social structure: An evolutionary theory of institutions.* Princeton, NJ: Princeton University Press.

Rasmusen, Eric. 1989. *Games and information: An introduction to game theory.* Oxford, UK: Basil Blackwell.

Reynolds, Jeremy. 2003. You can't always get the hours you want: Mismatches between actual and preferred work hours in the U.S. *Social Forces* 81:1171-97.

Ruhm, Christopher. 1998. The economic consequences of parental leave mandates: Lessons from Europe. *Quarterly Journal of Economics* 113:285-317.

Sanchirico, Chris, and Paul Mahoney. 2003. Norms, repeated games, and the role for law. *California Law Review* 91:1281.

Spence, Michael. 1973. Job market signaling. *Quarterly Journal of Economics* 87:355-74.

———. 1974. *Market signaling: Informational transfer in hiring and related screening processes.* Cambridge, MA: Harvard University Press.

Summers, Lawrence. 1989. Some simple economics of mandated benefits. *American Economic Review, Papers & Proceedings* 79:177-83.

Sunstein, Cass. 2001. Human behavior and the law of work. *Virginia Law Review* 87:205-76.

Wax, Amy L. 1999a. Caring enough: Sex roles, work, and taxing women. *Villanova Law Review* 44:495-523.

———. 1999b. Is there a caring crisis? A review of Shirley Burggraf's, *The feminine economy and economic man. Yale Journal on Regulation* 16:327-58.

———. 2003. Disability, reciprocity, and "real efficiency": A unified approach. *William and Mary Law Review* 44:1421-52.

Weiss, Andrew. 1995. Human capital vs. signalling explanations of wages. *Journal of Economic Perspectives* 9:133-54.

Wilkins, David, and G. Mitu Gulati. 1998. Reconceiving the tournament of lawyers. *Virginia Law Review* 84:1581-681.

Williams, Joan. 2000. *Unbending gender: Why family and work conflict and what to do about it.* New York: Oxford University Press.

———. 2002. "It's snowing down south": How to help mothers and avoid recycling the sameness/difference debate. *Columbia Law Review* 102:812-33.

Fast-Track Women and the "Choice" to Stay Home

Increasing attention has been given to high-achieving women who appear to be leaving their careers in favor of staying home full-time to raise children. Some commentators interpret this trend as reflecting these women's embrace of a "new traditionalism," a rejection of feminist goals in favor of more traditional gender roles. Based on intensive interviews with forty-three women, the authors find that participants' decisions to interrupt careers are highly conflicted and not grounded in a return to traditional roles. Although family concerns figure prominently, they are not the major reason behind most women's decisions. Work-based factors play a primary role, with characteristics of husbands playing an important secondary role. The authors conclude that by virtue of their occupational status and class membership, professional women are caught in a double bind between the competing models of the ideal worker and ideal parent. The authors discuss the policy implications for the organization of work-family life.

Keywords: professional women; work and family; career interruption; stay-at-home mothers

By
PAMELA STONE
and
MEG LOVEJOY

The phenomenon of women who leave professional careers to become so-called "stay-at-home moms" has generated considerable media attention and been the subject of numerous articles, editorials, on-air commentary (Stone 1998), and a best-selling novel, *I Don't Know How She Does It* (Pearson 2002). Recent high-profile examples include Bush administra-

Pamela Stone is an associate professor of sociology at Hunter College and the Graduate Center of the City University of New York. Her research is on women in the workforce, with a particular focus on sex segregation, earnings discrimination, and pay equity. She is currently writing a book based on her study of high-level

NOTE: This research has been supported by grants to the first author from the following: PSC-CUNY Faculty Grants Program, Hunter College Presidential Faculty Research Awards Program, Hunter College Gender Equity Program, and Radcliffe Institute of Harvard University's Public Policy Fellowship Program and Research Partner Program. The authors are grateful to Heidi Hartmann and Julia Wrigley for their insightful comments on a previous version of this article.

DOI: 10.1177/0002716204268552

tion staffers Karen Hughes and Victoria Clarke. Despite larger popular interest, there is little research on this phenomenon, a paucity noted by Ann Crittenden, author of *The Price of Motherhood* (2001, 30), who characterized it as a "conspiracy of silence" borne of a "feminist and corporate taboo."

Whether or not Crittenden (2001) is correct in claiming a taboo, the specter of highly trained women who have made significant professional investments "stepping off the fast track" potentially undermines the arguments of feminist advocates for women's advancement and challenges the rationale for, and/or effectiveness of, widely publicized corporate efforts to retain and promote women. Professional women's labor force departures to "stay home" are especially highly visible because many are still tokens in their fields and firms (Kanter 1977). When they quit, their actions can signal to supervisors and colleagues alike the perception that women are not committed to work, thereby setting in motion well-known processes of statistical discrimination.

The likelihood of deleterious stereotyping and ensuing discrimination is increased by what Joan Williams (2000) has called the "choice rhetoric" used to frame women's decisions to interrupt careers. Choice rhetoric attributes women's work status to their private and personal tastes and preferences and assumes that their decisions operate outside any system of constraints. A cover story in the *The New York Times Magazine* provides an especially vivid example of such an analysis. Titled "The Opt-Out Revolution," it asked "Why don't more women get to the top?" and answered "They choose not to" (Belkin 2003). In addition to Williams, a number of prominent analysts, including Susan Faludi (1991) and Rosalind Barnett (Barnett and Rivers 1996), have also challenged choice rhetoric, arguing that this portrayal of women's decisions about work and family is part of a broad backlash against feminism and gender egalitarianism.

Although the vast majority of women with professional degrees are working, they are out of the labor force at a rate roughly three times that of their male counterparts and overwhelmingly cite "family responsibilities" as the reason. In a 1993 national study of advanced-degree recipients ten years after graduation, 12.1 percent of women as compared to 4.0 percent of men in law were no longer in the labor force. Among MBAs, comparable figures were 7.8 versus 2.2 percent; and for those with an MD, the figures were 10.7 versus 3.7 percent (Baker 2002).

At the most elite echelons, there is anecdotal and accumulating evidence that these gender differentials may be even larger. Deloitte Touche, a leading professional services firm, for example, reported losing half the women in each incoming class during the five- to seven-year period from recruitment to partnership, a significantly higher rate than that seen for male recruits, until it took aggressive mea-

women who leave professional jobs to become full-time, at-home mothers that explores the processes leading up to and influencing this decision and its implications for the women themselves, their families, their communities, and the workplace.

Meg Lovejoy is a doctoral candidate in sociology at Brandeis University. Her research interest is on the impact of race, class, and gender on girls' and women's mental health. She has published in the area of ethnic differences in body image and eating disorders as well as on the impact of the women's studies curriculum in higher education on student development.

sures to stanch women's defections (McCracken 2000). Most of these women, moreover, were leaving the workforce, not the firm, findings echoed in studies of women graduates of leading business and professional schools. Swiss and Walker's (1993) study of the careers of women graduates of various Harvard professional schools found that about one-quarter were out of the labor force. The academy has long faced a "leaky pipeline" problem, with substantial numbers of women who have trained for scientific careers failing to pursue them (Preston 1994).

In addition to feeling time-pressured and emotionally torn, working part-time in jobs that were effectively full-time made many women feel inadequate.

The costs of career interruption are significant (see Crittenden [2001] for an especially good summary of the research literature on this point). Individually, women bear them directly in the form of lost salary and blocked or slowed advancement. Cumulatively, interruptions account for as much as one-third of the gender gap in earnings and partly explain the relative absence of women in the upper reaches of most professions. The costs to employers of replacing departing women professionals—high-priced talent in the so-called "talent wars"—are also considerable.

Married professional women, by virtue of the privileges their jobs confer as well as the demands they entail, are subject to numerous, competing pressures on their decision to quit jobs and exit the labor force. These pressures emanate from both the workplace (Jacobs and Gerson 1998) and from the home, where expectations about parenting are shaped by an ideology of intensive mothering (Hays 1996). The facile media depiction of these women's decisions as "choices" in favor of domesticity (Williams 2000) obscures our understanding of their actions and the complex decision making leading up to them. Nor does the limited information available from national surveys offer much insight. In this article, we seek to shed light on these issues by reporting the results of a qualitative study of professional women, married with children, who made the decision to quit their jobs and interrupt their careers—at least temporarily—by leaving the labor force. The goals of the article are threefold: (1) to develop a thematic analysis of the reasons behind professional women's decision to "go home" that is grounded in their experiences, (2) to explore the implications of our findings as they shed light on choice rhetoric, and (3) to inform the development of work-family (or as they are now more often called, work-life) policies and practices.

Data and Method

Study participants (N = 43) were women who were formally out of the labor force (neither at work nor actively looking for work) at the time of the interview. All were married, with at least one child younger than eighteen living at home, and all had formerly been employed in professional (which includes those in male-dominated professions such as law and medicine as well as female-dominated professions such as teaching) or managerial jobs. Participants resided in seven metropolitan areas throughout the United States and were recruited through referral or "snowball" sampling, primarily through alumnae networks of highly selective colleges. We confined the study to white women because cultural traditions vary significantly regarding work and family across different racial and ethnic groups.

Interviews were semistructured and conducted by the first author in the interviewee's home or a place of her choice and typically lasted about two hours. The interviews, which were audiotaped, explored women's work and family histories and elicited a detailed accounting of how and why these women made the decision to quit, including the work-family context in which this decision was made. To protect the identities of the women interviewed, we change their names and identifying information in the results presented here.

Women in the sample ranged in age from thirty-three to fifty-six, with a median age of forty-three. On average, they had worked thirteen years prior to dropping out and had been out of the labor force six years. Typically, they had two children, with just more than a third having preschoolers at the time of interview. Across all women in the sample, the youngest child was three months and the oldest fourteen years. All but one woman in the sample had a college degree, and half had an advanced degree. Two-thirds worked in male-dominated fields such as law, business, medicine, or the sciences; approximately one-fifth worked in mixed or transitional fields such as publishing, public relations, and health and educational administration; and the remainder worked in traditionally female-dominated professions such as teaching. Their husbands also worked as professionals or managers, typically in law, medicine, or finance, or owned businesses.

Because there is so little research on this group of women, it is difficult to assess the representativeness of our sample. As highly educated women, they had deferred childbearing, enabling most to become relatively well established in their careers. The majority worked in male-dominated professions. This may reflect a greater propensity for dropout among this group (as would plausibly be expected) or the vagaries of nonprobability sampling. As a result, we offer the caveat that our results may be more reflective of the experiences of women in male-dominated professions than of those in mixed or female-dominated professions. The nonrandom nature of our sample precludes generalization to a larger population.

The percentages we present are for descriptive purposes only and should be interpreted accordingly.

Interviews were coded using ATLAS-ti. Details of coding and analysis are available from the authors. We base our analysis of reasons for quitting both on the participants' directly stated reasons for doing so and on those implied from the circumstances and events surrounding the decision itself. Typically, multiple codes regarding women's motives for quitting were assigned to any given case, reflecting the fact that each woman's decision to quit was guided by numerous, varied, and complex factors.

Results

In the rhetoric of choice often invoked to explain why successful professional women exit the workforce, women's decisions are largely seen as an expression of their unfettered individual preferences for home and hearth over career. Our findings largely contradict this view. Approximately 90 percent of women in our sample expressed a moderate to high degree of ambivalence about the decision to quit their jobs, and for many the decision was protracted and agonizing. Claire Lott, a manager at a public utilities company, took a leave of absence from her job before finally quitting, a period during which she vacillated constantly:

> So at the end of that six months—I mean, it came down to literally the night before. What was again so hard was it was like a loss of identity. Ironically, that Sunday, after I made the decision, the sermon at church was "Loss of Identity because of Loss of Job or Loss of Spouse." That kind of clicked with me.

Quitting to "go home" was weighed against women's solid sense of identification with their careers and the heavy investments they had made in them, which for many included not only extensive work experience but postgraduate education. Women also found it hard to leave their jobs because they took pride in their professional accomplishments and derived intrinsic pleasure from their work. Nancy Yearwood, senior editor at a publishing house, voiced the difficulty many women felt in making the decision and reflected on the variety of losses it entailed:

> I would think about like well, "How could I do this?" I mean the financial was one aspect of it, but there are other aspects. Not to minimize that, but my whole identity was work. Yes, I was a mother and a wife and whatever, but this is who I was. And I would think like about the authors, and "Oh, my God, how can I leave this author?" And then the agents and these people I'd worked with for years and my books and the house and my colleagues. I mean just on and on and on. And I really thought long—I mean I just thought for a long time about it. And I would think like, "How could I do this?"

For only five women (representing 16 percent of the sample) can the decision to step off the career track be viewed as a reflection of a relatively unconstrained choice or preference to become full-time, stay-at-home mothers. Following Faludi

(1991), we call these women "new traditionalists." Like the classic traditionalists, they give full-time mothering precedence over working; however, in contrast to their earlier counterparts, they had successful and even high-powered careers in fields such as publishing, marketing, banking, and health care before starting their families. Unlike most of the women studied, they indicated that they had always planned to become full-time mothers and experienced no indecision or ambivalence in making the decision to interrupt their careers, quit their jobs, or be at home with their children. Also, unlike many of the women studied (as we will report later in the context of reasons for quitting), they made no efforts to reduce their work hours or enhance schedule flexibility to maintain their careers.

Women frequently used the word corporate *to connote a chill in the climate toward women as a result of restructuring.*

The new traditionalists were further distinguished from the other women by the value that they, and often their husbands, placed on having a full-time mother in the home, seeing own-mother care as irreplaceable in their children's lives. They often rejected unequivocally any form of child care, especially in the early years of their child's development. Vita Cornwall, who quit her job as a nonprofit executive after the birth of her first child, exemplified this perspective:

> The reason [I quit] is I want them to, for better or worse, interpret my values, our values, our moral system, speak in our cadence, with our grammatical errors or proper speech. I wanted them to be our children, and I don't think we would have been able to do that with me working full-time.

As exceptions, the new traditionalists highlight the many constraints faced by the majority of women in our sample. Our analysis of women's reasons for interrupting their careers brings into focus the nature of these constraints and how they impinged on the women's "choice" to go home. The analysis revealed three major themes around which women's motivations for leaving the workforce revolved: (1) work, (2) children, and (3) husbands. Identification of major themes is based both on the frequency with which particular reasons were invoked and our assessment of the weight each one carried in the larger context of women's decision making. These themes are described below along with the processes by which they operated.

Work-related factors in the decision to quit

Work-related reasons were the most frequently cited reasons for quitting, figuring as important considerations for 86 percent of the sample. Managers and professionals are, paraphrasing Schor (1992), the most overworked Americans (Jacobs and Gerson 1998). The women in our study dwelled squarely in the world of sixty-hour workweeks and 24/7 accountability. The time bind (Hochschild 1997) was an almost taken-for-granted feature of their lives—and had been even before they had children. Typical was Nathalie Everett's description of the high-technology industry in which she had worked as a marketing manager: "The high-tech workweek is really sixty hours, not forty. Nobody works 9 to 5 anymore." Added to this, many women were employed in settings where the pace and expectations were set by men with stay-at-home wives. Meg Romano, a trader at a large investment firm, was the only woman among a group of eleven men, men about whom she said, "Every single one, their wife stayed home . . . their wives handled everything."

The amount, pace, and inflexibility of work as well as the inadequacy of reduced-hour options led many women to quit. Economic restructuring played an important role in accelerating workplace demands but also operated in other ways to influence this outcome.

Workplace inflexibility

Upon becoming mothers, about half of the women in our sample expressed a desire to cut back on their work hours and/or to increase the flexibility of their schedules. Their efforts met with mixed results, however, as almost one-third of the sample (and 62 percent of those who had actually gone part-time) cited workplace inflexibility as a major factor in their decision to interrupt their careers. Romano's experience is illustrative. Having worked both part- and full-time over a fifteen-year period with the same firm, she took a leave of absence to attend to her child's medical problem. Ready to return to work,

> I went back to talk to them about what was next, and a part-time situation presented itself in the sales area, and I got all gung-ho for that. I got all the child care arrangements in place, started interviewing people to watch the kids, and at the last minute the big boss wouldn't sign off on it. So I was like, "Alright, whatever."

Romano and others like her tried and failed, but a number who would have liked to work part- time or job share knew better than to ask. More than one-third characterized their work as "all or nothing" and viewed their options as being either working forty-plus hours per week or quitting. Maeve Turner, a federal attorney, said of workplace accommodation, "It just wasn't in their [her superiors'] realm of reality." Nancy Yearwood encountered the same phenomenon, as illustrated by her account of telling her boss that she was quitting her job in publishing after ten years with the firm:

She was kind of shocked, and she said, "Is there *anything* [emphasis added] I can do to try to get you to stay?" I did bring up to her the fact that I thought about trying to get some kind of a part-time thing, but it's just not what they need. I know what they need. They need people who are there all the time, and working like dogs. And to work part-time in my business—I think you're going to end up working more than part-time. I wasn't willing to do that. I'd already been working time and a half. I raised it [part-time work] in this conversation, I guess, just to satisfy my curiosity about it. And she basically agreed with me.

Yearwood's belief that she would "end up working more than part-time" foreshadows the most frequent complaint among those who *were* able to arrange part-time work: for many, the nature of their jobs and the culture of their workplaces meant that they worked part-time in name only. Women spoke repeatedly about having full-time responsibilities on a part-time schedule, of doing a "job and a half" when they were supposed to be doing half a job. Diane Childs, a nonprofit CFO, observed that "when you have young babies, they leave you alone for a while," but when the honeymoon period ended, she was asked to "take more responsibility, do more, manage more." Making it difficult to limit work hours was the fact that many of these women were the only ones in their immediate work environment who were working part-time. "[My colleagues were] putting in fifty to sixty hours a week and I was working thirty" was how Elena Toracelli, a management consultant, described her situation.

Women's inability to limit their hours on a part-time schedule meant that they felt little relief from the spillover of work into their family lives. Bettina Mason, a real estate attorney, described the dilemma she faced:

Even though my children mean so much to me, I *listen* to someone who is paying me money, and I will then miss reviewing the math, reviewing the journal entry. I'll say "yes" to my employer. So then my hours were never twenty hours a week, they were much more than that—at least thirty hours a week.

In addition to feeling time pressured and emotionally torn, working part-time in jobs that were effectively full-time made many women feel inadequate. They struggled to perform to their own high standards in jobs where the demands so exceeded the time available that success was impossible. They also felt guilty, as if by working part-time they were shortchanging their employers. Mason's firm, where she described the people as "extremely nice" and the environment as "very fast paced," had no complaints about her working part-time, but from her perspective, "Things just had to get done and two days off just was not working out," adding, "I just felt that twenty hours was not going to give them all that they needed."

Mommy tracking and the maternal wall

Many of the women who worked part-time or job shared found themselves "mommy tracked," a career derailment that ultimately played a role in their decision to quit. Nancy Thomas, a marketing executive, used *Scarlet Letter*–like imagery to describe job sharing at her firm: "When you job share you have 'MOMMY' stamped in huge letters on your head." Reporting that "there were a dozen job sharers in the company and none were ever promoted," she recounted with triumph how she had finally succeeded in getting a promotion after a four-year campaign—a promotion, she observed somewhat incredulously, that "the chairman of the board of a six-thousand-person company had to approve."

Childs, the nonprofit executive, described the long-term prospects of continuing to work part-time, which eventually discouraged her from doing so:

> And I'm never going to get anywhere—you have the feeling that you just plateaued professionally because you can't take on the extra projects; you can't travel at a moment's notice; you can't stay late; you're not flexible on the Friday thing because that could mean finding someone to take your kids. You really plateau for a much longer period of time than you ever realize when you first have a baby. It's like you're going to be plateaued for thirteen to fifteen years.

Women were not only concerned about the loss of extrinsic rewards associated with the move to part-time but also bemoaned the loss of intrinsically interesting and engaging work. Toracelli, the management consultant, returned from maternity leave to a twenty-hour-a-week schedule, discovering when she did so that "I lost the vast majority of my interesting responsibilities and was really left with the more mundane modeling responsibilities that I wasn't nearly as interested in." Many felt marginalized. Paula Trottier, a marketing executive, described how her status and authority had been eroded when she went part-time, despite having considerable seniority, and how this played directly into her decision:

> So I decided to quit, and this was a really, really big deal . . . because I never envisioned myself not working. I just felt like I would become a nobody if I quit. Well, I was sort of a nobody working too. So it was sort of, "Which nobody do you want to be?"

Economic restructuring

The women in our sample worked in fields such as finance, marketing, professional services, law, and technology. Since the 1970s, these fields have experienced both an influx of female professionals and an economic restructuring brought about by consolidation in mature industries (e.g., finance and publishing) and extraordinarily high rates of growth in newly emerging ones (e.g., biotechnology). Reflecting this, stories of reorganization, mergers, takeovers, and rapid expansion recurred throughout our interviews, figuring prominently in the career interruptions of just less than half (42 percent) of our sample.

Speedup and disruption. Restructuring influenced women's decisions in a number of ways, most importantly by creating tremendous turbulence and speedup in the work environment, which in turn disrupted the complicated and fragile articulation of work and family that women had been able to achieve. Consolidation and rapid growth dramatically increased the scope and demands of women's jobs.

Nancy Taylor's experience as an executive with a company on an aggressive acquisition binge gives a flavor of what mergers meant for the people responsible for implementing them:

> There are forty-nine hundred branches, fifteen thousand ATMs, and all of the myriad things associated with that—capital budget of maybe 260 million dollars, about seventy-five people. And only five of them were in [the same city]. And that's where everything got out of control. We were scattered to the four winds. What that meant was I was traveling. I had to travel before, but this was just on a scale like . . . [gesturing with her hands and making sounds to indicate a nuclear explosion].

Women in high-growth industries such as biotechnology faced special challenges. Lynn Hamilton, an MD who was medical director of a start-up company, recalled continuously running fax machines and a grueling schedule of nonstop travel. She reflected on this life:

> I think the punch line is, there's a reason why people that tend to be funded by venture capitalists are twenty and live on Doritos in their basement. Because the pressure's on you when you have a start-up company like this. With these kinds of guys [the venture capitalists] expecting results, it's tough to be forty, with two young children and a husband with his own job.

Changes in corporate culture. Changes brought on by restructuring also prompted women to feel a growing disenchantment with their employers, often leading them to wonder aloud, "Why am I doing this?"—ultimately a question to which they had no answer. Restructuring was frequently linked to perceptions that the corporate culture was growing more hostile to women and more value divergent. "I think each of those changes [in ownership], it just became more and more corporate" was how Nancy Yearwood described what she observed as the publishing firm where she was an editor successively merged with others. Women frequently used the word *corporate* to connote a chill in the climate toward women as a result of restructuring. Edith Hortas, a Ph.D. scientist and biotechnology executive, recounted what she called "a turning point" that occurred when her firm replaced its female CEO with a male CEO brought on to "grow" the company:

> The company turned into a big corporation. And there were people there who became extremely corporate, who took a very hard-line financial view of things. And it became a much more male-run company. It was by no means a female-run company before, but it was a very inclusive kind of company.

Manager turnover. Restructuring was often associated with rapid turnover in the managers to whom these women reported, resulting in the loss of mentors and the collapse of family-friendly work arrangements. In domino-like fashion, turnover at the top contributed to women's own turnover, which occurred via one of two processes, either by disrupting the work-family equilibrium that women had achieved or by diminishing their career prospects through the loss of an important mentor.

Because schedule flexibility and the pace of work are to some extent a function of managerial style, women often saw their work lives transformed by what they considered to be the rather arbitrary dictates of new bosses. Lisa Bernard, an executive in the health care field who worked under four senior managers in rapid succession, remarked of her last one,

> This last person [who, she pointedly noted, had a wife, nanny, and mother-in-law at home] had a different approach to how to do certain things. I remember there was one time when he sent an e-mail to me on Sunday afternoon about a meeting that was 6:30 Monday morning and was just assuming that of course I would be reading my e-mail Sunday evening at home.

Sometimes losing a boss meant losing a supportive mentor. Kate Davenport, a public relations executive, said of her experience working for a highly successful, rapidly growing high-technology firm, "I had a new boss every three weeks." One in particular she described as having been "really cool" in encouraging her efforts to combine work and family. With her last boss, however, she hit the maternal wall:

> She didn't have much patience for the whole family scene. "If you're going to choose to have kids [and Kate at this point already had three], this is as far as your career is going to go, you're derailing, you're on the mommy track now."

Children's influence on the decision to quit

Seventy-two percent of the women we studied spoke of the pull of children as a factor in their decision to leave the workforce. Included among them are the five new traditionalist women in the sample. Three-quarters of women citing this reason quit when their children were in the baby or toddler years. Perhaps more surprising, a substantial number of women (32 percent)[1] who cited the pull of children were primarily compelled to leave the workforce by the needs of their older, school-aged children.

The pull of younger children

Women who cited the pulls of their younger, preschool children as an important reason for taking a pause in their careers experienced these pulls in two ways.

Primacy of parental care. One-third cited their belief in the importance of one parent playing a primary caregiving role in the life of a young child. Melanie Irwin, formerly a marketing manager in a computer software company, put it this way: "I guess in my heart I didn't really want a kid raised by a nanny." Kristin Quinn, a former teacher, said, "It was hard thinking who could take care of my kid better than me." For these women, parental care in the early years was important in providing consistency and enrichment. Maeve Turner, the government attorney, reflecting on why she and her husband decided that one of them (ultimately her) would be home after the birth of their first child, emphasized the constancy of parental care:

> The kids need especially—I think the kids need routine. They need a schedule. They need—I mean, not a schedule in the hourly sense, but they need a routine. They need to know that somebody is there connected to them who cares about them.

This theme more than any others cited by the women in the study reflects traditional notions of why women choose to stay home with their children rather than combining work and family. However, the new traditionalists and the nontraditionalists spoke about this issue in different ways. The nontraditionalists typically did not see full-time, mother-only care as the optimal or necessary solution, as the new traditionalists did. In fact, among nontraditionalists citing primacy of parental care, approximately one-third asked their employers if they could return to work on a reduced schedule but were denied this option.

The emotional pull of younger children. One-quarter of the women spoke of the emotional pull of younger children as a factor in their decision. For some women, this took the form of an intense feeling of attachment and bonding with their newborn baby or young child that made the return to a full-time work schedule difficult. Lauren Quattrone, formerly a lawyer, expressed it in this way: "I was just absolutely besotted with this baby. . . . I realized that I just couldn't bear to leave him." Regina Donofrio, a senior publicist for a large media corporation, decided to return to work full-time after the birth of her first child but described the anguish she felt in coping with her competing desire to be with her baby and to maintain a much-loved career:

> Then I began the nightmare of really never feeling like I was in the right place, ever. When I was at work, I should have been at home. When I was at home, I felt guilty because I had left work a little early to see the baby, and I had maybe left some things undone.

The pull of young children was also linked to their particular developmental phase and a desire not to "miss out" on it. Helena Norton, formerly an education administrator, commented, "I just don't want to miss this part because I know it does go by so fast." Three of the women who cited the emotional pull of younger children in their decision to leave work became first-time mothers in their early forties, and for these women, the desire to be fully present in the experience of motherhood was particularly keen since they did not expect to have any more children.

Among the nontraditionalist women who cited the emotional pull of young children, 40 percent tried to reduce their hours but were denied. Among this group, both Turner and Donofrio proposed job-sharing arrangements and left flourishing careers when their proposals were rejected.

The pull of older children

Older children were cited as having been a key factor in tipping the balance away from employment for one-quarter of our total sample and figured prominently for one-third of those who mentioned children as a factor in their decision to leave. Nancy Taylor echoed the sentiments of many of these women when she remarked with surprise, "It's funny. I always expected as they got older it would be easier." Instead, an increase in both the scope and complexity of the perceived needs and demands of older children relative to younger ones, as well as growing doubts about the capacities of their paid caregivers, played a role in women's career interruption.

Increased demands. Bearing in mind that the oldest child among the women we interviewed was only fourteen, women were often surprised to learn that homework started young. Diane Childs expressed an amazement shared by many:

> I don't know why this is happening, but elementary school kids get homework. These are children who can't read, who are in the first grade, and they have an assignment. And they'll be kind of sweet things, you know, "Use tally marks and count all of the pillows in your house." But if you come home from a frazzed-out day, . . . the last thing you want to do is find out that you have forty-two pillows in your house.

"[My husband] has always said to me, 'You can do whatever you want to do.' But he's not there to pick up any load."

After-school activities added to the stress of combining work and parenting. Childs noted that, like many professional women she knows who are now at home, a precipitating factor in her departure from work was an increasing awareness of her school-aged children's needs for extracurricular enrichment and the heightened demands that this placed on her as a parent, commenting dryly, "They can't drive themselves to piano lessons."

Lack of substitutability for own care. Women's perceptions about older children's increased demands were linked to their feelings that their children had "outgrown" their paid caregivers and that they themselves were increasingly needed at this point in their children's lives. Child care arrangements that had been regarded as highly successful were reevaluated as the more sophisticated needs of older children took precedence over the simpler, more straightforward "babysitting" needs of younger children. Elena Toracelli, the management consultant, expressed the satisfaction that most felt with their caregivers when children were younger:

> I had great child care. In some ways, I think babies, if they're in a loving environment, other nonparents can fulfill their basic needs in a way that parents can too. And I liked that

my kids got some tremendous socialization very early on in incredibly loving situations. And they are none the worse at all, if not the better for having been there.

As their children started entering school, however, these high-achieving women begin to question their caregivers' capacities and suitability, often comparing themselves directly with them. The premium placed on education and values transmission at this point in their children's lives served to widen the gap between themselves and their less well-educated caregivers, most of whom were from very different class, race, and ethnic backgrounds. Edith Hortas spoke of having "a sense that they were needing what I can provide and what the babysitter [her au pair] couldn't provide." Marina Isherwood, an HMO executive, elaborated this viewpoint:

> There isn't a substitute, no matter how good the child care. When they're little, the fact that someone else is doing stuff with them is fine. It wasn't the part that I loved anyway. But when they start asking you questions about values, you don't want your babysitter telling them. . . . Our children come home and they have all this homework to do, and piano lessons and this and this, and it's all a complicated schedule. And, yes, you could get an au pair to do that, to balance it all, but they're not going to necessarily teach you how to think about math. Or help you come up with mnemonic devices to memorize all of the counties in Spain or whatever.

Time and pleasure. For some women, watching their older children growing up created a heightened sense of urgency about quitting. These women saw childhood as a "little window" (as Nancy Yearwood put it) that was rapidly closing. Having worked a decade or more before quitting, many of them expressed a sense of "missing out" on their children's childhoods. Elena Toracelli described her feelings about the desirability of being home "when you sort of realize that time's running short. Paul's eight and tomorrow is going to be eighteen, and the same thing with Amanda. It's going to be over in a blink."

Complementing this sense of urgency, these women also found older children more *fun*, as Toracelli's observations convey:

> I've realized within myself that I am much more stimulated by older children than I am by babies. I loved my children as babies, they were my own, . . . but I thrive more in the interaction with the level that they are at now than I did when they were infants and toddlers. They reason. They're funny. You can have conversations with them. You can plan and dream and do all kinds of great activities with them. They are much more fun now.

Among this group whose children were older, 20 percent made efforts to navigate the demands of work and family by making part-time arrangements with their employers but had their requests refused.

Husbands' role in the decision to quit

The majority of the women in this study, roughly two-thirds, discussed their husbands as one of the key influences on their decision to leave the labor force. That husbands' involvement was not cited universally indicates the degree to which women perceived the work-family decision to be theirs alone to shoulder. Husbands' influence on women's decisions to quit operated through multiple channels.

Lack of husbands' help with parenting

The women in our study were married to men who worked in professional jobs much like their own, entailing long hours and extensive travel. Husbands' high-octane careers effectively precluded their willingness or ability to provide help with child care or household chores. Often women did not explicitly mention their husbands' lack of support, but it was clear from their narratives that their husbands were simply not around to share much if any of the "second shift" (Hochschild 1989) necessary to make their careers viable. Helena Norton, the educational administrator who characterized her husband as a "workaholic," described poignantly a scenario that many others took for granted:

> He was leaving early mornings; 6:00 or 6:30 before anyone was up, and then he was coming home late at night. So I felt this real emptiness, getting up in the morning to, not necessarily an empty house, because my children were there, but I did, I felt empty, and then going to bed, and he wasn't there.

Some women were more vocal in their estimation of how their husband's self-exemption from domestic labor affected their own career choices. Kristen Quinn observed about her husband, "He has always said to me, 'You can do whatever you want to do.' But he's not there to pick up any load."

Because these women had the resources to employ household help such as housekeepers, nannies, and babysitters, they rarely complained about "chore wars" occasioned by their husbands' failure to help with routine household tasks. Instead, the more profound impact of a husband's absence from the home was experienced by women in terms of his resulting inability to assist with the emotional labor of parenting. Many women were, like Helena Norton, the only parent available, and it fell to them to create a sense of family for their children. Leah Evans, a high-level medical administrator, highlighted this need when she described her decision to quit:

> So more than anything else it was just sort of what worked for the collective whole. Even though for Leah personally, I sort of feel like I'm the one who made the trade-off. Dick [her husband] certainly hasn't made any trade-off at this point and maybe eventually he will, but sort of realizing that it is a UNIT and you've got to do it [make your decision] based on what's best for the unit.

Toracelli found herself in a similar situation. Her husband's demanding career managing his own company in combination with her own near full-time work schedule meant that there was little time to create family:

> We had precious little family time, in part because, you know, here I am working like thirty hours. I have one day off, Friday, but my husband's not home Saturday and Sunday either. And so I am seven days a week, full-time, working with not too much of a break.

Another example of the "parenting vacuum" these women experienced as a result of their husbands' high-powered career came from Tricia Olsen, a former trader. Having herself once worked in the financial services industry, she was familiar with her husband's work world:

> My husband had taken a job three months earlier with a top investment bank, and we knew his life was going to go to hell because he was in the mergers and acquisitions department. So we knew that his life would be nonstop travel . . . and we decided that somebody should be home to be more attentive to the kids because now we had a second child. She was eighteen months old already, and we found that she was requiring more and more attention just because she was a child. So I decided, knowing his life was going to go to hell, we figured that somebody should be home, and that somebody was me.

Secondary income

Despite the high-powered nature of their own careers, the majority of women in the study did not explicitly broach the idea of their husbands cutting back. Instead, they seemed to implicitly accept that their career was secondary. This perception was based to some extent on husbands' higher earnings. Approximately one-quarter of the women whose husbands played a role in their decision to quit perceived their own income, however high, as secondary to their husbands' and/or as unnecessary to family welfare. Typically, women were correct in their perceptions because they worked in lower-paying, female-dominated occupations like teaching or publishing and/or lower-paying sectors such as government; they were already working part-time at the time of their quitting; or their own high earnings were far outstripped by their husbands'. Diane Childs, who worked in the nonprofit sector, said that as a couple she and her husband did not even consider having him cut back on his career in finance, despite increasing family strains, since, as she put it, "There's too much money at stake at this point in time that I couldn't approach his earning power."

Because many of these women and their husbands are midcareer, about half mentioned promotions or other significant career achievements (such as making partner) that led to dramatic increases in their husbands' salaries during the period when they were considering the need to reorder their work lives. Marina Isherwood reported that her husband's income went up fivefold before she quit:

> And mine wasn't going up fivefold, and so the amount of contribution I was making to our household dropped significantly. And then I thought, you know, taxes, what are we really bringing in? So the economics changed.

Husband's preference for wife to stay home

About one-quarter of the women whose husbands played a role in their decision to quit indicated that their husbands communicated to them, either explicitly or implicitly, that they expected their wife to be the one to sacrifice or modify her career to accommodate family responsibilities. A minority of husbands expressed this preference in traditionalist terms. For instance, Toracelli described the role her husband's attitude played in her decision to quit in the following way:

> My husband grew up in a very traditional household. His mother was home all the time. It's an Italian household in a very traditional sense of the word where, you know, there's always sort of a warm plate of food waiting for you on the table when you get home, and he relished the idea of having that kind of person.

[M]ost women who expressed interest in returning to work cited workplace flexibility as a critical feature of any future job.

More often, husbands professed an egalitarian stance toward women's decisions about whether to cut back on their careers, captured in the frequent refrain, "It's your choice," while tacitly indicating discontent with their wives' working. Women seemed to take their husbands' overt statements at face value, characterizing their husbands as "supportive" while recounting narratives that contradicted this assessment. For example, Bettina Mason described her husband in the following way: "He has always said do what I want. He would be supportive of whatever I chose." At another point in the interview, however, she admitted that part of her reason for quitting was that her husband, who was often out of town for weeks at a time, made it clear that he resented the fact that no one was around to "pick up the slack" when she worked full-time.

Some husbands simply refused to modify their careers in the face of mounting pressure on the home front. Lynn Hamilton, the MD turned medical director, described both herself and her husband as working "these killer jobs," a situation that was creating huge stress on their marriage and family life. They earned similar incomes and had similar credentials, and he was "admiring and supportive" of her work. When Hamilton repeatedly raised the need for them to "reconfigure" their work lives, however, he was nonresponsive, and she finally realized that "he wasn't going to."

Significantly, about one-third of the women who described their husbands' implicit or explicit preference for a stay-at-home wife as a factor in their quitting were earning comparable incomes or outearning their husbands at the time of their job departure. Thus, economics was not the only factor at play in these couples' perceptions that the wife's career was secondary.

Deference to husband's career

Under the duress of a dual-career lifestyle, some women's decisions to quit were influenced by a perception that their husbands' careers were more important or prestigious than their own or by an unspoken agreement with their husbands that husbands' careers took precedence. Two women accommodated their husbands' careers by deciding to step off the career track when their husbands' jobs required a geographical relocation. Feeling the mounting stress of juggling family and two careers—their own and their husbands'—some women simply weighed their own careers against their husbands' and decided that theirs were more dispensable. Moira Franklin, a former engineer whose husband was in the same field as her, describes her decision to quit as influenced by her perception that her own educational credentials were less than those of her husband and that her career was not as prestigious:

> I think if I had gone to get a Ph.D., then it would have been harder to quit. But master's was kind of a half-way, you're qualified, but you're not a hotshot yet. So it's not as if I was the faculty member . . . so I think it was easier for me to quit than stick it out and torture myself a little longer.

Future Work

While this article is concerned with the forces impinging on and reasons behind the decision to interrupt careers, in the larger study of which it is a part, we also asked women about their plans to return to work in the future. Two-thirds responded that they desired to reenter the workforce and discussed their intention to return with varying degrees of specificity. Significantly, the majority of women who desired to return to work said they would prefer to do so on a part-time basis that would accommodate their ongoing family responsibilities. Despite the difficulty many had encountered in arranging a part-time schedule in their former jobs, most women who expressed interest in returning to work cited workplace flexibility as a critical feature of any future job. In fact, some women planned to switch into traditionally female-dominated fields such as teaching, in part because they perceived them to offer more flexibility than the "all-or-nothing" style of the male-dominated careers they had left behind.

Discussion

For all but a handful of the women we studied, the decision to interrupt their careers was a reluctant and complex one, reached after taking into consideration myriad factors emanating from both the workplace and the family and often after having made efforts to reduce hours or otherwise maintain employment. For these women, there was no "Eureka!" moment, no final straw, but rather the gradual accumulation of often overlapping workplace pushes and family pulls that led them to quit their jobs. Women tracked their work lives against their family lives, frequently juxtaposing the two at critical junctures, for example, a company merger coinciding with their child's first year at school. Our results can only hint at the full complexity of these unfolding processes, but they do make clear three things. First, women faced enormous constraints in making their decision. Second, work-related considerations played a significant, arguably greater, role in their decision than did those related to family. Third, children were the primary focus of family-based pulls, with husbands playing a less visible but important role.

Although women couch their decisions to quit in the language of personal choice, the reasons they give are not consistent with choice rhetoric or with the idea that they are expressing "preferences." Our results undermine the notion that women are freely choosing family over work. Inflexible and highly demanding workplaces are the major barriers to their ability to exercise discretion in any meaningful way. With the exception of the small group of women we label (following Faludi 1991) new traditionalists, the women in our study made the "choice" to be at home not out of their preference for traditional gender roles but because of their experience of gendered realities. These realities are shaped by multiple factors that include economic restructuring, workplaces that assume the male model of work, the lack of real reduced-hours options that undermines women's efforts at work-family accommodation, husbands' exemption from household parenting obligations, and the ideology of intensive mothering at home. This confluence of pressures creates a kind of "perfect storm." That so many of the women we studied "weathered the storm" for as long as they did is testimony to their work commitment, ingenuity, and tenacity in the face of significant obstacles. The fact that so many women planned to return to work is further testimony to their commitment to work and to their desire to integrate career and family.

By virtue of their professional status, women face tremendous pressures as workers; by virtue of their upper-middle-class membership, they face equally tremendous pressures as mothers. They are called on to be not only the "ideal worker" (Williams 2000) but also the "ideal parent"—a double bind from which they effectively shield their husbands, owing primarily to the latter's superior earning power as well as the ideology of husband exemption.

Our findings illustrate the mirror-image processes by which women's careers become secondary to those of their husbands, who work in equally demanding jobs. Among these couples, as women attempt to shoulder the responsibilities of work and family, they accrue cumulating disadvantages at the same time that their husbands accrue advantages by "free riding" (Folbre 2001) on their wives' relatively weaker position in the labor market as well as on their desire to create family. The ascendancy of husbands' careers is driven not simply by higher earnings but also by the construction of gendered ideologies that privilege men's work in a process Pyke (1996) has called "the ideological hegemony of the male career." She

found this phenomenon to be especially characteristic of upper-middle-class families of the sort we studied. As we observed, even women with high-status jobs who
earned more than their husbands deferred to their husbands' careers and were
persuaded to accommodate to their husband's explicit, but more often tacit,
preference for them to bear the brunt of family work.

Policy implications

Our results highlight the importance of taking into account the perspectives of
women who are no longer employed for the development of effective work-family
policies by revealing the constrained context in which the majority of professional
women are actually making their decision to "go home" as well as the degree to
which their decisions are grounded in work, not family, considerations. The experiences of these women suggest several recommendations that would presumably
not only enhance the labor force attachment of women who might otherwise leave
it but improve the work and family lives of those who remain at work.

Some good news

The results reported here suggest that while the workplace remains less than
fully family friendly, there have indeed been meaningful improvements in the
work-family system. Consistent with research on the provision of family benefits
(Glass and Camarigg 1992), almost all the professional women in our sample had
access to generous maternity leave. Very little evidence among the women we studied showed the "trailing spouse" phenomenon or the "two-person career." Strik-
ingly, the burdens of corporate entertaining or other social supports for their husbands' high-powered careers were absent from these women's narratives. Also
notably missing were mentions of sexual harassment and overtly discriminatory
pay or promotion policies. If women encountered these problems, they did not
appear to play a role in weakening their career attachment in favor of family.

The family-friendly workplace: What women want

Hochschild (1997) cast doubt on the very need for work-family accommodations, arguing that workers are not interested in taking advantage of them. The
struggles of the women we studied to maintain their employment, primarily
through reduced hours, and their inability to obtain satisfactory part-time solutions
make clear that there exists among them a strong unmet demand for increased
workplace flexibility. Moreover, looking ahead to the future, the fact that they still
desired part-time work and expressed a willingness to change professions if necessary to obtain it, further testifies to the strong demand for workplace flexibility and
accommodation among this group. These findings underscore the importance of
policy recommendations that are receiving renewed attention (e.g., Hartmann,
Yoon, and Zuckerman 2000): first, to create meaningful part-time opportunities in
the professions that do not penalize workers who take advantage of them; and sec-

ond, to fully institutionalize these arrangements to shield them from arbitrary and individualized implementation.

The influence of children, especially school-age children, in women's decisions highlights the clash of family and occupational careers (Moen and Han 2001). Among professional women who defer childbearing, the birth of children and their entry into school and adolescence often coincides with a critical midcareer takeoff point, a period when women are assuming additional responsibilities and are poised for future earnings growth and advancement. To address this clash, work-life benefits are required beyond maternity leave to meet children's developing needs through the school years. The most progressive firms are already moving in this direction; however, broader societal-based changes might include synchronizing school and work schedules and more widespread provision of after-school programs. To overcome the reservations these women voiced about caregivers for their older children, strategies to professionalize the child care workforce via increased training and earnings are called for.

A number of the women in our study were employed by companies that were listed routinely by *Working Mother* magazine as "best places" to work (an irony not lost on some of them, but not reported to protect their identity). The professional women we studied did not work for "bad" companies; in fact, they worked for companies that are widely perceived to be highly desirable places of employment. Our analysis makes clear that to retain these women, employers must move beyond existing programmatic, human-resources-based approaches to reduce the hours of work and enhance its flexibility through work redesign.

To the extent that women disproportionately bear the burden of work speedup through the interruption, in many instances the termination, of once-flourishing careers, our results provide an additional equal-opportunity rationale for reducing work hours across the board among litigation-averse firms, in line with a strategy being developed by Joan Williams (2000) and other legal scholar/activists. They also give added impetus to reduced hours generally, as called for by the burgeoning "time movement" approach advanced by Schor (1992) and Hochschild (1997).

The striking degree to which the demands of husbands' careers cross over and influence women's decisions to interrupt their own careers underscores the importance of efforts already under way to position and implement work-family policies as gender neutral. Companies that bemoan their inability to retain highly talented professional women need to acknowledge that they are married to highly talented professional men. Not only men but employers too benefit from free riding on the coattails of women's career sacrifice. Only when both give up the free ride can women be freed from the double bind. Mounting evidence indicates that younger generations of men *are* increasingly interested in working less and devoting more time to life and family. Our results suggest that keeping work within reasonable bounds for *all* professionals and managers will be necessary to enable women in these fields to exercise their true choice, which is to maintain their careers and raise their families within the context of viable and sustained, supportive work-family structures.

Note

1. The percentages add up to slightly more than 100 percent here since there was some overlap between the categories of younger and older children. Specifically, one woman left the workforce when her youngest child was a preschooler and her oldest child was school aged and cited both types of reasons (the pull of younger and older children) as factors in her decision to quit.

References

Baker, Joe G. 2002. The influx of women into legal professions: An economic analysis. *Monthly Labor Review* 125:14-24.

Barnett, Rosalind C., and Caryl Rivers. 1996. *She works/he works*. New York: HarperCollins.

Belkin, Lisa. 2003. The opt-out revolution. *The New York Times Magazine*, October 26, pp. 42-47, 58, 85-86.

Crittenden, Ann. 2001. *The price of motherhood*. New York: Metropolitan Books.

Faludi, Susan. 1991. *Backlash: The undeclared war against American women*. New York: Crown.

Folbre, Nancy. 2001. *The invisible heart*. New York: New Press.

Glass, Jennifer, and Valerie Camarigg. 1992. Gender, parenthood, and job-family compatibility. *American Journal of Sociology* 98:131-51.

Hartmann, Heidi, Young-Hee Yoon, and Diana Zuckerman. 2000. *Part-time opportunities for professionals and managers: Where are they? Who uses them and why?* Washington, DC: Institute for Women's Policy Research.

Hays, Sharon. 1996. *The cultural contradictions of motherhood*. New Haven, CT: Yale University Press.

Hochschild, Arlie. 1989. *The second shift*. New York: Viking.

———. 1997. *Time bind*. New York: Metropolitan Books.

Jacobs, Jerry A., and Kathleen Gerson. 1998. Who are the overworked Americans? *Review of Social Economy* 56:442-59.

Kanter, Rosabeth Moss. 1977. *Men and women of the corporation*. New York: Basic Books.

McCracken, Douglas M. 2000. Winning the talent war for women: Sometimes it takes a revolution. *Harvard Business Review* 78 (6): 159.

Moen, Phyllis, and Shin-Kap Han. 2001. Gendered careers: A life-course perspective. In *Working families: The transformation of the American home*, edited by R. Hertz and N. L. Marshall, 42-57. Berkeley: University of California Press.

Pearson, Allison. 2002. *I don't know how she does it*. New York: Knopf.

Preston, Anne E. 1994. Where have all the women gone? A study of exits of women from the science and engineering professions. *American Economic Review* 84:1446-62.

Pyke, Karen. 1996. Class-based masculinities: The interdependence of gender, class, and interpersonal power. *Gender & Society* 10:527-49.

Schor, Juliet B. 1992. *The overworked American*. New York: Basic Books.

Stone, Pamela. 1998. Media myths about labor force dropout among professional and managerial women: Bringing some facts back in. Paper presented at the annual meetings of the Eastern Sociological Society, Philadelphia, March.

Swiss, Deborah J., and Judith P. Walker. 1993. *Women and the work/family dilemma: How today's professional women are confronting the maternal wall*. New York: John Wiley.

Williams, Joan. 2000. *Unbending gender*. New York: Oxford University Press.

SECTION TWO

Within the Professions

Marriage and Baby Blues: Redefining Gender Equity in the Academy

By
MARY ANN MASON
and
MARC GOULDEN

Traditionally, gender equity in the academy is evaluated in terms of women's professional success as compared to men's. This study examines gender equity not only in terms of professional outcomes but also in terms of familial outcomes, such as childbirth, marriage, and divorce. Using data from the Survey of Doctorate Recipients as well as data from a 2002 to 2003 survey of the work and family issues facing ladder-rank faculty in the nine campuses of the University of California system, the authors followed more than thirty thousand Ph.D.s in all disciplines across their life course and surveyed more than eighty-five hundred active University of California faculty. Results indicate that gender equity in terms of familial gains is as elusive as gender equity in terms of professional employment, raising the fundamental issue of what gender equity means in a university setting or in any fast-track employment setting.

Keywords: gender equity; academia; family; faculty

The traditional approach to issues of gender equity in the academy is to examine whether men and women have reached educational and employment parity, a fifty-fifty split, at each level of the academic enterprise. In recent years, the pipeline metaphor has been a popular way to depict the possible transitions from undergraduate matriculation to the achievement of full professor status (Camp 1997; Kulis, Sicotte, and Collins 2002; McBride 2002). Researchers concerned with problems in the pipeline to tenured faculty positions seek to determine, therefore,

Mary Ann Mason, JD, Ph.D., is dean of the Graduate Division and a professor in law and social welfare in the Graduate School of Social Welfare at the University of California, Berkeley. She publishes and lectures nationally on child and family law matters; the history of the American family and of childhood; and public policy issues related to work and family, child custody, children's rights, and stepfamilies. Among her publications are a major work on work/family issues, The Equality Trap, *and two major works on child custody,* From Father's Property to Children's Rights: A History of Child Custody in America *and* The Custody Wars: Why Children Are Losing the Legal Battles and What We Can Do about It. *Currently, she is engaged in a major*

DOI: 10.1177/0002716204268744

whether women disproportionately "leak out" of the pipeline at specific junctures (Cole and Zuckerman 1987; Ginther 2001; Jacobs 1996; Long 1990, 1992, 2001; Long, Allison, and McGinnis 1993; Perna 2001a, 2001b; Toutkoushian 1999; Valian 1998; Xie and Shauman 1998).

This approach has provided essential information to higher education policy makers and has led to the development of important policy interventions, particularly in the sciences. For example, the National Science Foundation's (NSF's) Advance Program seeks to aid women in pursuit of academic careers in the sciences (NSF 2002). The goal of this program is to facilitate women's progression through the academic ranks, building the necessary mechanisms—mentorship programs, funding opportunities, and so forth—to keep women in the sciences in the pipeline.

In our earlier work, we have sought to quantify the problems in the academic pipeline for women. Specifically, we have sought to determine what the effects of family formation are on the academic careers of men and women Ph.D. recipients (Mason and Goulden 2002; Wolfinger, Mason, and Goulden 2004). More recently, we have focused on an equally important, but neglected, approach to gender equity issues: assessing the effect of academic careers on the family outcomes of male and female academics—marriage rates, fertility, and divorce (Goulden, Mason, and Wolfinger 2004). This recent analysis has led us to conclude that programs and policies that are designed to promote gender equity in academia must take into account family outcomes as a measure of gender equity.

Gender Equity Problems in the Academic Pipeline, from Baccalaureate Degree to Tenured Professor

In the past thirty-five years, women's participation in undergraduate and graduate education has increased sharply and steadily. In 1966, women comprised 43 percent of bachelor's degree recipients, 34 percent of master's degree recipients, 5 percent of professional degree recipients, and 12 percent of doctorate degree recipients. In the academic year 2001-02, women constituted a clear majority of bachelor's and master's degree recipients, 57 and 59 percent, respectively; and were close to parity with men in the receipt of professional and doctorate degrees,

research study on the effects of family formation on the careers of men and women in the fast-track professions, the "Do Babies Matter?" study. She is also the co–principal investigator of a Sloan Foundation grant to implement family-friendly initiatives for ladder-rank faculty at the University of California.

Marc Goulden has a Ph.D. in social history and a background in life-course analysis. As a full-time academic researcher with the Graduate Division of the University of California, Berkeley, his work focuses on national research and policy issues related to graduate education and academia in general. He is also a coauthor of the "Do Babies Matter?" study as it relates to academic women and men.

constituting 46 and 45 percent of recipients, respectively (National Center for Education Statistics 2003a). Moreover, women now represent half of the full-time enrolled students in law schools and medical schools and at least half in doctoral programs in the life sciences, social sciences, and humanities (National Center for Education Statistics 2003b). Even in traditionally male-dominated fields such as the physical sciences and engineering, the representation of women has grown dramatically (NSF 2003).

Although women's obvious progress in the area of educational achievement is heartening, a less encouraging picture emerges if we examine the employment rates of men and women in the professorate. For example, in 1999, the most recent year of available data, women were just 29 percent of tenured faculty in the United States (National Center for Education Statistics 2001). At our institution, the University of California (UC), Berkeley, the situation is even less encouraging—women made up just 23 percent of tenured faculty in 2002, 259 out of the 1,126 associate and full professors (UC 2004).

One proposed explanation for why women have failed to progress to the upper ranks of academia is the rigid structure of the American workplace. The employment structures of the professions, proponents of this explanation argue, are configured for the typical male career of the nineteenth century, in which the man in the household was the single breadwinner and the woman was responsible for raising the children. According to this explanation, such rigid employment structures force women to choose between work and family. Rather than blatant discrimination against women, it is the long work hours and the required travel, precisely at the time when most women with advanced degrees have children and begin families, that force women to leave the fast-track professions (Crittenden 2002; Hochschild 1989, 1997; Mason 1988/2000; Williams 2000).

Many studies have shown that women have less time to devote to their careers than men because of domestic and caregiving responsibilities (Hochschild 1989; Press and Townsley 1998; Robinson 1988; Shelton and John 1996). Gary Becker (1991) has argued that the resources needed to meet professional responsibilities conflict directly with those needed for home duties. And more recent research confirms that this conflict extends to academics (Gatta and Roos 2002), with female professors spending considerably more time on domestic chores than their male counterparts (Suitor, Mecom, and Feld 2001).

Data Sources

With data from the Survey of Doctorate Recipients (SDR) (National Science Foundation 2004) and the University of California Faculty Work and Family Survey (Mason, Stacy, and Goulden 2003), we have tested the explanatory value of the work-family conflict explanation as it relates to career achievement in academia and problems in the pipeline to tenure for women.[1] What is more, these data sources have allowed us to do the opposite analysis: examine the effects of academic careers on familial outcomes of men and women doctoral recipients and ladder-rank faculty at the UC.

The SDR is a national biennial longitudinal study of U.S. doctoral recipients funded by NSF and others that started in 1973 and continues today (NSF 2004). For each biennial survey, the SDR includes (1) a nationally representative subsample of Ph.D. recipients drawn from the Survey of Earned Doctorates (SED), roughly 10 percent of the SED survey population; and (2) all individuals previously included in earlier SDR survey cycles who are younger than seventy-six years of age and live in the United States (NSF 1999). The overall response rate is high—nearly 87 percent of the surveyed population completed the survey in 1991 (NSF 1995); and to date, more than 160,000 doctoral recipients have participated in the study. Starting in 1981, the SDR included questions about both marriage and children younger and older than age six living in the household (Clark 1994). Thus, data from the SDR, since 1981, provide a full picture of career and family patterns over the life cycle and allow us to identify characteristics associated with career issues and family patterns and to measure their importance.

Our second data source, the University of California Faculty Work and Family Survey, includes the survey responses of 4,459 ladder-rank faculty who were working at one of the nine active UC campuses during the time of survey (Fall-Winter 2002-03 for UC Berkeley and Spring-Summer 2003 for the other eight active UC campuses). The fourteen-page survey focused on professional and family history, use of family-friendly policies, and work and family experiences while working as a faculty member at the UC (Mason, Stacy, and Goulden 2003). A total of 8,705 ladder-rank faculty with valid e-mail addresses were surveyed, with a 51 percent response rate. The results provide valuable information about work hours of UC faculty respondents, birth histories, attitudes toward childbirth, and issues of work and family conflict that augments our data findings from the SDR.

Assessing Family Formation Effects on the Tenure Rates of Men and Women Ph.D.s

In our initial analysis of data from the SDR, we sought to test the effect of children younger than six in the household at the time of career formation (up to five years post-Ph.D.), which we refer to as "early babies," upon the academic career progression of men and women doctorate recipients. We controlled broadly for discipline by conducting separate cohort analyses of Ph.D. recipients in (1) the sciences and (2) the social sciences and humanities. Among Ph.D. recipients from 1978 to 1984 who were still working in academia twelve to fourteen years out from Ph.D., we found that tenure rates for men with early babies in both the sciences and the social sciences and humanities were considerably higher (77 and 78 percent, respectively) than were the tenure rates of women with early babies in both the sciences and social sciences (53 and 58 percent, respectively). This finding led us to speculate that women with early babies were being pushed into, or choosing, second-tier jobs in academia (non–tenure track, part-time, and other similar positions) because of their family situation (Mason and Goulden 2002).

We also found that in both the sciences and the social sciences and humanities, women who had "late babies"—that is, the first child younger than six entering the household five or more years post-Ph.D.—or who had no children had somewhat higher tenure rates twelve to fourteen years out from Ph.D. than did women with early babies (65 and 71 percent, respectively). The tenure rates of women with late or no babies were still lower, however, than the tenure rates of men with early babies. We concluded, therefore, that gender-family effects were in part responsible for the lower tenure rates of women (Mason and Goulden 2002).

Rather than blatant discrimination against women, it is the long work hours and the required travel, precisely at the time when most women with advanced degrees have children and begin families, that force women to leave the fast-track professions.

To better test the validity of gender-family effects in accounting for women's lower rates of tenure achievement, we conducted a second series of analyses that were expressly designed to assess the exact location at which women Ph.D.s were leaking out of the pipeline to tenure (Wolfinger, Mason, and Goulden 2004). Using discrete-time event history analyses (Allison 1995), we modeled the effects of gender and family on the likelihood of individuals leaking out of the pipeline (1) from Ph.D. receipt to tenure-track job entry and (2) from tenure-track job entry to the receipt of tenure. Our analyses controlled for broad disciplinary field differences in sciences, social sciences, and humanities; age; ethnicity; Ph.D. calendar year; time-to-Ph.D. degree; and National Research Council (NRC) Ph.D. degree program reputation ranking (Wolfinger, Mason, and Goulden 2004).

Our findings from the second series of analyses provided us with a clearer understanding of the effects of gender and family on the pipeline to tenure for women and men academics. Specifically, we found significant interactions between gender and children younger than six in the household and between gender and marriage in estimating the likelihood of Ph.D.s entering a tenure-track position. Women with children younger than six were the least likely of all groups to secure a ladder-rank faculty position. In contrast, married men with children younger than six were the most likely of all groups to secure a tenure-track position. Married women without children younger than six were a little less likely than married men without children younger than six to enter a tenure-track job. And single women without children younger than six were a little more likely than single men without children younger than six to enter the ladder ranks. Thus, gender-family interactions are associated with the greater likelihood of women leaking out at the Ph.D. receipt to tenure-track entry stage (Wolfinger, Mason, and Goulden 2004).

When we tested statistically the relationships between gender-family interactions and movements through the portions of the pipeline from tenure-track job entry to tenure achievement, we found neither a "baby penalty" nor a "marriage penalty" for women. Rather, women were less likely than men, regardless of marriage or the presence of children younger than six in the household, to achieve tenure. Thus, we concluded that babies and marriage account for why women Ph.D.s disproportionately leak out of the pipeline prior to entering a tenure-track position; but these family effects do not explain completely why women, after securing a tenure-track position, are more likely than men to leave prior to achieving tenure (Wolfinger, Mason, and Goulden 2004).

Assessing the Effect of Academic Careers on Family Formation of Men and Women Ph.D.s

A great deal of scholarship analyzes the effects of gender and family on the academic career outcomes of men and women; considerably less research has been devoted to measuring the impact of academic careers on the family formation patterns of men and women. Women faculty have been observed to have overall lower rates of marriage and to have fewer children or dependents in the household than men faculty (Perna 2001a, 2003). But if they do marry, women academics are more likely than men to marry fellow academics, leading to the speculation that women academics are more likely to be professionally limited by dual-career couple constraints than are men (Astin and Milem 1997). There is also evidence that women faculty worry about the impact of family formation, particularly children, on their academic careers and that they may forgo or delay childbirth or time their births to occur during the summer months to avoid negative career consequences (Armenti 2004; Finkel and Olswang 1996). Delaying childbirth, however, can have adverse fertility consequences (Varner 2000).

With data from the SDR, we follow the cohort of Ph.D.s awarded between 1978 and 1983 and observe differences in the family status of men and women at different points after receipt of the Ph.D. by current employment situation. Figure 1 shows the family status of ladder-rank faculty women twelve years out from Ph.D. and the family status of two reference groups, ladder-rank faculty men and second-tier women—women Ph.D.s working in non-tenure-track faculty positions, working in part-time positions, or not working. Although a clear majority of ladder-rank faculty men, 69 percent, and second-tier women, 60 percent, are married with

FIGURE 1
FAMILY STATUS TWELVE YEARS OUT FROM PH.D.°

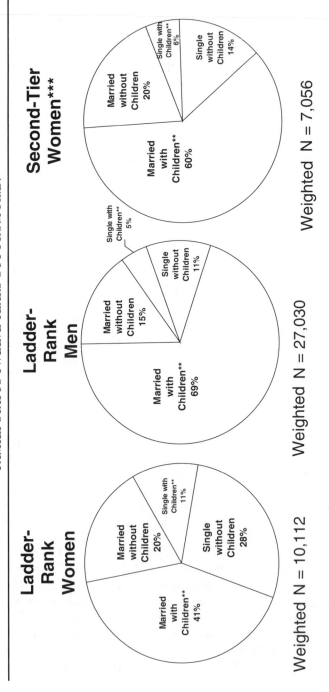

Ladder-Rank Women

Married with Children** 41%
Married without Children 20%
Single with Children** 11%
Single without Children 28%

Weighted N = 10,112

Ladder-Rank Men

Married with Children** 69%
Married without Children 15%
Single with Children** 5%
Single without Children 11%

Weighted N = 27,030

Second-Tier Women***

Married with Children** 60%
Married without Children 20%
Single with Children** 6%
Single without Children 14%

Weighted N = 7,056

SOURCE: Survey of Doctorate Recipients, Science and Humanities, 1979-95 (National Science Foundation 2004).

° Ph.D.s from 1978 to 1983 who are ladder-rank faculty twelve years out from Ph.D.

°° Had a child in the household at any point post–Ph.D. to twelve years out.

°°° Non–tenure track, part-time, or not working.

children (that is, currently married and having had children younger than eighteen in the household at some point after Ph.D. receipt), a minority of ladder-rank faculty women are married with children, 41 percent. Ladder-rank faculty women, in contrast, are more likely than both ladder-rank men and second-tier women to be single without children (28, 11, and 14 percent, respectively) and to be single with children (11, 5, and 6 percent, respectively). These findings suggest that men and women ladder-rank faculty have very different family formation patterns; it also shows that second-tier women are more similar to ladder-rank faculty men than they are to ladder-rank faculty women in their family patterns.

More recent cohorts may be postponing fertility until their careers are more firmly established.

Additional analyses using a larger cohort of Ph.D.s, all those with degrees awarded between 1978 and 1994, confirm that ladder-rank faculty women are different from ladder-rank men and second-tier women in their post-Ph.D. family formation patterns. Using logistic regression and controlling for broad disciplinary field, age, ethnicity, year Ph.D. awarded, time to Ph.D. degree, and program reputational ranking[2] (see Table 1), we find that women who are appointed as ladder-rank faculty within three years of receiving their Ph.D.s have a 50 percent lower probability of being married than do men and a 52 percent lower probability than do women appointed to second-tier positions.[3] These same ladder-rank faculty women also have a 61 percent lower probability of having a child younger than six in their households than do ladder-rank men and a 65 percent lower probability than do second-tier women.[4] In contrast, ladder-rank faculty women have a 144 percent greater probability of being divorced than do ladder-rank men and a 75 percent greater probability than do second-tier women.[5]

Based on a discrete-time event history analysis estimated with a complementary log-log regression (Allison 1995, 216-19) (see Table 2), we find that the probability of single women who are in ladder-rank positions within three years of receiving their Ph.D.s subsequently getting married is 32 percent lower than that of single ladder-rank men and 35 percent lower than that of single second-tier women.[6] Similarly, these same ladder-rank faculty women without children younger than six have a 35 percent lower probability of subsequently having a child younger than six enter their households than do ladder-rank men and a 61 percent lower probability than do second-tier women.[7] If these same ladder-rank faculty women are married within three years of their Ph.D.s, they are at a 35 percent greater risk of becoming divorced than are married ladder-rank men and at a 99 percent greater risk than are married second-tier women.[8]

TABLE 1

LOGISTIC REGRESSION OF MARRIED, CHILDREN YOUNGER THAN SIX IN
HOUSEHOLD, AND DIVORCED AT TIME OF CAREER FORMATION[a]

	Married	Child Younger than Six	Divorced
Female	.64°°°°	.68°°°°	−.16
Employment status			
Ladder-rank faculty	.61°°°°	.55°°°°	−.49°°°
Second tier[a]	—	—	—
Other full-time	.40°°°°	.37°°°°	−.22
Female × Ladder-Rank Faculty	−1.34°°°°	−1.61°°°°	1.05°°°°
Female × Second Tier[b]	—	—	—
Female × Other Full-Time	−1.15°°°°	−1.59°°°°	.80°°°°
Ethnicity			
White	—	—	—
African American	−.31°°°°	.23°°	.20
Asian American	.53°°°°	.45°°°°	.91°°°°
Latino	.07	.10	.04
Other/unknown	.17°	.06	−.11
Age	.02°°°°	−.07°°°°	.07°°°°
Year Ph.D. received	.00	−.01°°°	.01
Discipline			
Sciences	—	—	—
Social sciences	−.12°°°	−.11°°	.38°°°°
Humanities	−.19°°°°	−.22°°°°	.13
Rank of graduate program			
Best quartile	—	—	—
Second quartile	.15°°°	.25°°°°	.10
Third quartile	.20°°°°	.31°°°°	.09
Worst quartile	.28°°°°	.21°°°	−.17
Program unranked	.29°°°°	.23°°°	−.10
Field not ranked	.20°°°	.28°°°°	−.15
Time to degree			
Fastest quartile	—	—	—
Second quartile	.10°°	.34°°°°	−.07
Third quartile	.32°°°°	1.00°°°°	.04
Slowest quartile	.36°°°°	1.01°°°°	.02
Data missing	.36°°°	.70°°°°	.03
Constant	−5.51	23.38°°°	−24.07
Log-likelihood	−18,949.86	−16,221.10	−6,249.55

NOTE: Analyses are weighted. n = 30,874 for married, 27,870 for child younger than six, and 30,874 for divorced.

The data reported in Tables 1 and 2 also show that women Ph.D.s who are working full-time in other professional (nonfaculty) positions also experience lower

TABLE 2
DISCRETE-TIME EVENT HISTORY ANALYSES OF GETTING MARRIED,
HAVING A CHILD YOUNGER THAN SIX, AND GETTING DIVORCED
AFTER TIME OF CAREER FORMATION[a]

	Getting Married	Having a Child Younger than Six	Getting Divorced
Female	.46**	1.07****	−.39
Employment status			
Ladder-rank faculty	.42***	.56****	.00
Second tier[b]	—	—	—
Other full-time	.40***	.55****	−.23
Female × Ladder-Rank Faculty	−.85****	−1.50****	.69**
Female × Second Tier[b]	—	—	—
Female × Other Full-Time	−.85****	−1.35****	.81***
Ethnicity			
White	—	—	—
African American	−.20	−.04	.10
Asian American	.25**	.28***	−.54**
Latino	−.11	.13	.32
Other/unknown	−.06	−.14	−.05
Age	−.04****	−.10****	.01
Year Ph.D. received	.01	.03****	−.03***
Discipline			
Sciences	—	—	—
Social sciences	−.04	.05	.18*
Humanities	−.05	−.30***	.06
Rank of graduate program			
Best quartile	—	—	—
Second quartile	.09	.00	.11
Third quartile	.05	.08	.18
Worst quartile	−.15	−.02	.11
Program unranked	.08	.03	.22
Field not ranked	−.08	−.00	.39***
Time to degree			
Fastest quartile	—	—	—
Second quartile	.14*	.22***	.27**
Third quartile	.13	.29***	.27**
Slowest quartile	−.06	−.06	.23
Data missing	.36	.52**	−.31
Constant	−20.88	−64.86****	56.24***
Log-likelihood	−72,695.43	−96,378.11	−63,430.87

NOTE: Analyses are weighted. n = 6,366 for getting married (12,700 people biennial increments), 11,161 for having child younger than six (22,325 biennial increments), and 16,770 for
getting divorced (39,507 biennial increments).
a. At time of first Survey of Doctorate Recipients survey, within three years of Ph.D. receipt.
b. Working in non-tenure-track faculty positions, part-time employment, or not working.
*$p < .10$. **$p < .05$. ***$p < .01$. ****$p < .001$.

rates of marriage and fertility and higher rates of divorce than do ladder-rank faculty men, men employed in other jobs, and second-tier women. The effects of ladder-rank faculty positions on the family patterns of women Ph.D.s are not unique; other fast-track professional jobs have the same types of effects on the family outcomes of Ph.D. women. We observe, too, that Ph.D. recipients from lower-prestige programs and programs in the sciences and those taking a longer time to complete their degree show higher rates of marriage and children younger than six in their households within three years of their Ph.D.s than do individuals from higher-ranked programs, degree recipients in the social sciences and humanities, and faster degree completers, respectively. Asian American Ph.D. recipients consistently have higher rates of marriage and fertility and lower rates of divorce than do other ethnic groups. And there is evidence of a cohort shift in the fertility patterns of Ph.D. recipients, with more recent Ph.D. recipients showing lower rates of children younger than six in the household within three years of their degrees but higher subsequent rates of having children enter their households. More recent cohorts may be postponing fertility until their careers are more firmly established. These findings are discussed in greater detail in Goulden, Mason, and Wolfinger (2004).

Birth history data from the University of California Faculty Work and Family Survey provide further evidence that faculty men and women have different fertility patterns. As part of the survey, we asked respondents to provide us with the month and year of up to four children entering their household and their relationship to the child, biological or otherwise. Comparing the timing and rate of birth events in relationship to assistant professor start date for all UC faculty respondents, we observe clear differences in the fertility histories of UC men and women faculty. UC faculty women are more likely to have children prior to entry into graduate school or early on in their years of graduate school (see Figure 2). UC faculty men are considerably more likely than UC faculty women to have new babies at the critical time of career formation, from four years before to four years after assistant professor hire date. Moreover, from six years before hire date to twenty or more years after hire date, UC faculty men are more likely to have babies than are UC faculty women.

By taking the same birth history data and fixing it to respondent's age at birth of children, the differences in fertility patterns of UC women and men faculty are even clearer (see Figure 3). From age twenty-two to thirty-six, UC faculty men are more likely than UC faculty women to have babies. Women faculty, however, are more likely to have babies from age thirty-six to forty. This suggests that UC faculty women may be delaying childbirth until their mid- to late thirties. After age forty, men faculty are again more likely to have biological babies than are women faculty, no doubt because of biological constraints that disproportionately affect women after the age of forty.

Although many UC faculty women may have made a conscious decision to delay childbirth until their mid- to late thirties for career reasons, the longer-term consequences of doing so may not be readily apparent to aspiring faculty. Among faculty beginning their careers without children, the SDR data indicate that women lad-

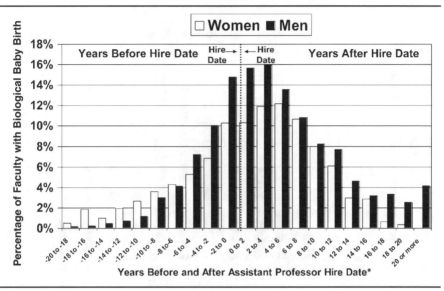

FIGURE 2
FERTILITY RATES OF UNIVERSITY OF CALIFORNIA FACULTY
IN PURSUIT OF TENURE

SOURCE: University of California Faculty Work and Family Survey (Mason, Stacy, and Goulden 2003).
NOTE: N = 2,340 men and 982 women.
*Year 0 represents assistant professor hire date.

der-rank faculty are less likely than men ladder-rank faculty to have children enter the household (30 percent in comparison to 50 percent, respectively) within twelve years of their hire.

UC faculty women are also more likely than UC faculty men to indicate that they had fewer children than they wanted to have. As seen in Table 3, 40 percent of UC faculty women aged forty to sixty indicate that they had fewer children than they wanted to have in comparison to 20 percent of UC faculty men aged forty to sixty. Among both men and women faculty, but particularly women faculty, individuals who had one child were the most likely to indicate that they had fewer children than they wanted, 42 and 64 percent, respectively. Thus, we observe that women faculty throughout the United States are less likely to have children than are men faculty, and UC faculty women are more likely than UC faculty men to indicate, after the age of likely fertility, that they had fewer children than they wanted.

Work and Family Conflict

Although there may be many reasons that ladder-rank women faculty forgo or delay childbirth, data from the University of California Faculty Work and Family

FIGURE 3
BIOLOGICAL BABY BIRTHS BY AGE OF UNIVERSITY OF
CALIFORNIA FACULTY

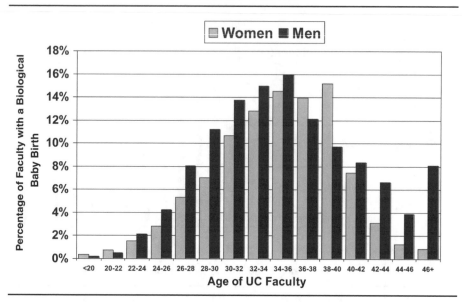

SOURCE: University of California Faculty Work and Family Survey (Mason, Stacy, and Goulden 2003).
NOTE: N = 2,809 men and 1,095 women.

Survey concerning total hours worked each week by faculty provide evidence that faculty mothers face what Arlie Hochschild (1997) referred to as a time bind. Among UC faculty aged thirty to fifty, women faculty with children self-report an average total of 101 hours per week engaged in professional, housework, and caregiving activities; men faculty with children report an average of 88 hours per week engaged in these activities; and men and women faculty without children report an average of 78 hours per week (see Figure 4). Caregiving activities take up a substantial portion of the time that women faculty with children devote to these activities, 35 percent of total hours, possibly to the detriment of their professional careers as seen in the lower number of hours, 51, that they report doing professional work each week.

UC faculty women with children are also more likely than UC faculty men to indicate they experience a great deal of tension or stress in their parenting as a result of certain work activities. As seen in Table 4, women with children are more likely than men with children to identify work activities that involve travel, field-work, conferences, and the time-consuming activity of writing and publishing as causes of stress in regard to their parenting. With the higher number of hours worked each week and greater parental stress as a result of work activities, UC faculty women with children seem to carry a heavier load than do UC faculty men and experience greater conflict in balancing professional and parenting demands.

TABLE 3

PERCENTAGE OF UNIVERSITY OF CALIFORNIA FACULTY, AGED
FORTY TO SIXTY, INDICATING THEY HAD FEWER CHILDREN THAN THEY
WANTED TO BY GENDER AND NUMBER OF CHILDREN

	n	%
Men		
No children	424	22
One child	239	42
Two children	514	13
Three or more children	236	8
All	1,413	20
Women		
No children	205	34
One child	153	64
Two children	224	32
Three or more children	50	24
All	632	40

SOURCE: University of California Faculty Work and Family Survey, 2002-03 (Mason, Stacy, and Goulden 2003).

FIGURE 4

UNIVERSITY OF CALIFORNIA FACULTY, AGED THIRTY TO FIFTY,
SELF-REPORTED HOURS PER WEEK ENGAGED IN PROFESSIONAL
WORK, HOUSEWORK, AND CAREGIVING

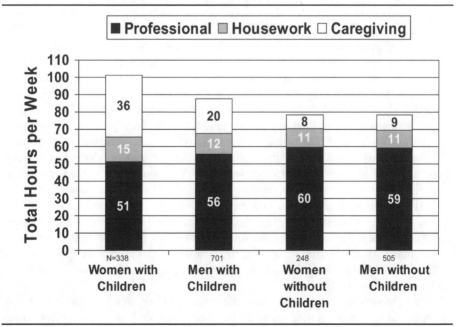

SOURCE: University of California Faculty Work and Family Survey (Mason, Stacy, and Goulden 2003).

TABLE 4

PERCENTAGE OF UNIVERSITY OF CALIFORNIA FACULTY
PARENTS EXPERIENCING A GREAT DEAL OF TENSION OR STRESS
IN THEIR PARENTING AS A RESULT OF SELECTED
WORK OBLIGATIONS, BY GENDER

	Doing Fieldwork or Field Research Away from Home		Writing and Publishing		Attending Conferences or Giving Conference Papers	
	n	%	n	%	n	%
Women with children	455	47	660	48	662	46
Men with children	1,148	27	1,782	29	1,772	22

SOURCE: University of California Faculty Work and Family Survey, 2002-03 (Mason, Stacy, and Goulden 2003).

Redefining Gender Equity

Our findings raise a host of cause-and-effect questions about family formation and academic success and the effect of academic careers on family formation. Although economists have asserted that there is a relationship between fertility and women's labor force participation, they have offered little consensus about the nature of causality (for an overview, see Macunovich 1996). Our first set of results relating to the pipeline to tenure shows that women may be more successful in obtaining academic careers if they forgo or delay marriage and childbirth.

Our second set of results relating to the effect of academic careers on family formation shows that women who successfully pursue ladder-rank faculty careers are quite different in their patterns of family formation from men who achieve ladder rank and also from women who drop out of the pipeline to tenure: ladder-rank faculty women are less likely to marry and have children and are more likely to divorce. We cannot determine with certainty the cause-and-effect relationships between these decisions. Women may be making conscious decisions to forgo or delay family formation to better their careers. Women may be choosing to drop out of the pipeline to marry, have children, or avoid divorce. Women who are dissatisfied with their rates of academic progress may be more likely subsequently to marry, have children, or stay married. Women may be forgoing academic careers or family formation for other reasons. We do know, however, that this pattern of low marriage and birth rates among many academic women is sharply at odds with the fact that most Americans desire both marriage and children (Thornton and Young-DeMarco 2001).

The life-course approach that we have taken in this article suggests that gender equity in terms of familial gains and losses is as unbalanced as gender equity in terms of professional gains, raising the fundamental issue of what gender equity means in a male-dominated profession. Thirty-odd years after the second-wave feminist revolution, equality in the workplace remains more of an aspiration than a reality. Yet the data presented above suggest that women, as compared to men, have significantly different family formation patterns when they pursue that elusive goal. Women aiming for high position in the professional academic world do not marry and have children in their early twenties, as their mothers did. They may be delaying these commitments because they consider a good boost up the career ladder the prudent preface to family formation. Meanwhile, in focusing solely on professional outcomes as the measure of gender equality, scholars have failed to acknowledge that the gap between the family outcomes of men and women, as measured by marriage, children, and divorce, is as wide as the gap in employment.

Notes

1. The Survey of Doctoral Recipients is sponsored by the National Science Foundation (NSF), the National Institutes of Health, and others for the sciences (including social sciences), and the National Endowment for the Humanities up through 1995. The use of NSF data does not imply NSF endorsement of research methods or conclusions contained in this report. Special thanks is due to the Association of Institutional Researchers and Alfred P. Sloan Foundation for funding our research.

2. Rankings are based on the National Research Council's ranks as reported in Goldberger, Maher, and Flattau (1995).

3. These probabilities can be computed from the Table 1 coefficients as follows: $50 = 100 \times [1 - \exp(0.64 - 1.34)]$ and $52 = 100 \times [1 - \exp(0.61 - 1.34)]$.

4. Computed as $61 = 100 \times [1 - \exp(0.68 - 1.61)]$ and $65 = 100 \times [1 - \exp(0.55 - 1.61)]$.

5. Computed as $144 = 100 \times [1 - \exp(1.05 - 0.16)]$ and $75 = 100 \times [1 - \exp(1.05 - 0.49)]$.

6. Computed as $32 = 100 \times [1 - \exp(0.46 - 0.85)]$ and $35 = 100 \times [1 - \exp(0.42 - 0.85)]$.

7. Computed as $35 = 100 \times [1 - \exp(1.07 - 1.50)]$ and $61 = 100 \times [1 - \exp(0.56 - 1.5)]$.

8. Computed as $35 = 100 \times [1 - \exp(0.69 - 0.39)]$ and $99 = 100 \times [1 - \exp(0.69)]$.

References

Allison, Paul D. 1995. *Survival analysis using the SAS system: A practical guide*. Cary, NC: SAS Institute, Inc.

Armenti, Carmen. 2004. May babies and posttenure babies: Maternal decisions of women professors. *Review of Higher Education* 27:211-31.

Astin, Helen S., and Jeffrey F. Milem. 1997. The status of academic couples in U.S. institutions. In *Academic couples*, edited by M. A. Ferber and J. W. Loeb, 128-55. Urbana: University of Illinois Press.

Becker, Gary S. 1991. *A treatise on the family*. Cambridge, MA: Harvard University Press.

Camp, Tracy. 1997. The incredible shrinking pipeline. *Communications of the ACM* 40:103-10.

Clark, Sheldon B. 1994. Variations in item content and presentation in the survey of doctorate recipients, 1973-1991. Working Paper, National Science Foundation, Washington, DC.

Cole, Jonathan R., and Harriet Zuckerman. 1987. Marriage, motherhood and research performance in science. *Scientific American* 255:119-25.

Crittenden, Ann. 2002. *The price of motherhood: Why the most important job in the world is still the least valued*. New York: Owl Books.

Finkel, Susan Kolker, and Steven G. Olswang. 1996. Child rearing as a career impediment to women assistant professors. *Review of Higher Education* 19:129-39.

Gatta, Mary L., and Patricia A. Roos. 2002. Balancing without a net in academia: Integrating family and work lives. Manuscript, Center for Women and Work, Rutgers University, New Brunswick, NJ.

Ginther, Donna. 2001. Does science discriminate against women? Evidence from academia, 1973-97. Working Papers 2001-2002. Atlanta, GA: Federal Reserve Bank of Atlanta.

Goldberger, Marvin L., Brendan A. Maher, and Pamela Ebert Flattau, eds. 1995. *Research doctorate programs in the United States: Continuity and change.* Washington, DC: National Academy Press.

Goulden, Marc, Mary Ann Mason, and Nicholas Wolfinger. 2004. Alone in the ivory tower: The hidden cost of academic success for women. Manuscript.

Hochschild, Arlie (with Anne Machung). 1989. *The second shift.* New York: Avon Books.

Hochschild, Arlie. 1997. *The time bind: When work becomes home and home becomes work.* New York: Metropolitan Books.

Jacobs, Jerry. 1996. Gender inequality and higher education. *Annual Review of Sociology* 22:153-85.

Kulis, Stephen, Diane Sicotte, and Shawn Collins. 2002. More than a pipeline problem: Labor supply constraints and gender stratification across academic science disciplines. *Research in Higher Education* 43:657-91.

Long, J. Scott. 1990. The origins of sex differences in science. *Social Forces* 68:1297-316.

———. 1992. Measures of sex differences in scientific productivity. *Social Forces* 71:159-78.

———, ed. 2001. *From scarcity to visibility: Gender differences in the careers of doctoral scientists and engineers.* Washington, DC: National Academy Press.

Long, J. Scott, Paul D. Allison, and Robert McGinnis. 1993. Rank advancement in academic careers: Sex differences and the effects of productivity. *American Sociological Review* 58:703-22.

Macunovich, Diane J. 1996. Relative income and price of time: Exploring their effects on US fertility and female labor force participation. *Population and Development Review*, suppl.: "Fertility in the United States: New Patterns, New Theories," 22:223-57.

Mason, Mary Ann. 1988/2000. *The equality trap.* Somerset, NJ: Transaction Books.

Mason, Mary Ann, and Marc Goulden. 2002. Do babies matter? The effect of family formation on the lifelong careers of academic men and women. *Academe* 88 (6): 21-27.

Mason, Mary Ann, Angelica Stacy, and Marc Goulden. 2003. *The UC faculty work and family survey.* http://ucfamilyedge.berkeley.edu/workfamily/htm.

McBride, Helen. 2002. The academic pipeline is a choice, not an obligation. *Science: Next Wave*, July 19. http://nextwave.sciencemag.org/cgi/content/full/2002/07/16/7.

National Center for Education Statistics (NCES). 2001. *The Integrated Postsecondary Education Data System (IPEDS) Salaries, Tenure, and Fringe Benefits of Full-Time Instructional Faculty Survey.* Washington, DC: NCES.

———. 2003a. *The Integrated Postsecondary Education Data System (IPEDS) Completions Survey.* Washington, DC: NCES.

———. 2003b. *The Integrated Postsecondary Education Data System (IPEDS) fall enrollment.* Washington, DC: NCES.

National Science Foundation (NSF). 1995. Changes to the survey of doctorate recipients in 1991 and 1993: Implications for data users. Presentation to the National Science Foundation, April 12.

———. 1999. *Characteristics of doctoral scientists and engineers in the United States: 1997.* Arlington, VA: NSF.

———. 2002. *Advance: Increasing the participation and advancement of women in the academic science and engineering careers: Program solicitation.* Arlington, VA: NSF.

———. 2003. *Survey of graduate students and postdoctorates in science and engineering.* Washington, DC: NSF.

———. 2004. *Survey of doctorate recipients.* http://www.nsf.gov/sbe/srs/ssdr/start.htm.

Perna, Laura. 2001a. The relationship between family responsibilities and employment status among college and university faculty. *Journal of Higher Education* 72:584-611.

———. 2001b. Sex and race differences in faculty tenure and promotion. *Research in Higher Education* 42:541-67.

———. 2003. Sex differences in faculty tenure and promotion: The contribution of family ties. Paper presented at the annual meeting of the Association for the Study of Higher Education, Portland OR.

Press, Julie E., and Eleanor Townsley. 1998. Wives' and husbands' housework reporting: Gender, class, and social desirability. *Gender & Society* 12:188-218.

Robinson, John. 1988. Who's doing the housework? *American Demographics* 10:24-28.

Shelton, Beth Anne, and Daphne John. 1996. The division of household labor. *Annual Review of Sociology* 22:299-322.

Suitor, J. Jill, Dorothy Mecom, and Ilana S. Feld. 2001. Gender, household labor, and scholarly productivity among university professors. *Gender Issues* 19:50-67.

Thornton, Arland, and Linda Young-DeMarco. 2001. Four decades of trends in attitudes toward family issues in the United States: The 1960s through the 1990s. *Journal of Marriage and Family* 63:1009-37.

Toutkoushian, Robert. 1999. The status of academic women in the 1990s: No longer outsiders, but not yet equals. *Quarterly Review of Economics and Finance* 39:679-98.

University of California. 2004. *Ladder and equivalent rank faculty, years 1989 to 2002, universitywide and by campus.* Oakland: University of California, Office of the President.

Valian, Virginia. 1998. *Why so slow?: The advancement of women.* Cambridge, MA: MIT Press.

Varner, Amy. 2000. *The consequences and costs of delaying attempted childbirth for women faculty.* University Park: Department of Labor Studies and Industrial Relations, Pennsylvania State University.

Williams, Joan. 2000. *Unbending gender: Why family and work conflict and what to do about it.* Oxford, UK: Oxford University Press.

Wolfinger, Nicholas, Mary Mason, and Marc Goulden. 2004. Problems in the pipeline: Gender, marriage, and fertility in the ivory tower. Manuscript.

Xie, Yu, and Kimberlee A. Shauman. 1998. Sex differences in research productivity: New evidence about an old puzzle. *American Sociological Review* 63:847-70.

Overworked Faculty: Job Stresses and Family Demands

Do professors put in very long workweeks solely out of a love of their work, or do expectations for teaching and publishing essentially require a sixty-hour workweek for the successful completion of the job? How do faculty members reconcile the demands of an academic career with the realities of family life? Drawing on a large national survey of postsecondary faculty conducted in 1998, the authors examine the length of the workweek by analyzing its relationship to faculty dissatisfaction with their workload. The authors find evidence that many professors are dissatisfied with their workload. Moreover, dissatisfaction increases among those working the longest hours. The data also indicate that very long hours on the job greatly contribute to research productivity. The very long hours demanded by faculty jobs thus pose a dilemma for parents who want to spend time with their children and their families. The authors conclude by suggesting that the challenge is to create a set of expectations for academic employment that are compatible with responsible parenting in dual-career couples.

Keywords: working time; faculty jobs; work-family conflict; working women; working parents

By
JERRY A. JACOBS
and
SARAH E. WINSLOW

As a way to commemorate the thirtieth anniversary of the Women's Studies Program at the University of Pennsylvania, Janice Madden organized a conference in October 2003 titled "Mommies and Daddies on the Fast Track." Given that occasion, we began by taking a step back and putting today's questions in context. Women have made major strides in entering many prominent professions during the thirty

Jerry A. Jacobs is Merriam Term Professor of Sociology at the University of Pennsylvania. He has been an active member of the American Sociological Association and Sociologists for Women in Society. He has just completed a term as president of the Eastern Sociological Society and is starting a three-year term as editor of the American Sociological Review, *the leading sociology journal in the United States. He has written extensively on opportunities for working women over the past two decades. His research has addressed a number of aspects of women's employment, including authority, earnings, working conditions, part-time work, and entry into male-dominated occupations. Jacobs is the author of*

DOI: 10.1177/0002716204268185

years since Penn's Women's Studies program was established. Since 1973, we have seen so many firsts—the first woman morning news anchor, the first woman on the Supreme Court, the first woman astronaut, the first woman secretary of state, the first woman president of an Ivy League university, the first woman CEO of a Fortune 500 technology company—that the very idea of female firsts is almost old news. In some areas, women's advances have gone well beyond the successes of a few pioneers. In 1973, no one would have dared to predict that within thirty years, students in law school and medical school would be able to count as many female as male classmates (American Association of Medical Colleges 2004). For all the complicated issues of gender inequality that remain for our society, we do believe that it is useful to remind ourselves of how much has changed in so short a time.

Many feminists and other interested observers are coming to the conclusion, however, that in recent years, the progress women have made in entering the professions has begun to stall. Arlie Hochschild (1989), who has coined so many memorable phrases, has referred to the current period as "a stalled revolution" in gender roles. The gender gap in earnings appears to be stagnating (Padavic and Reskin 2002). In an earlier paper, we found evidence of a plateau in gender segregation of occupations (Jacobs 1999). The disparity in attainment seems most evident at the highest echelons of business corporations. For example, at present, only eight women head Fortune 500 companies.[1]

At the same time as scholars raise serious questions about maintaining the momentum toward economic advances on the part of women, concern is growing about the ability of parents, especially working mothers, to balance commitment to their jobs and families. This body of research generally focuses on the ways work spills over into the rest of life, although we must take into account spillovers in both directions. Work-family conflict results from the competition between families and employers for the time and energy of individuals; it is a form of interrole conflict that emerges whenever the demands of one role make it difficult to fulfill the requirements of another (Greenhaus and Beutell 1985). Tension between work and family can result from three major sources: the demands of work (e.g., working

---

three books, Revolving Doors: Sex Segregation and Women's Careers *(1989)*; Gender Inequality at Work *(1995); and* The Time Divide: Work, Family and Gender Inequality, *with Kathleen Gerson (forthcoming). His current research projects include a study of women's entry into the medical profession, funded by the Macy Foundation, and a study of working time and work-family conflict among college and university faculty.*

Sarah Winslow is a Ph.D. candidate in sociology at the University of Pennsylvania. Her research interests focus on gender, the intersections of work and family, and the life course. She has written about trends in work-family conflict from the 1970s through the 1990s and about the relationship between welfare reform and women's enrollment in postsecondary education. Her publications include "Welfare Reform and Enrollment in Postsecondary Education," The Annals of the American Academy of Political and Social Science, *vol. 586 (with Jerry A. Jacobs); "The Academic Life Course, Time Pressures and Gender Inequality," in* Community, Work, and Family, *with Jerry A. Jacobs (forthcoming); and "Work-Family Conflict, Gender, and Parenthood, 1977-1997,"* Journal of Family Issues *(forthcoming). Her dissertation examines wives' contributions to couples' income over time and its relationship to the timing and incidence of childbearing and women's postbirth employment.*

time, schedule inflexibility, and so on), the demands of home (e.g., the gendered division of household labor), and normative and/or cultural expectations (e.g., the ideals of appropriate parenting and successful career achievement). In earlier work (see Winslow forthcoming), we have shown that reported levels of work-family conflict have increased in recent decades; furthermore, the rise in experiences of conflict between employment and family life has been concentrated among parents.

[T]he best jobs have become more demanding over time.

We feel that these two sets of issues—gender equity and family compatibility— need to be considered together. The goal should be to have family-friendly institutional arrangements in our society that also promote equal opportunities for women and men. Too many inquiries focus on one-half of this set of paired concerns. In other words, it is easy enough to address the family-friendly side of this equation—women can drop out of the labor market or the creation of more part-time jobs can be encouraged in organizational and occupational contexts where these remain the exception. But in the absence of broader institutional reforms, expanding part-time options will just make the gender disparities bigger. So as we see it, the real question is how to maintain and enhance women's access to the best jobs while making it possible for successful workers to be responsible and caring parents.

One key to understanding this dilemma is to recognize that the best jobs have become more demanding over time.[2] Long hours on the job are expected in many professional and managerial settings, far in excess of the forty-hour workweek that was established as the national standard more than sixty years ago. Moreover, smaller staffs are expected to get more done in less time as the pace of business has sped up. In other words, many jobs are more demanding in terms of effort as well as time. As a result, a significant fraction of respondents in national surveys report that they often feel used up at the end of the workday (Jacobs and Gerson 2004). Thus, "having it all" becomes especially difficult in the context of increased expectations at work.

Exacerbating the increased expectations on the job are increased expectations at home. While we often think of caring for children as a natural response of parents, closer consideration reveals that parenting is a socially constructed set of practices. Hays (1996) has suggested that middle-class parents are increasingly expected to cultivate every aspect of their children's social and intellectual facilities. Declining family size means that there are fewer children on the street to play with, resulting in more one-on-one time expected from parents (see also Lareau 2002).

Workplace demands in some occupations, inflexibility in others, and increased expectations of parents result in a set of work-family dilemmas that face many working families. These challenges call for a national discussion and for some institutional changes. The expectations of the typical job need to be brought more into line with the needs of the typical family, even while we recognize the diversity in both jobs and family arrangements (Jacobs and Gerson 2004).

In this article, we focus on the work side of these issues for one interesting occupation: faculty members employed in academia. University faculty members resemble incumbents in other high-profile occupations in some ways but are distinctive in others. Professors work long hours for less pay than many other professionals but have more autonomy regarding the substance of their work and more flexibility in their daily schedules. What of the prospects for women's employment in academia? Large numbers of women are training for academic positions, but a large gender gap in professional success remains. Women are overrepresented in part-time positions that are paid very low wages. Women are also overrepresented at the rank of assistant professor. One might expect this during an initial period when women are entering a profession in large numbers, but this pattern has persisted for quite some time. In other words, it is clearly the case that waiting for more women to work their way up the academic ladder will not lead to parity in employment any time soon.

Among the major pluses of academic employment is the flexibility of these jobs. The evidence indicates that workplace flexibility is a key factor in reducing work-family conflict (Galinsky, Bond, and Friedman 1996; Glass and Camarigg 1992). A key problem, however, is that academic jobs are very demanding. Professors often complain that the demands of their jobs never end. Furthermore, a long, continuous stretch of full-time commitment is expected for successful entry into the ranks of tenured faculty.

Female academics tend to have full-time employed husbands, and this has the potential to add to the time pressures they experience. Because jobs in academia pay less than other prominent professions, such as law and medicine, dual-earner careers will become increasingly common for men as well as women.

This article is organized as follows: First, we review the findings of several companion papers on the nature of academic careers. Second, we outline two views of the nature of academic work. Then we develop specific research questions regarding whether professors' long work hours are self-imposed. Third, we present our analysis of data on dissatisfaction with workload as well as an analysis of faculty research productivity, drawing on data from the 1998 National Survey of Post-Secondary Faculty (NSOPF). We show that many faculty members who put in long workweeks tend to be dissatisfied with their workload. Finally, we conclude with a discussion of some ways in which academia might become a more family-friendly institution.

Work and Family in Academia

This is the third article in a series on the work demands of faculty employed in colleges and universities. In two previous articles (Jacobs 2004; Jacobs and Winslow 2004), we documented a number of facets of faculty work time. We showed that the average workweek for full-time faculty exceeds fifty hours. These long workweeks are characteristic of all groups of faculty, irrespective of rank and institutional type. In other words, assistant, associate, and full professors all work in excess of fifty hours per week, as do faculty at research, liberal arts, and comprehensive institutions. We suggested that these long hours present a challenge to faculty trying to juggle the demands of having young families and the requirements of an academic position.

A second notable finding is that the timing of tenure decisions collides with that of family formation. Many assistant professors are in their late thirties and early forties. Indeed, we found that the average age of assistant professors was just over forty. As a result, the strategy of waiting until after one earns tenure to have children is not a viable one for large numbers—perhaps even the majority—of assistant professors.

Dual-earner careers are prevalent among academic families, especially among female academics. Of married faculty in 1990, just more than half of men and nearly 90 percent of women are married to other full-time workers (Jacobs 2004). A significant minority are married to other academics (18.2 percent of female faculty and 12.5 percent of male faculty). Thus, the long workweeks experienced by faculty need to be understood in the context of busy families.

Faculty Workload: Two Views

How can we make sense of the long workweeks put in by faculty? To clarify the issues here, we juxtapose two views, which we label the self-imposed or optimistic view and the structural constraints or pessimistic view.

The optimistic view holds that academia is a context in which devotion to work is self-imposed. Professors do not punch a time clock. Time spent in class is limited. Even at the most teaching-intensive institutions, classroom time rarely exceeds fifteen hours (authors' calculation from NSOPF data), and all other work time is allocated based on a professor's own concept of the time necessary to perform at an acceptable level. Thus, time demands experienced by faculty are in some sense discretionary. In any event, faculty members love their work. They deeply identify with their professional role. In this sense, academia represents a secular "calling" in the sense employed by Max Weber (1918/1946). This perspective on faculty working time would be consistent with the "work devotion" schema outlined by Blair-Loy (2003). Professors keep working diligently into retirement as long as their strength and stamina allow. While one can raise questions about exploitation of professional workers in some positions (such as junior associates in law firms, software engineers expected to work around the clock to make a tight deadline on the next application, and so on), faculty fall into a different category of worker. If the faculty workweek seems excessive to some, it certainly does not to faculty because it is what they chose to do.

In contrast to the view that faculty work time is self-imposed, an alternative view is that professors often find themselves caught in a set of institutional and professional expectations. Adherents to this second, more pessimistic, view would point to a number of other facets of academic life to support their position. For example, the pessimist would note that the life of assistant professors, who often slave away to meet high and imprecisely defined tenure standards, does not easily fit into the story of the self-imposed workweek. While the institutional demands perspective would acknowledge the many attractions of academia, such a view stresses the practical challenges that large numbers of faculty confront at both elite and less selective colleges and universities. The leading research institutions set high expectations for research, while at less well-endowed institutions, faculty struggle to keep up with preparing many different courses. And the optimistic picture certainly does not apply to increasingly cash-strapped institutions where state budget cuts mean more teaching with less support. Endless committee meetings, posttenure reviews, and a relentless stream of e-mails make today's faculty work experience less than the idealized world of academia suggested by the self-imposed viewpoint outlined above.

The rosy portrait of faculty life also fails to acknowledge the family context of faculty lives outside of their academic institutions. Academia demands a great deal of effort on a consistent basis for many years before the rewards of tenure are bestowed on anxious candidates. In this way, academia is an excellent example of what Phyllis Moen (2003) referred to as the "lock step life course," namely, jobs that do little to accommodate a variety of entry and exit points over the course of one's career.

Professors, especially female faculty, often delay having children as long as possible to meet tenure demands. In an earlier work (Jacobs and Winslow 2004), we have shown that this delay strategy may result in childlessness, given that the tenure decision, for the majority of faculty, occurs in one's early forties to midforties (see also Mason and Goulden 2004 [this volume]). Furthermore, the modest salaries of faculty (at least by middle-class standards) mean that many are partners in dual-earner couples. This is because the lower the husband's income, the more likely the wife is to work, other things being equal (Blau, Ferber, and Winkler 2002). As a result, today's faculty cannot count on a full-time homemaker to provide them uninterrupted time to focus on reading and writing as did their counterparts in the 1950s and 1960s.

If professors' long workweeks are due to "structural constraints," what are these structures, and what are the sources of these constraints? There are four main sources of growing time pressures on faculty (Jacobs 2004).

First, the rising cost of higher education has brought renewed public scrutiny and, with it, calls for more emphasis on teaching. The general public wonders why professors do not spend more time in the classroom. As a result, pressure to increase the quantity and quality of time devoted to teaching has been evident in public and private institutions of higher education. In public institutions, the concern is to justify the tax dollars spent on universities. In the private context, the $30,000 or $40,000 price tag of a year of college focuses parents and university administrators alike on how much faculty attention students actually receive.

[Time pressures on faculty] thus include organizational forces, professional norms, and technological changes.

Second, the increased emphasis on teaching has been accompanied by rising expectations for research productivity. Both the form and the content of the tenure review system formerly most developed in the elite schools have been adopted by colleges and universities at all levels of higher education. Dimaggio and Powell's (1983) notion of institutional isomorphism may be useful here. They suggested that institutions obtain legitimacy by adopting the organizational forms of high-prestige organizations. In the academic context, this means that second- and third-tier colleges and universities adopt the tenure review apparatus of the more elite schools. On the other hand, posttenure reviews represent a form of increased publication standards that did not originate in the elite universities (American Association of University Professors 2001). In short, high research expectations are no longer the restricted province of elite schools but have diffused throughout higher education.

Third, technological changes associated with the information economy have paradoxically increased the time demands and intensity of faculty jobs. Ruth Schwartz Cowan (1983) has explained how labor-saving technologies often result in a dramatic increase in the quality and quantity of a product that is produced but do not actually save time. We feel that computers represent a classic example of this pattern. It is much faster to produce a short letter on e-mail than it is to write and mail a letter. As a result, more time is spent reading and responding to e-mail messages than was formerly spent in hard copy correspondence. The adoption of computers was also accompanied by a decline in secretarial support among faculty.

Finally, we have suggested that the rise of part-time employment in academia increases the pressures on full-time faculty members (Jacobs 2004; Gappa and Leslie 1993). Part-time employment in academia has risen sharply over the past thirty years as extremely low-paid part-time faculty are available to teach for a small fraction of the cost of full-time members of the standing faculty. In 1999, more than two in five (42.5 percent) postsecondary faculty were employed part-time, a substantial increase from the 21.9 percent found in 1970 (U.S. Department of Education 2002).[3] The growth in the number of part-timers increases pressures on full-timers in two ways. First, the reduction in the number of full-time positions makes entry into the ranks of full-time faculty that much more competitive. Furthermore, since part-timers are rarely asked to serve on committees and take on other administrative roles, the growth of part-time employment means that a smaller fraction of faculty are saddled with a growing amount of administrative responsibilities.

These four factors thus include organizational forces, professional norms, and technological changes. Employers (colleges and universities) are the principal source of teaching requirements, and employers' cost-cutting concerns are the reason for the expansion in part-time employment. Publication expectations can probably be best understood as a set of professional norms, although the Dimaggio and Powell (1983) perspective acknowledges the organizational role in institutionalizing these arrangements. Finally, the technological changes associated with computers have also contributed to this trend.

Which of these views fits the data more closely? We are able to shed some light on this question with data from the NSOPF, which asked respondents a series of job satisfaction questions (a more complete description of these measures appears below). While it is clear that faculty overwhelmingly report being satisfied with their jobs, they do voice complaints about salary, benefits, and their workload. Here we focus on whether faculty report dissatisfaction with their workload because it allows us to assess the extent to which the length of the faculty workweek is self-imposed and willingly chosen. If the optimistic perspective is correct, then we would expect that those who put in the longest hours express few if any complaints about their workload since these faculty love teaching and research and cannot get enough of it. On the other hand, the pessimistic view suggests that some professors are not satisfied with their workload. If one's workload is largely driven by institutional and professional demands such as increasing course loads and expectations for publishing, then we may find a significant number of professors who are not satisfied with their jobs. A key question, then, is whether satisfaction with workload increases with time on the job. If so, then those working the longest may not be doing so completely voluntarily. Instead, work patterns may be the result of many pressures, some stemming from the institution and others from normative expectations set by other faculty.

We are also interested in the connection between working time and research productivity. Do long workweeks play a key role in contributing to success in publishing? If so, this relationship may give us insights into the reasons for the amount of time faculty spend on the job.

Our analysis begins by examining levels of workload dissatisfaction. We assess whether a connection exists between the length of the workweek and the likelihood of reporting workload dissatisfaction. We then examine variation in the length of the faculty workweek. Next, we model workload dissatisfaction in a multivariate context. Our analysis concludes with an assessment of the link between the length of the faculty workweek and research productivity.

Data

The data analyzed in this article were drawn from the 1998 NSOPF administered by the National Center for Education Statistics (NCES) of the U.S. Department of Education (U.S. Department of Education, NCES 2002). The survey is part of an ongoing series of cross-sectional surveys of faculty. This survey has been administered three times: during the 1987-88, 1992-93, and 1998-99 academic years. A fourth wave is currently in progress. In 1998, a nationally representative sample of faculty was drawn from 819 colleges and universities. The response rate was 83.2 percent, yielding a total of 17,600 responses.

For the present analysis, the sample was restricted to those faculty members at four-year institutions who considered their academic appointment to be their primary job and who did not spend the majority of their time in administrative activities. This resulted in a final sample size of 10,116 full-time faculty members.[4]

Measures of work dissatisfaction used in the analyses come from respondents' answers to a series of job satisfaction questions. Specifically, respondents were asked, "How satisfied or dissatisfied are you with the following aspects[5] of your job at this institution?" Responses to this question were measured on a 4-point scale consisting of *very dissatisfied, somewhat dissatisfied, somewhat satisfied*, and *very satisfied*. We focus our analyses on the questions regarding workload and reverse-code the responses to focus on the issue of workload dissatisfaction.

Our principal independent variable of interest is the amount of time spent working at the institution. (Time spent in other roles, such as consulting, is not included in our analysis, although we do include a measure of whether the faculty member does consulting work.) We tried a number of different specifications of working time, including hours as a continuous measure and hours squared. We present results with two dummy measures: those working fifty to fifty-nine hours and those working sixty hours or more. For most of our analyses, this specification captured the majority of the hours effects. These measures are also easily interpretable and allow for consistency with our earlier research in this area.

Control Variables

While the NSOPF data are not as systematic about family measures as we would like, we nonetheless were able to construct family-related variables in our analysis. Respondents were asked to indicate their marital status during the fall 1998 term according to the following four categories: single, never married; married; living with someone in a marriage-like relationship; and separated, divorced, or widowed. Those indicating that they were married or were living with someone in a marriage-like relationship are considered married for the purposes of our analyses.

Since respondents were asked to indicate their spouse or significant other's gross income in the 1998 calendar year, we were able to create a dummy variable indicating whether the respondent's spouse was employed in the reference year (i.e., if the respondent reported his or her spouse's income to be zero, he or she was considered to have a nonemployed spouse). A (proxy) measure of whether the respondent's spouse is also a faculty member was created using a survey question in which respondents were asked to indicate whether their "spouse or significant other [was] employed in a professional position at a higher education institution."

[A]ssistant professors were less likely to report dissatisfaction with their workload. Perhaps this is due to their expectation of extensive job commitment associated with being an assistant professor.

The collection of data on children in the NSOPF is even more limited. The measure we use is a proxy measure, obtained using responses to the question, "For the 1998 calendar year, how many persons lived in your household including yourself?" Single individuals were coded as having children if they reported two or more total household members, while married respondents were coded as parents when reporting three or more household members. The NSOPF unfortunately does not include questions on work-family conflict or stress. This is a major limitation that we hope other data collection projects will be able to address.

The NOSPF has a range of measures of job attributes that are relevant to our analysis of work dissatisfaction. In the regression models predicting hours worked and workload dissatisfaction discussed below, we control for a number of potentially influential covariates. Age is measured using a variable created by the NCES (survey respondents are asked to provide their month and year of birth). Our education measure is a dummy variable in which those with a first professional degree (M.D., D.O., D.D.S., J.D., etc.) or a doctoral degree (Ph.D., Ed.D., etc.) are coded as one, with all others coded as zero. Faculty rank is obtained from answers to the question, "Which of the following best describes your academic rank, title, or position at this institution during the 1998 Fall Term?" Institution type represents a Carnegie classification schema and is drawn from a variable created by the survey administrators. Our academic field variable comes from responses to the question, "What is your principal field or discipline of teaching?" The numerous potential response options listed for respondents to choose from were grouped into twelve larger categories: biological sciences, physical sciences, medicine and dentistry, nursing, other health fields, architecture and engineering, business, computer science and math, social science, education, arts and humanities, and vocational and other fields.

We also include several other job-related variables in our multivariate analyses. We assess the distribution of faculty work time by including measures of the percentage of time spent on teaching (undergraduate and graduate students) and research. We also control for whether the respondent was a department or division chair, whether the respondent's current appointment was temporary, and the respondent's union membership status. Finally, we control for respondents' employment outside the institution with two dummy variables, one for outside consulting work and another for outside employment other than consulting.

Results

Faculty workload dissatisfaction

Professors are largely quite satisfied with their jobs. In the 1998 NSOPF survey, 84.8 percent of male and 81.8 percent of female full-time faculty report being somewhat or very satisfied with their jobs (results not shown).[6] But that does not mean that faculty are happy with all aspects of their jobs. One common area of dissatisfaction has to do with faculty workload.

Tables 1 and 2 display the mean responses to the question of workload dissatisfaction for male and female faculty, respectively. A significant minority of faculty report being dissatisfied with their workload. Specifically, 30.4 percent of male faculty and 35.5 percent of female faculty report being dissatisfied with their workload. Dissatisfaction with workload may well be related to another faculty concern, not being able to keep current with one's field, which is the most common complaint voiced by faculty in the NSOFP survey. This problem is reported by 44.6 percent of male and 51.5 percent of female faculty.

In additional analyses (results not reported here), we found that concerns expressed over workload are a powerful determinant of overall job satisfaction. In fact, workload dissatisfaction rivaled concerns over salary and benefits as predictors of overall job satisfaction. When we predicted overall job satisfaction, we found that workload dissatisfaction and concern with not being able to keep current in one's field had effects similar in size and explanatory power to those of concerns over salary and benefits.[7]

As reported in Tables 1 and 2, faculty dissatisfaction with workload increases with hours on the job. Of male faculty working fewer than fifty hours per week, only 24.0 percent report being dissatisfied with their workload. The level of dissatisfaction rises to 38.2 percent for men putting in sixty or more hours per week. The same association can be found for female faculty. Nearly one in three (30.3 percent) of those working fewer than fifty hours per week report being dissatisfied

TABLE 1

DISSATISFACTION WITH WORKLOAD, BY WORK HOURS,
FAMILY STATUS, AND AGE FOR FULL-TIME MALE FACULTY

	Percentage Dissatisfied	Percentage Very Dissatisfied
All	30.4°°	8.6°°
<50 weekly hours	24.0°°	5.2°°
50+ weekly hours	34.3°°	10.1°°
60+ weekly hours	38.2°°	12.5°°
Married with children	32.7	8.7°°
Married without children	27.8°°	7.6°°
Single with children	34.6	9.5
Single without children	35.6	12.0
Married, employed spouse	31.8°°	8.4
Married, nonemployed spouse	27.2	7.8
Married, faculty spouse	34.2°°	9.3
Married, nonfaculty spouse	29.9	8.1
Age		
<35	27.6°°	8.3
35-44	38.0	11.0
45-54	35.8	9.5
55-64	26.3°°	7.2°°
65+	14.0°°	4.5°°

NOTE: "All" comparison assesses the gender gap. Fifty-plus and sixty-plus t-tests compare those who work fifty (sixty) hours or more each week to those of the same gender who work less. All other comparisons are within gender (with single nonparents as the reference category for the four-category marital/parental status variable and thirty-five to forty-four the reference age category).
°°$p < .01$.

with their workload, compared with more than two in five (44.1 percent) of those working more than sixty hours per week.

Thus, the evidence suggests that the more hours that faculty report working, the more likely they are to complain about an excessive workload. This is a simple and perhaps not surprising idea, but it runs counter to the notion that people working the longest hours are all doing so simply out of a love of their job.

Tables 1 and 2 also display dissatisfaction with faculty workload by marital and parental status. The results on this score are somewhat surprising. We expected that those people experiencing the greatest nonwork demands on their time, that is, individuals who are married and who have children at home, would report the highest levels of dissatisfaction with their workload on the job. We expected this to be particularly true for mothers, who continue to shoulder a larger share of the housework and child care burden than do fathers. The results indicate, however, that both married fathers and married mothers report lower levels of dissatisfaction with their workload than do those in other statuses.

We considered two explanations for this result. The first is that the question only focuses on workload and not overall work-family stress. Perhaps a broader mea-

TABLE 2

DISSATISFACTION WITH WORKLOAD, BY WORK HOURS,
FAMILY STATUS, AND AGE FOR FULL-TIME FEMALE FACULTY

	Percentage Dissatisfied	Percentage Very Dissatisfied
All	35.5	10.8
<50 weekly hours	30.3°°	7.6°°
50+ weekly hours	41.5°°	12.9°°
60+ weekly hours	44.1°°	15.2°°
Married with children	35.7°°	9.3°°
Married without children	37.3	11.7
Single with children	35.6°	10.7
Single without children	41.3	12.8
Married, employed spouse	36.6	10.4
Married, nonemployed spouse	32.3	12.8
Married, faculty spouse	38.9°°	12.8°°
Married, nonfaculty spouse	34.9	9.4
Age		
<35	31.6°	6.7
35-44	38.3	9.7
45-54	40.2	13.6°°
55-64	36.1	10.2
65+	22.3°°	9.0

NOTE: "All" comparison assesses the gender gap. Fifty-plus and sixty-plus t-tests compare those who work fifty (sixty) hours or more each week to those of the same gender who work less. All other comparisons are within gender (with single nonparents as the reference category for the four-category marital/parental status variable and thirty-five to forty-four the reference age category).
°$p < .05$. °°$p < .01$.

sure would yield a different result. The other possibility is that married parents find ways to limit the time they spend at work and, therefore, experience somewhat less overload on the job. We consider this latter possibility in more detail below when we examine the determinants of hours on the job.

Other aspects of faculty's marital status do impact dissatisfaction with workload in the expected directions. Men whose wives work for pay are more likely to experience dissatisfaction with their workload than those whose wives stay at home. And those men whose wives are themselves faculty report higher levels of workload dissatisfaction. This should not be surprising because their wives are likely themselves to be working fifty or more hours per week.

For female faculty, the presence of an employed spouse increases workload dissatisfaction, but the gap is not quite statistically significant. This is likely due to the fact that so few husbands are not employed. We do see higher levels of workload dissatisfaction for female faculty whose husbands are faculty as well.

The age patterns are also somewhat surprising. There is a curvilinear pattern of workload dissatisfaction for both male and female faculty. The highest levels of workload dissatisfaction occur between the ages of thirty-five and fifty-four for both groups. We were particularly surprised that assistant professors were less likely to report dissatisfaction with their workload. Perhaps this is due to their expectation of extensive job commitment associated with being an assistant professor. In other words, perhaps they feel that long workweeks are built into the job, and perhaps they expect the situation to be temporary.

[Faculty perception of workload] is not just how many hours one works but whether one is doing the kind of work one finds most satisfying.

One important pattern that connects Tables 1 and 2 is the many commonalities in the reports of male and female faculty. In other words, while overall workload dissatisfaction is higher among women than among men, the correlates that we consider in Tables 1 and 2 generally have similar effects for men and women. This evidence supports the premise that work-family issues are not restricted to women.

Determinants of working time

Workload dissatisfaction increases with time on the job, so we now turn to the determinants of the faculty workweek. In our previous work, we stressed the long workweeks common to faculty of all stripes. For each group of full-time faculty we considered—whether they were assistant, associate, or full professors and whether they were working at research universities, liberal arts colleges, or comprehensive institutions—working hours exceeded fifty per week. Here we focus on variation among faculty since variability around this high mean is of interest and may be related to the likelihood of reporting dissatisfaction with one's workload.

Table 3 presents separate regression analyses for men and women. We first examine the determinants of working time, treating work hours as a continuous variable. We then present results for models that analyze the odds of working more than sixty hours per week.

The first notable finding in Table 3 is that both married mothers and fathers work less than those in other marital and parental statuses. On average, married mothers work four hours less per week than do single women without children, while for married fathers, the gap is two hours per week. The gap is especially pronounced in the analysis of the odds of working more than sixty hours per week.

TABLE 3
REGRESSION ANALYSES OF HOURS WORKED, BY GENDER

	Ordinary Least Squares Regression, Hours Worked, Women	Ordinary Least Squares Regression, Hours Worked, Men	Logistic Regression, Hours Sixty-Plus, Women	Logistic Regression, Hours Sixty-Plus, Men
Intercept	42.307**	42.627**	0.491**	0.642**
Married with kids	−4.132**	−2.033**	0.769**	0.715**
Married without kids	−1.506*	−1.373*	0.715**	0.809
Single with kids	−2.224**	−0.486		
Single without kids (reference)				
Nonemployed spouse	0.767	0.991*	1.286	1.240**
Faculty spouse	0.840	0.540	1.057	1.177*
Rank				
Full	0.593	2.006**	1.172	1.424**
Associate (reference)				
Assistant	−0.393	1.562**	0.845	1.323**
Instructor/lecturer	−3.279**	−1.248	0.618**	0.909
Other/ no ranking	−3.042**	0.555	0.528**	1.030
Institution type				
Research	1.297*	2.287**	1.065	1.388**
Doctoral	−0.088	1.524**	0.913	1.198
Liberal arts	1.213	1.183*	1.209	1.232*
Comprehensive (reference)				
Other	−0.617	0.179	0.749	1.127
Percentage of time spent on research	−0.026*	−0.002	0.999	1.000
Age	0.502**	0.458**	1.049	1.031
Age squared	−0.006*	−0.006**	0.999*	0.999*

Education				
Ph.D.	1.693**	0.371	1.366**	0.977
Professional degree	2.440*	1.959*	1.614**	1.072
Department chair	1.639*	2.097**	1.179	1.354**
Temporary appointment	−0.019	−0.962*	1.080	0.898
Union member	−0.642	−0.358	0.920	0.989
Outside employment				
Consulting	4.668**	3.727**	1.686**	1.501**
Other employment	0.966*	0.795*	1.240**	1.192**
Field				
Biological sciences	2.514*	2.961**	1.548**	1.455**
Physical sciences	0.764	2.391**	1.246	1.213
Medicine/dentistry	3.218**	3.995**	1.712**	1.820**
Nursing	2.549**	4.903	1.267	2.695
Other health	1.807*	3.276**	1.183	1.685**
Architecture/engineering	2.936	2.058**	1.474	1.268*
Business	−1.000	−0.328	0.744	0.867
Computer science/math	0.240	0.195	0.918	0.927
Social science	0.711	0.285	0.954	0.927
Education	2.484**	1.058	1.372*	0.991
Arts and humanities (reference)				
Vocational and other fields	3.793**	3.049**	1.644**	1.502**
R-squared	.079	.066	.055	.038

$^*p < .05. \ ^{**}p < .01.$

Married mothers are about half as likely as single childless women to work more than sixty hours per week, while married fathers are about two-thirds as likely to do so than are their single, childless counterparts.

This pattern helps to explain the findings reported in Tables 1 and 2. Married mothers and fathers report less dissatisfaction with their workload because they work less. As we will see, working more than sixty hours per week is a powerful predictor of dissatisfaction with workload, and married mothers and fathers are much less likely to work these extremely long hours.

For female faculty, the average workweek does not vary significantly between assistant, associate, and full professors, while male associate professors report a small slump in working time. Faculty report working the longest hours in research universities, compared to comprehensive institutions, but the gap is not large (just more than one hour per week for women faculty and just more than two hours per week for male faculty).

The results in Table 3 indicate that male or female faculty who spend a larger proportion of their work time on research do not have a longer workweek. This result runs counter to the idea that the race for scientific stardom is the driving force behind the long workweeks of faculty. Having controlled for institution type, devoting a larger fraction of one's time to research is not the principal determinant of long workweeks. (We return to the issue of time devoted to research when we consider the issue of faculty research productivity below.)

Being a department chair increases the length of the workweek by one to two hours. Outside employment, including consulting, has a more significant effect on the length of the faculty workweek. Note that time spent consulting is not included in the hours measure we use in this study. In other words, those who do consulting work also devote more time to their institution, all other factors being equal.[8] Union members do not work different hours.[9] Age and age squared impact the average work week but have less impact on the odds of working more than sixty hours per week.

Determinants of workload dissatisfaction

Table 4 presents the results of our models of workload dissatisfaction. We group somewhat dissatisfied and very dissatisfied together into a single category of workload dissatisfaction. We conducted additional analyses of being very dissatisfied, and the results largely mirror those reported here. We initially present a pooled analysis of male and female faculty. Results for a series of nested models are presented. Table 5 presents separate models for men and women.

The first notable result in Table 4 is that those faculty working fifty to fifty-nine hours are more likely to report being dissatisfied with their workload than those working fewer than fifty hours per week. In the final model, those working fifty to fifty-nine hours per week are about one-third more likely to report workload dissatisfaction than those working fewer than fifty hours per week. Similarly, the odds of reporting workload dissatisfaction rise again for those working sixty hours per week. Here we find that professors who work more than sixty hours per week are

TABLE 4

LOGISTIC REGRESSION OF WORKLOAD DISSATISFACTION
(ODDS RATIOS REPORTED)

	Model 1	Model 2	Model 3	Model 4	Model 5
Female	1.478°°	1.367°°	1.327°°	1.306°°	1.344°°
Hours 50-59	1.391°°	1.332°°	1.338°°	1.333°°	1.337°°
Hours 60+	1.470°°	1.921°°	1.952°°	1.946°°	1.955°°
Age		1.227°°	1.208°°	1.204°°	1.212°°
Age squared		0.998°°	0.998°°	0.998°°	0.998°°
Highest degree		1.186°°	1.173°°	1.227°°	1.232°°
Married with kids		0.761°°	0.770°°	0.770°°	0.780°°
Married without kids		0.872°	0.878	0.873°	0.879
Single with kids		0.864	0.870	0.873	0.873
Single without kids (reference)					
Nonemployed spouse		0.908	0.910	0.917	0.902
Faculty spouse		1.046	1.079	1.091	1.083
Rank					
Full			0.818°°	0.827°°	0.816°°
Associate (reference)					
Assistant			0.950	0.944	0.954
Instructor/lecturer			0.769°°	0.741°°	0.754°°
Other/no ranking			0.699°°	0.710°°	0.714°°
Institution type					
Research			0.632°°	0.887	0.879
Doctoral			0.947	0.954	0.952
Liberal arts			1.006	0.936	0.942
Comprehensive (reference)					
Other			0.799°°	0.778°°	0.765°°
Percentage of time spent on research				0.992°°	0.992°°
Percentage of time spent teaching				1.001	1.001
Department chair				1.204°°	1.212°°
Temporary appointment				1.020	1.024
Union member				1.043	1.052
Outside employment					
Consulting				0.951	0.964
Other employment				1.061	1.058
Field					
Biological sciences					0.889
Physical sciences					0.933
Medicine/dentistry					0.964
Nursing					0.812
Other health					0.745°°
Architecture/engineering					1.220
Business					0.688°°
Computer science/math					0.869
Social science					0.884
Education					0.766°°
Arts and humanities (reference)					
Vocational and other fields					0.682°°
Pseudo R-squared	.019	.034	.041	.045	.048

°p < .05. °°p < .01.

TABLE 5
LOGISTIC REGRESSION OF WORKLOAD DISSATISFACTION,
BY GENDER (ODDS RATIOS REPORTED)

	Men	Women
Hours 50-59	1.345°°	1.345°°
Hours 60+	2.051°°	1.856°°
Age	1.207°°	1.220°°
Age squared	0.998°°	0.998°°
Highest degree	1.213°	1.267°°
Married with kids	0.779°°	0.811°
Married without kids	0.898	0.884
Single with kids	0.940	0.837
Single without kids (reference)		
Nonemployed spouse	0.914	0.860
Faculty spouse	1.147	0.989
Rank		
Full	0.750°°	0.999
Associate (reference)		
Assistant	0.866	1.079
Instructor/lecturer	0.788	0.804
Other/no ranking	0.596°°	0.871
Institution type		
Research	0.923	0.787
Doctoral	0.976	0.916
Liberal arts	0.933	0.950
Comprehensive (reference)		
Other	0.776°	0.746°
Percentage of time spent on research	0.991°°	0.993°°
Percentage of time spent teaching	1.002	1.000
Department chair	1.249°°	1.166
Temporary appointment	1.098	0.944
Union member	1.145	0.952
Outside employment		
Consulting	1.000	0.921
Other employment	1.102	0.997
Field		
Biological sciences	0.803	1.062
Physical sciences	0.967	0.759
Medicine/dentistry	0.950	0.977
Nursing	0.486	0.876
Other health	0.775	0.719°
Architecture/engineering	1.248	0.886
Business	0.644°°	0.746
Computer science/math	0.862	0.865
Social science	0.795°	1.001
Education	0.752°	0.800
Arts and humanities (reference)		
Vocational and other fields	0.691°°	0.666°°
Pseudo R-squared	.051	.040

°$p < .05$. °°$p < .01$.

nearly twice as likely to report workload dissatisfaction as those working fewer than fifty hours per week.

The effects of the length of the workweek on workload dissatisfaction are robust across the nested models we present. The only notable change that occurs is that the effect of working sixty hours or more increases once age is controlled. In other words, the effect of hours worked is obscured by age, and once this association is controlled, the effect of working very long workweeks becomes even stronger.

What factors affect workload dissatisfaction besides time on the job? Women report more workload dissatisfaction than men. Workload dissatisfaction increases with age in a curvilinear manner.

Those reporting having the highest appropriate degree report more workload dissatisfaction than those with fewer credentials. (In most cases, this is the Ph.D., but in some professional settings such as law school, the highest appropriate degree may not be a Ph.D.) This suggests that those who are fully certified feel the full brunt of academic expectations. Those with fewer credentials may be less committed to the academic calling and are, thus, less susceptible to professional norms regarding research productivity. Those with fewer credentials may also be less likely to be called upon to serve on committees and thus have fewer obligations regarding academic governance.

We expected assistant professors to have the most complaints about workload. But the results suggest that it is associate professors who have the most complaints. The odds ratios for assistant professors are less than one, indicating lower levels of dissatisfaction, but these differences are not statistically significant. Full professors and those in other ranks report statistically lower levels of dissatisfaction with workload. Perhaps assistant professors accept the high workload expectations set by their institutions, and perhaps they view their heavy workload as a temporary accommodation needed to obtain tenure. Full professors are less likely to report workload dissatisfaction, as are those in nonstandard faculty positions.

We found few differences across institutional type. Those in research, liberal arts, and comprehensive institutions were equally likely to report being dissatisfied with their workload, all other factors being equal.

Teaching, research, and administration have somewhat different effects on faculty's perception of workload. Thus, it is not just how many hours one works but whether one is doing the kind of work one finds most satisfying. Those spending a larger fraction of their time on research are less likely to complain about their workload. (Of course, these are average effects, and there may be a significant subset with different views about the relative satisfactions of teaching and research.) In contrast, spending a larger fraction of time on teaching is not clearly differentiated from spending more time on administration in terms of its effect on workload dissatisfaction.

Department chairs report higher levels of workload dissatisfaction than do other faculty. This effect is obtained even when we control for the number of hours they put in on the job. It is clear that these positions demand a certain kind of time that professors tend to feel is especially onerous. Faculty members who are union members do not report any less dissatisfaction with workload.

We expected that marital and parental status would be powerful predictors of faculty workload dissatisfaction, but this was not the case. As we noted above, married individuals were not more likely to report dissatisfaction with their workload. While this does not surprise us for husbands, the result does not conform to our expectation for wives. We expected that wives' increased housekeeping responsibilities at home would make them more likely to complain about their workload on the job.[10]

Recall that married women without children worked about 1.5 hours less per week than their single counterparts. While this slight reduction in work is surely not sufficient to compensate for the extra unpaid work that they are taking on, there were more sizable effects of being married at the high end of the distribution. Married women were only 70 percent as likely to work more than 60 hours per week as were single women, and thus these women may be cutting back on the very longest hours that generate the most dissatisfaction with workload. Perhaps married faculty members were able to achieve a better balance in their work lives and, as a result, were no more likely to report being dissatisfied with their workload.

Similarly, parents did not report higher levels of dissatisfaction with their workload than did those with no children. Recall that married mothers work about four fewer hours per week than do single women without children. Married fathers reported working about two hours less than single childless men. As we saw with married individuals, there was more evidence of cutting back on working time among those putting in more than sixty hours per week. Here we find that married mothers were about half as likely to work more than sixty hours per week, and married fathers were about 60 percent as likely to work more than sixty hours per week. Again, by cutting back on the most onerous hours, married parents are able to keep complaints about their workload at a level comparable to other faculty. Thus, the lack of an effect of marital and parental status appears to be due to a combination of the facts that the questions did not elicit information about overall stress levels and that professors in these roles reduce the hours they devote to their academic work, especially by cutting back once they reach sixty hours per week. These reductions in working time, however, are not costless, as we will see in the following discussion of publishing patterns. If cutting back on working time means jeopardizing research productivity, which is essential to securing tenure, then the efforts of parents to balance work and family come with a substantial price tag.

Research productivity

We remained curious about the connection between time devoted to research and workload satisfaction. We found that the percentage of time spent on research was not the driving force behind long work hours. There is no statistically significant increase in working time associated with a larger fraction of time spent on research. On the other hand, those who spent a larger fraction of their time on research were less likely to voice dissatisfaction with their workload. Are those who put in the longest workweeks the most productive in terms of research?

Table 6 presents results of regression analyses on research productivity. We define research productivity as the sum of articles published to date. We convert books into this measure by multiplying the number of books by five. (The results are broadly similar when we consider just books, just articles, and different book-to-article translation scores.) Controls in the model for academic specialty capture important differences in publication rates between different academic fields. Given the nature of these data, we are unable to control for differences in quality among published articles and books.

The results make it clear that those who put in the longest workweeks are likely to publish more books and articles. The differences between those putting in more than fifty hours per week versus those putting in fewer than fifty hours per week are substantial. However, the impact of working more than sixty hours per week is even more dramatic. Working sixty hours per week seems especially critical for women since the coefficient on working fifty to fifty-nine hours per week is not significant for them.[11] If research productivity is indispensable for success in academia, and if a sixty-hour workweek is key for success in publishing, then working sixty or more hours per week essentially becomes a requirement of academic jobs.

As a final step in our analysis, we took these productivity results into account in our analysis of dissatisfaction with workload. We considered whether those scholars who are highly productive researchers are less likely than others to be dissatisfied with their workload. In other words, it is clear that many who work very long hours are not fully satisfied with this situation. But perhaps the complaints are concentrated among those who are less successful in publishing. We found no such association in the NSOPF survey. Specifically, among those working the most hours, dissatisfaction with workload is equally evident among scholars with high research productivity and those with shorter academic vitae.

Conclusion

While academia may appear to be a setting in which work effort is completely self-imposed, the analyses we have presented here begin to flesh out a more complicated picture. Those who work the most hours are the most likely to express dissatisfaction with their workload. Furthermore, while professors often express concerns about the extent of their workload, the brief responses to fixed-choice survey questions are likely to *understate* the breadth and depth of concerns about the voracious time demands of academic life.

So why do faculty work so much? The data indicate that very long workweeks significantly contribute to success in publishing. Those who work sixty or more hours per week are substantially more likely to publish than those who work fewer hours. Since continued research productivity has become a central expectation of faculty at all types of colleges and universities, it is not hard to see why many faculty consider a very long workweek to be a requirement of their job.

We view these data as providing considerable support for the structural constraints perspective on the faculty workweek. While some faculty members would

TABLE 6

ORDINARY LEAST SQUARES REGRESSION
OF PUBLICATION PRODUCTIVITY, BY GENDER

	All	Men	Women
Intercept	−26.126°	−44.903°	−28.151°°
Female	−5.127°°	—	—
Hours 50-59	4.550°°	7.733°°	0.691
Hours 60+	12.123°°	16.894°°	5.191°°
Age	0.520	0.666	1.295°°
Age squared	0.002	0.003	−0.010°
Highest degree	2.681°	1.919	4.584°°
Married with kids	3.071°	4.597	−1.006
Married without kids	2.706	3.385	−0.085
Single with kids	1.822	3.930	−0.566
Single without kids (reference)			
Nonemployed spouse	4.117°°	4.184°	−1.330
Faculty spouse	1.116	1.641	1.681
Rank			
Full	24.551°°	25.873°°	16.338°°
Associate (reference)			
Assistant	−3.987°	−3.720	−5.866°°
Instructor/lecturer	−0.053	−1.374	−3.789°
Other/no ranking	−1.177	2.034	−7.213°°
Institution type			
Research	9.638°°	9.147°°	8.690°°
Doctoral	0.725	0.818	1.113
Liberal arts	−9.462°°	−13.106°°	−3.757°
Comprehensive (reference)			
Other	−5.630°°	−7.864°°	−1.871
Percentage of time spent on research	0.303°°	0.381°°	0.187°°
Percentage of time spent teaching	−0.058°°	−0.060	−0.047°
Department chair	2.038	3.008	1.000
Temporary appointment	−4.258°°	−5.231°	−1.564
Union member	−3.897°°	−5.137°	−1.486
Outside employment			
Consulting	12.862°°	16.307°°	6.727°°
Other employment	1.761	2.721	0.772
Field			
Biological sciences	8.454°°	10.276°°	4.871°
Physical sciences	18.458°°	22.327°°	3.400
Medicine/dentistry	13.773°°	18.842°°	3.465
Nursing	4.802	−0.953	3.233
Other health	13.105°°	21.572°°	3.436
Architecture/engineering	35.967°°	39.523°°	14.934°°
Business	−0.424	−0.350	0.655
Computer science/math	2.574	4.847	0.662
Social science	4.727°°	5.280°	3.577°
Education	1.811	1.688	1.566
Arts and humanities (reference)			
Vocational and other fields	8.946°°	12.055°°	5.553°°
Pseudo R-squared	.256	.247	.193

°$p < .05.$ °°$p < .01.$

surely spend all of their free time on job-related reading and writing, a significant minority indicate that they feel constrained to work longer than they would like.

It is difficult to sustain a sixty-hour-per-week schedule over the course of an entire career. And as we have seen, parents (especially mothers) are less likely to put in these very long hours. It is exceedingly challenging to be a responsible parent while maintaining this extent of work commitment, even if academic jobs are highly flexible. These effects are far-reaching—the tension between work and family does not end with young children; nor does it end with tenure.

We maintain that work and family are compatible when the expectations of work are not excessive. The data presented here suggest that the demands of academic life are becoming excessive and are making it difficult for individuals to succeed at work while having the time to be caring and responsible parents. This suggests that efforts to promote a better balance between work and family should go beyond parental leave policies for newborns and try to establish limits on the apparently limitless demands of academic jobs.

Notes

1. Catalyst (2003a, 2003b). Women's representation on corporate (Fortune 500) boards of directors has been inching up, from 8.7 percent in 1995 to 15.7 percent in 2002.

2. In this discussion, we focus on the work-family issues confronting workers employed in professional and managerial positions. Workers in less elite jobs often face a somewhat different set of challenges. These jobs tend to have less flexibility even when workers are not routinely expected to work fifty or sixty hours per week. And because those with modest incomes have fewer financial resources to draw on, their work-family dilemmas may be even more daunting than those facing professional families. The variety of work-family issues confronting different segments of American society is one of the themes of *The Time Divide* (Jacobs and Gerson 2004).

3. We considered whether part-time faculty teach substantially fewer courses and consequently fewer students than full-time faculty. Recent evidence finds, however, that part-timers account for 39 percent of faculty and 40 percent of courses and students taught (National Education Association 2001).

4. Many important issues confront academics in part-time positions who find themselves on the other side of the "faculty time divide" (Jacobs 2004). But here we focus on the issue of overworked full-timers.

5. The job aspects in question were as follows: "my work load; my job security; opportunity for advancement in rank at this institution; time available for keeping current in my field; the effectiveness of faculty leadership at this institution (e.g., academic senate, faculty councils, etc.); freedom to do outside consulting; my salary; my benefits, generally; my job here, overall." An additional question, regarding "spouse or partner employment opportunities in this geographic area," was included in the survey but excluded from the present analyses as it was not asked of the entire sample.

6. It is important to keep in mind that responses to job satisfaction questions tend to inflate the reported level of job satisfaction. In the survey context, respondents in most jobs tend to volunteer that they are satisfied with their employment.

7. Salary and benefits were slightly better predictors of overall job satisfaction for men, but workload was a better predictor for women.

8. Among full-time faculty, a sizable minority of men (34.4 percent) and women (27.0 percent) do some paid consulting work.

9. We believe that faculty unions have focused more on wages and benefits than on working time, but we have not found a positive effect of union membership on wages (Jacobs 2004).

10. Because, as discussed above, we were forced to impute the presence of children based on the size of the household, it is possible that our results are affected by measurement errors.

11. These analyses reveal a negative effect of gender on research productivity. A full discussion of productivity in terms of teaching, administration, and research is beyond the scope of this article, but see Allen (1998) for a useful overview.

References

Allen, Henry L. 1998. Faculty workload and productivity: Gender comparisons. *The 1998 NEA Almanac of Higher Education*. http://www.nea.org/he/healma98/workload.pdf (accessed April 5, 2004).

American Association of Medical Colleges. 2004. AAMC facts: Applicants, matriculants and graduates. http://www.aamc.org/data/facts/ (accessed April 2, 2004).

American Association of University Professors. 2001. *Post-tenure review*. Washington, DC: American Association of University Professors. http://www.aau.edu/reports/PostTenure4.01.pdf, accessed April 5, 2004.

Blair-Loy, Mary. 2003. *Competing devotions: Career and family among women executives*. Cambridge, MA: Harvard University Press.

Blau, Francine D., Marianne A. Ferber, and Anne E. Winkler. 2002. *The economics of women, men and work*. 4th ed. Upper Saddle River, NJ: Prentice Hall.

Catalyst. 2003a. *Census of women corporate officers and top earners*. New York: Catalyst.

———. 2003b. *Census of women directors of the Fortune 100*. New York: Catalyst.

Cowan, Ruth Schwartz. 1983. *More work for mothers: The ironies of household technology from the open hearth to the microwave*. New York: Basic Books.

Dimaggio, Paul, and Walter W. Powell. 1983. The iron cage revisited: Institutional isomorphism and collective rationality in organizational fields. *American Sociological Review* 48 (2): 147-60.

Galinsky, E., J. T. Bond, and D. E. Friedman. 1996. The role of employers in addressing the needs of employed parents. *Journal of Social Issues* 52 (3): 111-36.

Gappa, Judith M., and David Leslie. 1993. *The invisible faculty: Improving the status of part-timers in higher education*. San Francisco: Jossey-Bass.

Glass, J., and V. Camarigg. 1992. Gender, parenthood, and job-family compatibility. *American Journal of Sociology* 98 (1): 131-51.

Greenhaus, J. H., and N. J. Beutell. 1985. Sources of conflict between work and family roles. *Academy of Management Review* 10 (1): 76-88.

Hays, Sharon. 1996. *The cultural contradictions of motherhood*. New Haven, CT: Yale University Press.

Hochschild, Arlie. 1989. *The second shift*. New York: Viking.

Jacobs, Jerry A. 1999. Sex segregation of occupations: Prospects for the 21st century. In *Handbook of gender in organizations*, edited by Gary Powell, 125-41. Thousand Oaks, CA: Sage.

———. 2004. The faculty time divide. *Sociological Forum* 19 (1): 3-27.

Jacobs, Jerry A., and Kathleen Gerson. 2004. *The time divide: Work, family and gender inequality*. Cambridge, MA: Harvard University Press.

Jacobs, Jerry A., and Sarah E. Winslow. 2004. The academic life course, time pressures and gender inequality. *Community, Work and Family* 7 (2): 143-61.

Lareau, Annette. 2002. Invisible inequality: Social class and childrearing in black families and white families. *American Sociological Review* 67 (5): 747-76.

Mason, Mary Ann, and Marc Goulden. 2004. Marriage and baby blues: Redefining gender equity in the academy. *Annals of the American Academy of Political and Social Science* 596:84-103.

Moen, Phyllis, ed. 2003. *It's about time: Couples and careers*. Ithaca, NY: ILR Press.

National Education Association. 2001. *Part-time faculty*. NEA Update vol. 7, no. 4. Washington, DC: National Education Association Higher Education Research Center. http://www.nea.org/he/heupdate/vol7no4.pdf (accessed April 5, 2004).

Padavic, Irene, and Barbara Reskin. 2002. *Women and men at work*. 2nd ed. Thousand Oaks, CA: Pine Forge Press.

U.S. Department of Education. 2002. *Digest of education statistics*. Washington, DC: Government Printing Office. http://nces.ed.gov/programs/digest/ (accessed April 5, 2004).

U.S. Department of Education, National Center for Education Statistics. 2002. *1999 National Study of Postsecondary Faculty (NSOPF:99) methodology report*. NCES 2002-154. By Sameer Y. Abraham,

Darby Miller Steiger, Margrethe Montgomery, Brian D. Kuhr, Roger Tourangeau, Bob Montgomery, and Manas Chattopadhyay. Project officer, Linda J. Zimbler. Washington, DC: Government Printing Office.

Weber, Max. 1918/1946. Science as a vocation. In *From Max Weber: Essays in sociology*, edited by Hans Gerth and C. Wright Mills, 12-156. New York: Oxford University Press.

Winslow, Sarah. Forthcoming. Work-family conflict, gender, and parenthood, 1977-1997. *Journal of Family Issues*.

The Mommy Track and Partnership: Temporary Delay or Dead End?

By

MARY C. NOONAN
and
MARY E. CORCORAN

Using unique data from University of Michigan Law School graduates, the authors examine sex differences in promotion to partnership among lawyers. The authors investigate three steps in the partnership process: (1) the decision to attrite early from private practice, (2) the attainment of partnership among those who do not attrite, and (3) determinants of partners' earnings. Results show that men are less likely than women to leave private practice and more likely than women to become partners, even after controlling for a number of individual characteristics. Among partners, men earn significantly more than women. There is no evidence of a direct marriage or parenthood penalty, but lawyers who have taken time out of the labor force to attend to child care responsibilities are less likely to become partners and earn less if they do become partners. These findings provide strong indirect evidence that women lawyers face multiple glass ceilings in the workplace.

Keywords: lawyers; promotion; gender; work-family conflict

M ore than 40 percent of recent law school graduates are women, and almost 40 percent of associates in large firms are women (Epstein et al. 1995; *Harvard Law Review* 1996). In 2003, women made up 63 percent of Berkeley Law School's graduating class, 51 percent of Columbia Law School's graduating class,

Mary C. Noonan is an assistant professor in the University of Iowa's Department of Sociology. She received her Ph.D. in sociology and her master's in public policy from the University of Michigan. Her research interests include gender, work, and family issues. Past research has examined the effect of time spent in housework on men's and women's wages. She is currently examining employment outcomes of former welfare recipients. Other research examines the relationship between work-family policies and time spent in housework, men's and women's employment behavior around childbirth, the sex-based earnings gap among lawyers, and the impact of welfare reform on the employment of single mothers.

Mary E. Corcoran is a professor of political science, public policy, social work, and women's studies at the University of Michigan. She received her Ph.D. from the Massachusetts Institute of Technology. Her research focuses on the effects of discrimination on economic status and on welfare and employment policies.

DOI: 0.1177/0002716204268773

and 47 percent of Harvard Law School's graduating class (Belkin 2003). Despite the rapid feminization of law since the 1970s, women associates are far less likely than male associates to become partners. According to a recent American Bar Association Commission report, the most pervasive underrepresentation of women lawyers is among partners in law firms (Rhode 2001, 23). Only 16 percent of partners in law firms are women (Belkin 2003). Rhode (2001, 23) contended that "the disparities are even more pronounced for equity and managing partners . . . only about 5 percent of managing partners . . . are women."

Women now graduate from top law schools and enter prestigious law firms at roughly the same rates as do men. As Belkin (2003, 44) put it, women "start strong out of the gate." But after leaving law school and entering firms, women increasingly fall behind men. Why is this? Epstein et al. (1995) asserted that women associates make partner at lower rates than do male associates because women face "multiple glass ceilings" that men do not at many stages of the career hierarchy. One such stage is the decision to remain in a firm long enough to be considered for partnership. Partnership typically occurs after six to eight years at a firm, but many women associates drop out of large law practices by their fourth year (Epstein et al. 1995). Donovan (1990, 142) claimed that "the single most important element of women's inability to make partner is the high attrition rate of women from firms . . . women cannot make partner if they have left the firm." Foster (1995, 1658) stated that "attrition perpetuates the glass ceiling as fewer women are available for promotion and more men remain in decision-making positions as a result."

High attrition in the first years after joining firms is not the only reason offered for women's underrepresentation in partnership ranks. Epstein et al. (1995), Kay and Hagan (1999), and Rhode (2001) have claimed that glass ceilings operate at other career stages as well—resulting in lower promotion chances for women associates who remain in firms and in lower earnings and equity shares for women who become partners.

Epstein et al. (1995) identified the following as institutional factors that may marginalize women associates: "rainmaking" demands (i.e., generating new clients for the firm), lack of mentors, sexual harassment and discrimination, high work hours, and part-time work tracks that permanently derail lawyers from partnership tracks. Kay and Hagan (1999) listed many of the same factors when they argued that female associates have fewer opportunities than male associates to develop "social capital" within law firms. Researchers who interview women lawyers find that many report experiencing sex discrimination within the firm. Chambers (1989) reported that both men and women lawyers identify sex discrimination as one of the main reasons for women's early attrition from private firms and lower rates of promotion to partnership. Rosenberg, Perlstadt, and Phillips (1993) noted that women lawyers report lower levels of discrimination at the "front door" (hiring) than on the job (salary, promotion, and assignments).

NOTE: We thank Janice Madden, Cynthia Epstein, and the participants of the "Mommies and Daddies on the Fast Track" conference for their helpful comments.

The primary personal factor identified by these authors as constraining women's partnership chances is that some cut back labor supply (e.g., work part-time for a period, take a family leave, work fewer hours per year) to balance the demands of motherhood with the demands of practicing law. As Donovan (1990, 142) put it, "The most notorious reason for women to leave [a firm] is motherhood." Brockman (1994) found that child care responsibilities and family leave policies play a significant role in career decisions—jobs, specialties, cases, and work hours—for women but not for men. Common reasons women report for leaving the field of law are the lack of flexibility offered by law firms, long hours, child care commitments, and the stressful nature of the work. Men are less likely to cite "work-family conflict" as a reason for leaving law and are more likely to state the desire to use different skills (Brockman 1994).

As these authors noted, the distinction between institutional and personal constraints is fuzzy. For instance, a woman associate may "choose" to work part-time for several years, and this choice may reduce her chances of making partner. But this choice may be a response to discrimination within a firm, or this choice may be all that is available in a firm. Furthermore, the "choice" itself may be strongly conditioned by the expectations of others—family, colleagues, the larger culture—expectations that do not constrain men's labor supply choices (Epstein et al. 1995).

Past Research

Most authors cited above hypothesized that work-family conflicts lead women to reduce their labor supply in ways that increase their chances of exiting law firms and reduce their chances of becoming partners. Two studies of attrition from law firms (Kay 1997; Spurr and Sueyoshi 1994) and several studies of partnership (Hagan and Kay 1995; Hull and Nelson 2000; Kay and Hagan 1998, 1999; Spurr 1990; Spurr and Sueyoshi 1994) have used relatively recent data on lawyers' outcomes to test this hypothesis.

What do these researchers find? First, sex strongly predicted exits from law firms and promotion to partnership even when controlling for law school quality, academic distinction in law school, *potential* work experience (i.e., years since called to the bar, years since law school graduation), legal specialization, having taken a leave for child care, marital status, children, current work hours, and measures of social capital (Hagan and Kay 1995; Hull and Nelson 2000; Kay 1997; Kay and Hagan 1998, 1999; Spurr 1990; Spurr and Sueyoshi 1994). Second, labor supply matters. Having taken a family leave was more common among women and reduced chances of partnership in Hagan and Kay's (1995) sample of Toronto lawyers. A work-family constraint lowered women's but not men's chances of partnership in Hull and Nelson's (2000) sample of Chicago lawyers. Current work hours positively predicted partnership.

The usefulness of this research in assessing for the extent to which women's labor supply choices reduce their chances of becoming partners is limited given the relatively weak measures of labor supply used. No study had a measure of years worked part-time to care for children. Yet Epstein et al. (1995) and Rhode (2001) have argued that choosing to work-part time on a "mommy track" can stigmatize women as "not serious" and permanently damage chances of becoming partners. Hagan and Kay (1995), Hull and Nelson (2000), and Kay and Hagan (1998) had measures of whether lawyers had taken family leaves but no data on the length of those leaves. No study had a measure of years practicing law. Instead, all of these prior studies included a measure of potential experience (years since called to the bar or years since law school graduation), but actual years practiced is likely lower for women than for men. Hagan and Kay (1995), Hull and Nelson (2000), and Kay and Hagan (1998, 1999) had measures of current work hours, but current work hours are likely endogenous since partners are expected to work long hours. Those who do not make partner might well cut back work hours.

Researchers who interview women lawyers find that many report experiencing sex discrimination within the firm.

Given the limitations of the labor supply measures used in past research, it may be surprising to learn that even with these weak controls for labor supply, mothers are no less likely than childless women to become partners (Hagan and Kay 1995; Hull and Nelson 2000; Kay and Hagan 1998, 1999). This does not mean that *sex* does not matter for partnership; mothers and childless women are equally *less* likely than men to become partners.

We use detailed information on the fifteen-year careers of graduates of the University of Michigan Law School to investigate sex differences in promotion to partnership. Because women may be disadvantaged relative to men at multiple career stages, we examine three steps in the partnership process: (1) the decision to attrite early from private practice, (2) the attainment of partnership among those who do not attrite, and (3) determinants of partners' earnings. Because we have direct measures of the labor supply choices made to handle child care responsibilities (e.g., months time out for kids, months worked part-time for kids, and years worked in law), we can more precisely estimate the extent to which cutbacks in labor supply are associated with reduced chances of becoming partner for women who start out in private practice than have past researchers. If, after controlling for sex differences in these precise measures of labor supply, women still have higher early attrition rates from private practice than men, women who stay in private practice are still less likely to be promoted than men, and women who become partners still have lower earnings than men, then this is strong indirect evidence that glass ceilings such as those outlined by Epstein et al. (1995) constrain women's opportunities at multiple points in their legal careers. In addition, if after controlling for labor supply, motherhood has no further effects on early attrition, partnership among stayers, and wages of partners, then it seems unlikely that parenting concerns account for the remaining sex differences in early attrition, partnership, and earnings.

Examining women's experiences at multiple stages of their careers after they first enter firms is important because the experiences of women long-termers in a firm likely inform the career decisions made by new women entrants. If cutting back on labor supply has derailed the partnership of older women, then new entrants who are concerned about balancing work and family may quit private practice for another legal setting. If older women who have not cut back labor supply are less likely than men with similar work histories to become partners, and if women partners earn less than men partners with similar work histories, then even new women entrants who are not concerned about balancing family demands may decide their opportunities are restricted and leave.

Data

We use a sample of University of Michigan Law School graduates to examine these questions. The law school surveys all graduates fifteen years after graduation about their earnings, work hours, work histories (including interruptions and years worked part-time), work settings, and families. These survey data are matched with law school records, giving additional information on graduates' performance while in law school.

The sample includes the graduating classes of 1972 to 1985. Outcomes are observed from 1987 to 2000. The average response rate across all years was 60 percent for women and 64 percent for men. We exclude women and men with missing data on the variables used in the analyses (about 18 percent of the total sample). We use three samples in our analyses: those who spent at least one year in private practice (433 women and 1,876 men), those who spent at least four years in private practice (354 women and 1,694 men), and those who were partners in their fifteenth year (144 women and 1,116 men).

Measures

We constructed three dependent variables. The first is a dummy variable equal to one if the respondent has less than four years of private practice experience but has worked in private practice for at least one year (i.e., an "early attritor" or "leaver"). The second is a dummy variable equal to one if the respondent is a partner in a firm with two or more members at year fifteen. The third is the log of annual earnings in year fifteen.

Independent variables are in six groups: demographics, law school performance, family characteristics, work experience, connections/support, and personal satisfaction. Demographic variables include a dummy variable for whether a respondent is male and another for whether the respondent is white. Law school performance is measured by grade point average (GPA) in law school. Family variables include dummy variables for whether the respondent has ever been married and ever had children. Measures of work experience include years practiced law, months since law school during which the respondent worked part-time to care for children, and months since law school during which the respondent did not work at all to care for children. Connections/support are measured by dummy variables that indicate whether the respondent's spouse is a lawyer and whether the respondent has a mentor. We include a dummy variable equal to one if the respondent is satisfied with his or her balance of family and professional life. All the above variables are used in the analyses predicting partnership. In the attrition analyses, we exclude the spouse is lawyer variable. In the earnings analyses, we exclude the spouse is lawyer and satisfaction variables and include measures of firm size (small, medium, and large) and the log of annual hours worked in year fifteen.

Method

First, we present statistics showing the percentage of women and men in private practice for varying lengths of time; the percentage who are partners, using varying samples based on time in private practice; and the means of predictor measures. Next, we estimate models predicting early attrition (i.e., leaving private practice within four years) for those who have at least one year of private practice experience and predicting partnership for those who have at least four years of private practice experience. Because these dependent variables are binary, the models are estimated using logistic regression. We estimate models for all lawyers and for men and women separately to see if the effects of the predictor variables differ significantly by sex. We then estimate models predicting annual earnings for those who are partners in their fifteenth year using ordinary least squares (OLS) regression. We also reestimated models predicting early attrition and partnership including the log of annual hours worked as a predictor variable and report results in the text.

Results

Table 1 reports the private practice experience of law school graduates and the percentages of graduates who make partner. The vast majority of graduates had spent at least one year in private practice, and a smaller but still sizeable majority had spent four or more years in private practice. Women were less likely than men to have tried out private practice for at least one year (82 vs. 87 percent), to have stayed in practice for four or more years (67 vs. 79 percent), and to have made part-

TABLE 1

UNIVERSITY OF MICHIGAN LAW SCHOOL DATA
(GRADUATION YEARS 1972-85)

	Men	Women	Gender Gap
Percentage in private practice			
At least one year	87	82	5
At least four years	79	67	12
At year fifteen	57	35	22
Percentage partner			
Of total sample	52	27	25
Of those in private practice at least one year	59	33	26
Of those in private practice at least four years	65	40	25
n (total sample)	2,150	531	

FIGURE 1

ATTRITION FROM PRIVATE PRACTICE, BY SEX,
OR THOSE IN PRIVATE PRACTICE FOR AT LEAST ONE YEAR,
UNIVERSITY OF MICHIGAN LAW SCHOOL GRADUATES

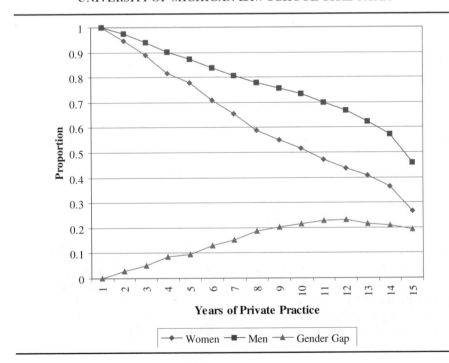

ner (27 vs. 52 percent). Among graduates who did not attrite early (those with four or more years' of private practice), 40 percent of women and 65 percent of men were partners.

Figure 1 shows attrition from private practice over time for graduates who have worked at least one year in private practice. At three years of experience, the gap between the percentage of men and women still in private practice is minor—94 versus 89 percent, respectively. The gap widens to approximately 10 percentage points after four and five years of work experience. We suspect that this is the period when women become discouraged about their chances of making partner. Between five and eight years, the years in which partnership decisions are typically made, the gap widens another 10 percentage points, reaching nearly 20 percent at year eight. It seems likely that women leave private practice at higher rates after five to eight years of practice either because they expect not to make partner or they do not make partner. The gender gap in attrition is constant over the period from eight to fifteen years.

Table 2 reports the means of the variables used in the analyses for graduates with one or more year of private practice. The means for graduates with four or more years of private practice experience are not shown but are very similar to the means presented here. Means that differ significantly by sex are in bold, and those that differ by parenthood status within sex are underlined. Sex differences in family characteristics were large: women were more likely to be childless, less likely to be married, and more likely to be married to a lawyer. Women, on average, also worked significantly fewer hours than men—1,966 hours versus 2,493 hours. Women and men were equally likely to have had a mentor and were equally satisfied with the balance of family and work in their lives.

Sex differences in the labor supply of parents are striking (see Table 3). Only 19 of the 1,574 fathers in our sample had worked part-time, and only 17 had taken a leave from work to care for children. In contrast, 47 percent of mothers had worked part-time and 42 percent had taken a leave from work. Mothers who had worked part-time averaged forty-two months of part-time work over the fifteen years since law school graduation, and those who took a leave from work averaged twenty-four months not working. Fathers worked more hours in year fifteen than did mothers—2,519 versus 2,005 hours. These differences in mothers' and fathers' labor supply are consistent with Epstein et al.'s (1995) observation that while both fathers and mothers report family and work conflicts, only mothers reduce their labor supply to respond to these conflicts.

Although women lawyers were more likely than men lawyers to cut back labor supply, 56 percent of women lawyers *never* worked part-time or took a leave. This 56 percent consists of childless women (29 percent of the sample) and mothers who never worked part-time or took time out to care for children (27 percent of the sample). Women who had not worked part-time or dropped out worked high hours—roughly twenty-four hundred at year fifteen.

Results of estimating the multivariate models predicting early attrition and partnership are reported in Table 4. The first three columns in Table 4 report results from logistic regressions predicting early attrition for lawyers with at least one year

TABLE 2

DESCRIPTIVE STATISTICS USED IN REGRESSION ANALYSES,
BY SEX AND PARENTHOOD STATUS, IN PRIVATE PRACTICE
FOR AT LEAST ONE YEAR, UNIVERSITY OF MICHIGAN LAW SCHOOL DATA
(GRADUATION YEARS 1972-85)

Variable	Men			Women		
	All	Childless	Fathers	All	Childless	Mothers
Partner	**0.59**	0.49	0.61	**0.33**	0.31	0.34
	(0.49)	(0.50)	(0.50)	(0.47)	(0.46)	(0.48)
Less than four years'	**0.10**	0.12	0.09	**0.18**	0.19	0.18
of private practice	(0.29)	(0.32)	(0.29)	(0.38)	(0.39)	(0.38)
At least four years'	**0.90**	0.88	0.91	**0.82**	0.81	0.82
of private practice	(0.30)	(0.32)	(0.29)	(0.39)	(0.39)	(0.38)
White	**0.95**	0.93	0.95	**0.91**	0.90	0.92
	(0.22)	(0.26)	(0.21)	(0.29)	(0.31)	(0.28)
Grade point average	3.19	3.14	3.20	3.16	3.13	3.18
	(0.40)	(0.41)	(0.40)	(0.42)	(0.43)	(0.41)
Family						
Ever married	**0.90**	0.53	0.97	**0.78**	0.44	0.92
	(0.30)	(0.50)	(0.17)	(0.41)	(0.50)	(0.27)
Ever had children	**0.84**	0.00	1.00	**0.71**	0.00	1.00
	(0.37)	(0.00)	(0.00)	(0.45)	(0.00)	(0.00)
Experience						
Years practiced law	**13.99**	13.74	14.03	**13.06**	13.10	13.05
	(2.68)	(2.83)	(2.67)	(3.45)	(3.73)	(3.39)
Months part-time	**0.29**	0.00	0.34	**13.95**	0.00	19.68
for kids	(3.72)	(0.00)	(4.06)	(29.18)	(0.00)	(33.00)
Months not worked	**0.10**	0.00	0.11	**7.04**	0.00	9.94
for kids	(1.82)	(0.00)	(2.00)	(20.79)	(0.00)	(24.12)
Annual hours worked[a]	**2,493**	2,414	2,508	**1,966**	2,370	1,800
	(455)	(493)	(446)	(860)	(643)	(884)
Mentor (1 = yes)	0.60	0.55	0.61	0.61	0.62	0.61
	(0.49)	(0.50)	(0.49)	(0.49)	(0.49)	(0.49)
Spouse is a lawyer (1 = yes)	**0.11**	0.10	0.11	**0.31**	0.17	0.36
	(0.31)	(0.31)	(0.31)	(0.46)	(0.37)	(0.48)
Satisfied with work-family	0.57	0.54	0.58	0.56	0.49	0.59
balance (1 = yes)	(0.49)	(0.50)	(0.49)	(0.50)	(0.50)	(0.49)
n	1,876	302	1,574	433	126	307

NOTE: Standard deviations in parentheses. Values in bold are significantly different by sex ($p <$ .10). Values that are underlined are significantly different by parenthood status within sex ($p <$ .10).

a. For those employed in year fifteen.

of practice; the next three columns report results of logistic regressions predicting partnership for lawyers who had been in private practice for four or more years. In each set of three regressions, we present results for all lawyers, then for male law-

TABLE 3

DESCRIPTIVE STATISTICS ON PARENTS' WORK
HISTORIES BY SEX, IN PRIVATE PRACTICE FOR AT LEAST
ONE YEAR, UNIVERSITY OF MICHIGAN LAW SCHOOL DATA
(GRADUATION YEARS 1972-85)

Work History	Fathers (n = 1,574)		Mothers (n = 307)	
	%	Mean Months	%	Mean Months
Ever worked part-time	1	28.41 PT	47	41.67 PT
Ever nonwork	1	10.54 FT	42	23.83 FT
Only worked part-time	1	26.93 PT	20	44.69 PT
Only nonwork	1	6.31 FT	14	28.20 FT
Worked both part-time and nonwork	0.25	41.29 FTE	27	41.28 FTE
Worked part-time or nonwork	2	14.04 FTE	62	32.13 FTE

NOTE: All statistics are significantly different by sex (p < .10), except for the "mean months" value for mothers and fathers who both worked part-time and nonwork. PT = part-time months; FT = full-time months; FTE = full-time equivalent months.

yers, and then for female lawyers. Coefficients that differ significantly by sex are in bold.

We begin by discussing early attrition (i.e., leaving a firm by the fourth year). Many of the predictor variables are measured over the fifteen years after graduation, and most of the "leavers" likely exited private practice prior to year fifteen. As a result, the findings on attrition are not interpreted within a causal framework but instead within an "associative" framework. That is, the findings simply tell us whether those who left private practice by the fourth year differ significantly on a set of characteristics compared to those who remained in private practice beyond the fourth year.

Women are more likely than men to exit, even after controlling for GPA, marriage, children, labor supply, mentoring, and satisfaction (see Table 4). GPA and years practiced law are significantly associated with lower rates of leaving for both men and women. Marriage, children, time out, and part-time work are not significantly associated with rates of leaving for women or men. Even when the experience measures are removed from the model, marriage and children remain unrelated to rates of leaving for both women and men. Men who have a mentor are less likely to exit. Only one coefficient is significantly different in the male and female regressions. Men who left are more likely than men who stayed to be satisfied with their work-family balance at the fifteenth year; this is not true for women. Further analyses show that, for women, having children, taking time out of work, and working part-time are all positively associated with work-family satisfaction. Women who leave private practice are more likely to take time out of work, women who stay in private practice are more likely to work part-time, and both groups are equally likely to have children. Therefore, it appears that both women "leavers" and "stayers" have balanced their work and family lives in different ways, but both

TABLE 4

SUMMARY OF REGRESSION RESULTS, UNIVERSITY OF MICHIGAN LAW
SCHOOL DATA (GRADUATION YEARS 1972-85)

Variable	Predicting Early Attrition[a]			Predicting Partnership[b]		
	Total	Men[c]	Women[c]	Total	Men[c]	Women[c]
Male	−0.568***			0.690***		
	(0.181)			(0.152)		
White	−0.540**	−0.444	−0.805*	0.212	**0.478***	**−1.005***
	(0.264)	(0.345)	(0.431)	(0.235)	(0.265)	(0.519)
Grade point average	−0.589***	−0.473**	−0.873**	0.636***	**0.530***	**1.201***
	(0.185)	(0.219)	(0.360)	(0.135)	(0.149)	(0.349)
Family						
Ever married	0.023	0.315	−0.369	0.388**	0.301	0.486
	(0.239)	(0.324)	(0.366)	(0.181)	(0.211)	(0.372)
Ever had children	−0.101	−0.280	0.190	0.284*	0.307*	0.278
	(0.206)	(0.247)	(0.364)	(0.153)	(0.175)	(0.327)
Experience						
Years practiced law	−0.208***	−0.221***	−0.168***	0.398***	0.399***	0.403***
	(0.018)	(0.020)	(0.037)	(0.038)	(0.042)	(0.104)
Months part-time for kids	−0.007	0.008	−0.007	−0.006	−0.018	−0.007*
	(0.006)	(0.017)	(0.007)	(0.004)	(0.023)	(0.004)
Months not worked for kids	0.002	−0.033	0.006	−0.066**	**−0.797***	**−0.053***
	(0.005)	(0.060)	(0.006)	(0.026)	(0.375)	(0.025)
Mentor	−0.215	−0.312*	0.111	0.296***	0.281**	0.517**
	(0.143)	(0.167)	(0.283)	(0.102)	(0.113)	(0.260)
Spouse is a lawyer	—	—	—	0.244	**0.089**	**0.787***
				(0.150)	(0.177)	(0.291)
Satisfied with work-family balance	0.453***	**0.645***	**−0.062**	−0.511***	−0.536***	−0.643**
	(0.150)	(0.183)	(0.276)	(0.103)	(0.114)	(0.257)
n	2,309	1,876	433	2,048	1,694	354

NOTE: Standard errors in parentheses.
a. Sample includes those with at least one year in private practice.
b. Sample includes those with at least four years in private practice.
c. Coefficients in bold are significantly different by sex ($p < .10$).
*$p < .10$. **$p < .05$. ***$p < .01$.

approaches are equally satisfying. Since very few men who remain in private practice actually work part-time, it may be that—for men—work-family satisfaction only comes through leaving the stressful world of private practice for other less demanding lines of work.

Sex also affects promotion rates for lawyers who remain in firms for at least four years. Women are less likely than men to be promoted to partner, even when GPA, race, years practiced law, months part-time, months nonwork, marital status, number of kids, mentorship, and satisfaction are controlled (see Table 4). There is no evidence of a marriage or parenthood penalty for women either when experience is controlled or when experience measures are excluded from the models (results not shown). In fact, marriage and children are *positively* associated with the probability of becoming partner when experience measures are included. Marriage remains positively associated with partnership for women when experience measures are excluded, but the coefficient on children drops to zero. GPA, years practiced law, and having a mentor are positively associated with partnership, and months not worked is negatively associated with partnership. The effects of time out on partnership are significantly larger for men, and the effects of GPA on partnership are significantly larger for women. Part-time work significantly decreases the likelihood of becoming a partner for women but not for men; however, the difference in the effect is not large enough to be statistically different by sex. Having a lawyer as a spouse increases women's but not men's chances of becoming a partner.

We suspect that this [after four or five years of work experience] is the period when women become discouraged about their chances of making partner.

There is a lot of consistency across the two sets of results. Men are less likely to attrite and more likely to make partner. Lawyers with high GPAs, a mentor, and more legal work experience are less likely to attrite and more likely to make partner. Taking time off from work decreases the chance of partnership (significant) and increases the chances of attrition (insignificant). There is no evidence of a direct marriage or motherhood penalty for women. Male stayers are less satisfied with their work-family balance than males who left private practice early in their careers, and men and women who make partner are less satisfied with work-family balance than those who do not.

Because logistic coefficients do not show how much the probability of an event changes when the predictor variables change, we translate the estimated coefficients into predicted probabilities. We calculate the predicted probability of exiting private practice/becoming partner for an individual with fixed characteristics and then recalculate probabilities changing those characteristics one at a time. We report these predicted probabilities in Table 5. The first column in Table 5 reports predicted probabilities of early attrition based on coefficients from the early attrition regressions analyzed for all lawyers. The next two columns report probabilities based on the coefficients in the attrition regressions analyzed for men and women separately. The last three columns in Table 5 report predicted probabilities of part-

TABLE 5

PREDICTED PROBABILITIES, UNDER DIFFERENT
SCENARIOS, UNIVERSITY OF MICHIGAN LAW SCHOOL DATA
(GRADUATION YEARS 1972-85)

Scenario	Probability of Early Attrition			Probability of Becoming a Partner		
	All[a]	Men[b]	Women[b]	All[a]	Men[b]	Women[b]
1. Male, white, 3.2 grade point average, married, kids, 13.5 years practiced law, 0 part-time months, 0 break months, mentor, satisfied with work-family balance, spouse not a lawyer	.09	.09	.14	.57	.58	.35
2. Sex ("become female")	**.15**			**.40**		
3. Grade point average increases by 0.5	**.07**	**.07**	**.09**	**.65**	**.64**	**.49**
4. Never married	.09	.07	.18	**.48**	.50	.24
5. No kids	.10	.12	.11	**.51**	**.50**	.29
6. Never married/no kids	.10	.09	.16	.41	.43	.20
7. One additional year practicing law	**.08**	**.08**	**.12**	**.67**	**.67**	**.44**
8. Forty-two part-time months	.07	.13	.10	.51	.39	**.28**
9. Twelve break months	.09	.06	.14	**.38**	**.00**	**.22**
10. Eighteen break months	.10	.05	.15	**.29**	**.00**	**.17**
11. No mentor	.11	**.12**	.12	**.50**	**.51**	.24
12. Not satisfied with work-family balance	**.06**	**.05**	.14	**.69**	**.70**	**.50**
13. Spouse "becomes" a lawyer	—	—	—	.63	.60	**.54**

NOTE: Figures represent predicted probability when only the given variable is changed. Bolded values represent changes for variables that are statistically significant.
a. Using same coefficients for both sexes.
b. Using sex-specific coefficients.

nership based on the coefficients from the partnership regressions. Predicted probabilities that are based on significant coefficients are in bold.

The "base" lawyer in Table 5 is a white man who is married with children, has an average GPA, 13.5 years of private practice experience, no leave, no part-time experience, a mentor, is satisfied with his work-family balance, and has a spouse who is not a lawyer. This "base" lawyer has a 9 percent chance of leaving private practice before his fourth year and a 57 percent chance of making partner if he remains in private practice for at least four years (see Table 5, scenario 1). A woman with these same characteristics has a 15 percent chance of leaving practice within four years and a 40 percent chance of making partner if she remains in private practice for at least four years (see Table 5, scenario 2). Thus, "being female" increased the predicted chances of attrition by 6 percentage points and reduced the chances of becoming partner by 17 percentage points.

Only GPA, years practiced law, having a mentor, and lack of satisfaction with family/work balance were significantly associated with early attrition. An increase of 0.5 in one's GPA (roughly a rise from a B+ to an A average) reduced the predicted probability of early attrition from .09 to .07 for the "base" man and from .14 to .09 for the "base" woman (see Table 5, scenario 3). An additional year of law practice reduced the "base" man's predicted probability of early attrition from .09 to .08 and the "base" woman's predicted probability of attrition from .14 to .12. Men who had mentors had a lower predicted probability of early attrition than did men without mentors—.09 versus .12. Men who were satisfied with work-family balance had a lower predicted probability of early attrition than did those who were not satisfied—.09 versus .05.

GPA and time out to care for children had modest to large effects on partnership chances, depending on whether predicted probabilities were calculated using coefficients from the male or female regressions. An increase of 0.5 in law school GPA would raise the "base" man's predicted probability of partnership from .58 to .64 and the "base" woman's predicted probability from .35 to .49. If a "base" man were to take a one-year leave from work for child care responsibilities, his predicted probability of becoming a partner plummets from .58 to .00 (see Table 5, scenario 9). If the "base" man were to work part-time for forty-two months, his predicted probability of becoming partner drops from .58 to .39. These drops, while theoretically large, have little practical import since virtually no men drop out or work part-time. The predicted effects of labor supply for women's partnership chances, while smaller than those of men, are by no means trivial. A year leave of absence reduces the "base" women's predicted probability of partnership from .35 to .22, and working part-time for forty-two months reduces her predicted probability of partnership from .35 to .28 (see Table 5, scenarios 9 and 8). Since large minorities of women lawyers do take family leave and/or work part-time, these predicted drops in chances of partnership have practical as well as theoretical implications.

There is little evidence in Table 5 of a marriage or motherhood penalty. If the "base" woman were never married (versus married), her predicted probability of partnership drops from .35 to .24. If the "base" woman were childless (versus being a mother), her predicted probability of partnership drops from .35 to .29.

Mentorship and satisfaction significantly predicted partnership for both men and women, and having a spouse who is a lawyer predicted partnership for women but not men. Not having a mentor reduced the "base" man's predicted chances of becoming a partner from 58 to 51 percent and reduced the "base" woman's chances even more from 35 to 24 percent. Having mentors for women within firms may be effective in improving chances of partnership. If we simulate our "base" case to be unsatisfied with his or her work-family balance, the "base" man's predicted chances of becoming partner rises from 58 to 70 percent, and those of the "base" woman rises from 35 to 50 percent. This should not be interpreted causally; it shows that partners are less likely than other lawyers to be satisfied with their work-family balance. Having a spouse who is a lawyer increases the "base" woman's chance of becoming partner from 35 to 54 percent.

We did not control for work hours in the attrition and partnership regressions because of endogeneity concerns; work hours are measured in year fifteen, and attrition and partnership likely occur prior to year fifteen. As a specification check, we added measures of hours worked in year fifteen to these regressions. When we did so, the coefficients on the sex dummy drop slightly. The "base" woman's probability of attriting drops from 15 to 14 percent, and her probability of making partner rises from 40 to 43 percent (scenario 2 in Table 5). Work hours, as expected, are lower for those who attrite and are higher for partners.

Rhode (2001) argued that women who become partners are less likely than men partners to hold equity shares and to become managing partners. We examine the sex difference in earnings for lawyers who have become partners by their fifteenth year after graduation in Table 6. The first two columns of Table 6 report means on earnings and individual characteristics for men and women partners. The difference between men's and women's mean log earnings is .28. This means that men's average earnings are 32 percent higher than those of women (i.e., $[\exp(.28) - 1] \times 100 = 32$ percent). Women partners are less likely than men partners to be married and more likely to be childless. There are no sex differences in years practiced law, but there are modest differences in part-time work and family leave. On average, women partners have worked part-time for one year and have spent 1.7 months out of the labor force. In comparison, men partners average only two to three days of part-time work experience and no time away from work. Men partners' annual work hours are 10 percent higher than those of women—a difference of about 224 hours more per year. Both sexes are equally likely to have had a mentor and are equally distributed among firms of different sizes.

The third column of Table 6 reports results of a regression predicting partners' annual earnings. When we reran this regression separately by sex, only the coefficients on part-time work and firm size significantly differed by sex. The fourth column of Table 6 reports results from an earnings regression that includes interactions of sex with part-time work and with the firm size dummies. The male earnings advantage is halved from 32 to 16 percent (i.e. $[\exp(.15) - 1] \times 100 = 16$ percent) when race, GPA, marital status, children, work experience, work hours, mentoring, and firm size are controlled (Table 6, third column). Sex differences in annual work hours at year fifteen and in time out account for most of this drop.

Taking time out to care for children has a big effect on partners' earnings. Earnings drop by 2.3 percent for each additional month of family leave. Thus, a single year of family leave over the fifteen years since leaving school would lower a woman partner's expected earnings in year fifteen by 27.6 percent. Part-time work experience has no effect on women partners' earnings, but male partners with part-time work experience pay a large earnings penalty. For every additional month of part-time work experience, men's annual earnings drop by 3.4 percent. There is no evidence of a marriage or parenthood penalty; marriage and parenthood have positive but insignificant effects on earnings.

Table 6

**DESCRIPTIVE STATISTICS AND REGRESSION RESULTS
FOR ANALYSIS PREDICTING LN EARNINGS AMONG PARTNERS,
BY SEX, UNIVERSITY OF MICHIGAN LAW SCHOOL DATA
(GRADUATION YEARS 1972-85)**

Variable	Mean		Coefficient	
	Men	Women	Model 1	Model 2
ln annual earnings	**12.19**	**11.92**		
	(0.55)	(0.70)		
Sex (1 = male)	**1.00**	**0.00**	0.145°°°	0.434°°°
			(0.048)	(0.089)
White	**0.97**	**0.92**	−0.013	−0.018
	(0.18)	(0.28)	(0.075)	(0.075)
Grade point average	3.24	3.28	0.219°°°	0.207°°°
	(0.39)	(0.38)	(0.039)	(0.039)
Ever married	**0.92**	**0.85**	0.017	0.019
	(0.27)	(0.36)	(0.056)	(0.056)
Ever had children	**0.87**	**0.73**	0.062	0.068
	(0.34)	(0.45)	(0.045)	(0.045)
Years practiced law	14.73	14.69	0.034°°	0.030°°
	(0.90)	(1.02)	(0.015)	(0.015)
Months part-time for kids	**0.10**	**12.06**	−0.002	−0.001
	(1.87)	(29.60)	(0.002)	(0.002)
Months part-time for Kids × Sex				−0.033°°°
				(0.008)
Months not worked for kids	**0.00**	**1.71**	−0.022°°	−0.023°°
	(0.09)	(4.36)	(0.010)	(0.010)
ln annual hours	**7.84**	**7.73**	0.648°°°	0.661°°°
	(0.14)	(0.27)	(0.091)	(0.090)
Mentor (1 = yes)	0.63	0.67	0.050°	0.046
	(0.48)	(0.47)	(0.029)	(0.028)
Small firm	0.26	0.24	Omitted	Omitted
	(0.44)	(0.43)		
Medium firm	0.21	0.24	0.328°°°	0.583°°°
	(0.41)	(0.43)	(0.041)	(0.118)
Medium Firm × Sex				−0.289°°
				(0.125)
Large firm	0.53	0.52	0.516°°°	0.873°°°
	(0.50)	(0.50)	(0.035)	(0.100)
Large Firm × Sex				−0.406°°°
				(0.105)
R-squared			.286	.303
n	1,116	144	1,260	1,260

NOTE: Standard deviations/standard errors in parentheses. Values in bold are significantly different by sex ($p < .10$).
°$p < .10$. °°$p < .05$. °°°$p < .01$.

Conclusion and Discussion

In this article, we use data on graduates of the University of Michigan Law School, a highly ranked law school that provides specialized training and access to well-paid jobs, to examine sex differences in the path to partnership. These men and women started off on an equal footing in the legal marketplace. Despite this, men were almost twice as likely as women to become partners.

How did this happen? The pattern is one of cumulating disadvantages. Women fell behind men in each stage in the progression to partnership. Women were slightly less likely than men to try out private practice (82 vs. 87 percent). Women who entered private practice were 1.8 times as likely as men to leave within four years (18 vs. 10 percent). And among those who remained for four or more years, men were 1.6 times more likely to be promoted to partner (65 vs. 40 percent). Even among the select group of those who made partner, men's mean annual earnings were 32 percent higher than those of women.

Some argue that women are more likely than men to select themselves out at each stage of the partnership process because men and women handle family responsibilities differently. Certainly, a large minority of women in our sample cut back labor supply to deal with family responsibilities, and virtually no men did so. These cutbacks in labor supply were negatively associated with partnership chances and with partners' earnings. But we found large gaps between the early attrition rates, chances of partnership, and annual earnings of men and women partners with the *same* work histories. When we control for labor supply, marriage, and children, the gap between men's and women's early attrition rates drops from 8 to 6 percentage points, the gap in promotion rates drops from 25 to roughly 17 percentage points, and the gap in partners' mean earnings decreases from 32 to 16 percentage points. At most, one-quarter to one-third of the male/female differences in early attrition and promotion and one-half of the earnings gap between men and women partners are due to labor supply differences. These estimates of reductions may be on the high side since women's labor supply choices are likely influenced by the options firms offer and by women's perceptions of sex differences in promotion opportunities.

A family leave of one year reduced women's chances of making partner by one-third and reduced women partners' earnings by 28 percent. But law school performance and connections had equally strong effects on women lawyers' careers. A woman with a B+ average GPA in law school was 1.5 times as likely to attrite early as was one with an A average (14 vs. 9 percent) and was less likely to make partner (35 vs. 49 percent). Women with mentors were almost 1.5 times as likely to become partners as were those without mentors (35 vs. 24 percent), and women married to lawyers were 1.8 times as likely to make partner as women who were not married to lawyers (54 vs. 35 percent).

The few male lawyers who reduced their labor supply to care for children fared badly economically. A year of leave reduced men's predicted chances of making partner from 58 to 0 percent, and a year of part-time work reduced male partners' predicted earnings by 41 percent. The meaning of these drops is unclear. These could be very unusual men, or it could be that male lawyers who behave in nontraditional ways face high penalties. If the latter were true, it is not surprising that so few male lawyers reduce labor supply. Among fathers in our sample, only six had taken at least one year of leave, and only thirteen had one year or more of part-time work experience. None of the six fathers who had taken a year or more of leave, and only three of the fathers who worked part-time for a year or more were partners.

One could argue that parenting responsibilities reduce women's productivity at work in ways not captured by these analyses. But controlling for labor supply, mothers had the same early attrition rates, promotion rates, and earnings as did childless women; and ever-married women were more likely to be promoted than never-married women. It seems implausible that women's commitment to home and hearth accounts for the remaining sex-based gaps in early attrition, partnership, and partners' earnings.

This brings us to sex-based differences in the ways women are treated in law firms. Epstein et al. (1995) posited that direct discrimination and sexual harassment, as well as a wide array of embedded institutional practices, marginalize women within law firms. We could not directly test this proposition since our data set does not include measures of sexual harassment and discrimination and only has two institutional measures—firm size and mentoring. But our finding of large sex differences at each stage of the progression to partnership, controlling for labor supply differences, suggests that women are disproportionately selected out and discouraged at each of these stages. This is strong indirect evidence that women face multiple glass ceilings.

Researchers who have conducted in-depth, in-person interviews with associates and partners in law firms describe two sets of mechanisms that could systematically disadvantage women. One set constrains associates' labor supply choices and determines the effects these choices have on partnership. For instance, although firms offer part-time tracks, official policies differ on whether part-time work counts for partnership and on whether part-timers can return to partnership tracks (Epstein et al. 1995). Even when the official policy is that family leaves and part-time work do not disqualify women from partnership, several studies find that some women reported being assigned less important cases and being labeled as less motivated after having worked part-time (Epstein et al. 1995; Gannon 2003). This social stigma and fear of not being taken seriously likely keeps many lawyers from pursuing part-time options. For instance, a study of 1,305 law offices nationwide in 2003 found that while 96 percent of those firms offered part-time positions, only 4.1 percent of attorneys took advantage of reduced schedules (National Association of Law Placement 2003). This 4.1 percent rate of part-time work is markedly lower than the 13 percent rate for individuals in professional specialties in 2002 (National Association of Law Placement 2003). A second set of mechanisms can systematically disadvantage women in ways that are unrelated to their actual labor supply choices. Epstein et al. (1995) and Rhode (2001) claimed that high rainmaking demands, a lack of mentoring, sex discrimination, disproportionate shares of pro bono work, and mixed messages about personal style all may reduce women's chances of making partner.

It is easy to describe institutional arrangements that might make law firms more family-friendly. A report in the *Harvard Law Review* (1996) suggested reducing "billable hours" requirements, billing approaches that move away from reliance on billable hours to other indicators of performance, officially counting part-time work toward partnership, developing a work climate in which individuals who work part-time and take family leaves are not stigmatized, part-time partnership, employer-assisted emergency day care, and mixed compensation (compensation consisting partly of time and partly of money).

The few male lawyers who reduced their labor supply to care for children fared badly economically.

It is equally easy to list approaches that can change institutional barriers to women's mobility. To the extent that sex discrimination and sexual harassment limit women's chances, there may be legal avenues to pursue. Of course, the individual costs of pursuing such strategies may be high. Other strategies include programs that improve the mentoring women associates receive, broaden the criteria for partnership, and reduce the extent to which women's personal styles are viewed as less effective in a legal setting. We find mentoring has a big impact on women's partnership chances.

Implementing family-friendly policies and changing embedded institutional policies that disadvantage women may require shifts in law firm culture. This is the rub. The *Harvard Law Review* study (1996, 1381) warned that such changes can "conflict with (firms') institutional norms" and that "law firms and their clients are understandably reluctant to challenge deeply ingrained business practices." Epstein et al. (1995) asserted that three social processes—traditionalism, stereotyping, and ambivalence—contribute to this institutional inertia.

The *Harvard Law Review* study (1996, 1376) succinctly summed up the dilemma facing women associates: "Women cannot reach true equality within firms as large numbers of women are considered atypical because they fail to conform to the male-based definition of the ideal worker." Despite this gloomy assessment, the *Harvard Law Review* study and Rhode (2001) have contended that the benefits to changing firm culture may be powerful enough to overcome inertia. The *Harvard Law Review* report argues that high hour demands have led to a "time famine" among lawyers and that this "lack of time" can adversely affect health by increasing stress and can inhibit professional development by reducing available time for community service, pro bono work, scholarship, and education. The *Harvard Law Review* study and Rhode agreed that the current emphasis on high billable hours and constant availability is likely inefficient as well—that lawyers who are stretched too far are more likely to make mistakes. They also agreed that the current rigid set of expectations in law firms is likely related to disaffection and attrition among lawyers—both male and female. Our results show that partners are less satisfied with their work-family balance than are lawyers who do not make partner. To the extent that these arguments are correct, programs that change law firms' cultures to be open to a wider range of work and personal styles have the potential to reduce disaffection, raise morale, enhance professional development, increase efficiency, and improve productivity. These could be powerful incentives for change.

References

Belkin, Lisa. 2003. The opt-out revolution, *The New York Times* October 26.

Brockman, Joan. 1994. Leaving the practice of law: The wherefores and the whys. *Alberta Law Review* 32 (1): 116-80.

Chambers, David L. 1989. Accommodation and satisfaction: Women and men lawyers and the balance of work and family. *Law & Social Inquiry* 14:251-87.

Donovan, Kathleen. 1990. Women associates' advancement to partner status in private firms. *Georgetown Journal of Legal Ethics* 4:135-52.

Epstein, Cynthia Fuchs, Robert Saute, Bonnie Oglensky, and Martha Gever. 1995. Glass ceilings and open doors: Women's advancement in the legal profession. *Fordham Law Review* 64:306-449.

Foster, S. Elizabeth. 1995. The glass ceiling in the legal profession: Why do law firms still have so few female partners? *UCLA Law Review* 1597:1631-89.

Gannon, Joyce. 2003. A growing number of law firms let attorneys work part-time. *Pittsburgh Post-Gazette,* December 7.

Hagan, John, and Fiona Kay. 1995. *Gender in practice: A study of lawyers' lives*. New York: Oxford University Press.

Harvard Law Review. 1996. Why law firms cannot afford to maintain the mommy track. Unsigned Student Note. 109 (6): 1375-92.

Hull, Kathleen E., and Robert L. Nelson. 2000. Assimilation, choice or constraint? Testing theories of gender differences in the careers of lawyers. *Social Forces* 79 (1): 229-64.

Kay, Fiona M. 1997. Flight from law: A competing risks model of departures from law firms. *Law and Society Review* 31 (2): 301-35.

Kay, Fiona M., and John Hagan. 1998. Raising the bar: The gender stratification of law firm capital. *American Sociological Review* 63:728-43.

———. 1999. Cultivating clients in the competition for partnership: Gender and the organizational restructuring of law firms in the 1990s. *Law and Society Review* 33:517-55.

National Association of Law Placement. 2003. Part-time attorney schedules still widely available, but remain rarely used by partners, associates. http://www.nalp.org/press/p_t2003.htm (accessed November 7, 2003).

Rhode, Deborah. 2001. *The unfinished agenda: Women in the legal profession*. Chicago: American Bar Association Commission on Women in the Profession.

Rosenberg, Janet, Harry Perlstadt, and William R. F. Phillips. 1993. Now that we are here: Discrimination, disparagement, and harassment at work and the experience of women lawyers. *Gender & Society* 7:415-33.

Spurr, Stephen J. 1990. Sex discrimination in the legal profession: A study of promotion. *Industrial and Labor Relations Review* 43:406-17.

Spurr, Stephen J., and Glenn T. Sueyoshi. 1994. Turnover and promotion of lawyers: An inquiry into gender differences. *Journal of Human Resources* 29:813-42.

Mothers in Finance: Surviving and Thriving

MARY BLAIR-LOY
and
AMY S. WHARTON

This article explores two dimensions of well-being among five hundred finance managers and professionals in a large firm: higher income, which we regard as a proxy for career success, and work-family balance. These dimensions are partially incompatible: longer work hours are associated with higher earnings and with intensified conflict. Mothers are more likely than fathers to experience work-family conflict. Work that is overwhelming and unpredictable can exacerbate conflict, while workplace flexibility can alleviate it. Among men, using dependent care policies is associated with lower earnings. We find an earnings gap between men and women in the sample but no earnings penalty for mothers relative to other female respondents. Although women are less likely than men to combine parenting with careers at this firm, the mothers still at the firm may be unusually successful compared to their female coworkers.

Keywords: work-family conflict; gender and work; income; inequality

Work-family balance is a salient issue for professionals and managers in financial services. On one hand, these elite workers have traditionally enjoyed autonomy and high salaries, which offer resources in balancing work and family. On the other hand, managers and professionals have seen work hours increased in recent years (Jacobs and Gerson 2004), and they are expected to demonstrate commitment by making work the central focus of their lives (Blair-Loy 2003; Bailyn 1993). In the financial services sector, deregulation, consolidation, new technologies, unstable markets, and a twenty-four-hour global economy create a fast-

Mary Blair-Loy is an associate professor of sociology at the University of California, San Diego. She is the author of Competing Devotions: Career and Family among Women Executives *(Harvard University Press, 2003).*

Amy S. Wharton is a professor of sociology at Washington State University. Her teaching interests are sociology of gender; sociology of work; social inequality; race, class, gender, and sexuality; and sociology of sport.

NOTE: We thank Janice Madden, Jerry A. Jacobs, and Akos Rona-Tas for helpful comments.

DOI: 10.1177/0002716204268820

changing and demanding environment. Moreover, the increase in mothers' labor force participation and rise in dual-earner couples has exacerbated the time squeeze for families (Jacobs and Gerson 2001; Clarkberg and Moen 2001). How do mothers maintain full-time careers in this demanding environment? What factors facilitate their success and well-being?

This article explores these issues among managers and professionals in a firm we call International Finance (a pseudonym). Rather than studying these processes among typical or representative workers, we selected an extreme case of employees especially likely to face the pressures of work alongside the opportunity for high rewards.

International Finance is one of the largest multinational financial service institutions in the world in a turbulent industry strongly affected by global competition (Powell 2001; Fraser 2001). Following the trend of other global banks, it completed a merger in the late 1990s, followed by a massive layoff. International Finance is a "high-commitment" firm (Osterman 1995), which expects long hours and dedication from managers and professionals in return for high salaries, advancement opportunities, and a generous set of official work-family policies (Blair-Loy and Wharton forthcoming). In the sample analyzed here, the mean hours worked a week is 52.5 and the mean years of organizational tenure is 10.62. A conservative estimate of mean income (1998) is $101,547. Women and men put in similar numbers of hours worked and have devoted a similar number of years to International Finance.

How do employees maintain full-time careers in this demanding environment? We focus particularly on mothers, who tend to shoulder much of the weight of family caregiving.

We examine two aspects of well-being: salary (which we regard as a proxy for career success) and work-family conflict. Some studies suggest that these two features of well-being are somewhat incompatible because employees pursuing work-family balance are penalized with slower career advancement and lower salaries (Hochschild 1997; Fried 1998; Blair-Loy 2003). Our previous research on this firm has found that some employees perceive the use of corporate work-family policies to be risky and to come with career penalties attached (Blair-Loy and Wharton 2002). This perception is supported by Glass's (2002) longitudinal analysis, which followed a broad sample of mothers over a nine-year period and found that those who took advantage of work-family policies were penalized with reduced earnings growth compared to other mothers in the sample.

An extensive literature using large, representative samples explains earnings variation, and an emerging literature on large, representative samples explains variation in work-family conflict. Our goal is not to try to replicate these broad studies. Instead, we analyze detailed data on managers and professionals in one firm to assess the extent to which patterns apparent in broad data sets do or do not characterize full-time elite workers in the demanding and lucrative finance industry. In our sample, women work similar hours and have similar levels of organizational tenure to men. Our contribution is to identify factors that reduce or enhance the well-being of professional women who are mothers.

We present our findings as exploratory for several reasons. First, although our research questions and models are informed by previous research on these issues in broader populations, the literature does not yet provide a clear menu of inductive hypotheses. Relatively few studies investigate these processes in stressful, high-earning, professional and managerial occupations. The studies that do exist are generally qualitative and focus on one or a small number of workplaces, which could be idiosyncratic (Hochschild 1997; Fried 1998; Bailyn 1993; Perlow 1997; Blair-Loy 2003). Second, our cross-sectional data do not allow us to definitively sort out the direction of causality among the factors associated with salary or work-family conflict. Third, by definition our sample includes only those employees who have maintained careers at International Finance. This sample does not allow us to net out the selection effects that may have kept people at the firm or encouraged them to combine full-time careers with motherhood. We are able to fruitfully analyze these issues by using a valuable data set that provides detailed information on personal, family, and workplace characteristics and work-family policy use for a homogeneous group of professionals in a high-commitment organization.

Earnings, Family Responsibilities, and Gender

Research on broad samples has documented that, net of other factors that should affect earnings, marriage and children are associated with higher incomes for men and lower incomes for women. For example, a study of a broad sample of organizationally employed men found that, controlling for other factors, married men and fathers enjoy a wage premium (Hersch and Stratton 2000). Other studies on managerial and professional men in a broad array of occupations and industries have shown that the marriage wage premium is higher for men with homemaking wives than for those with employed wives (Hotchkiss and Moore 1999; Pfeffer and Ross 1982; Bellas 1992).

In contrast, studies of national populations of employed women have found a wage penalty associated with motherhood (Budig and England 2001; Waldfogel 1997; Hersch and Stratton 2000), with higher penalties for ever-married than for single mothers (Budig and England 2001). A study of Wall Street investment bankers found that longer hours worked increased earnings but that women earned less than men even when hours and other job and organizational factors were controlled for (Roth 2003). These empirical patterns are consistent with characterizations of the preferred elite organizational worker as someone who manifests singular "devotion to work" (Blair-Loy 2003), unencumbered with family responsibilities (Acker 1990). If this characterization applies to the present case, then what are the implications for parents' and especially mothers' perceptions of work-family conflict?

Work-Family Conflict

We explore one facet of the overarching phenomenon of "work-to-family conflict" (Thompson, Beauvais, and Lyness 1999), in which the demands of work interfere with one's life outside of work (Voydanoff 1988).[1] Specifically, we study parents' concerns that their jobs interfere with time needed for family and children. This is a salient measure of work-family conflict for the full-time, elite workers in our sample. This high-commitment firm (Osterman 1995; see also Pfeffer 1997) promotes a strong culture of work involvement and promises high dividends for elite employees' career investment.

We are particularly interested in mothers as compared to fathers, so we examine work-family conflict among a subsample of parents with children younger than sixteen at home. Concerns about jobs draining too much time from family may be most pressing for mothers since employed women generally take on more responsibility for family caregiving and domestic work than do employed men (Spain and Bianchi, 1996). Prior studies have found higher levels of work-family conflict among women (Galinsky, Bond, and Friedman 1996; Galinksy, Kim, and Bond 2001; Rothbard 2001) and among parents (Galinsky, Bond, and Friedman 1996).

Previous research on broad samples has shown that scheduling flexibility reduces work-family conflict (Golden 2001; Glass and Camarigg 1992). In addition, International Finance offers a generous array of corporate work-family policies, which are promoted as helping employees balance work and family responsibilities (Blair-Loy and Wharton 2002). However, employees may be worried about career penalties associated with the use of certain work-family policies and avoid using them, even if they are available on paper (Jacobs and Gerson 2004). In her qualitative study of one firm, Hochschild (1997) found that workers were reluctant to take advantage of policies that reduced work hours and that men were extremely unlikely to take officially available parental leaves.

Longer hours on the job (Voydanoff 1988; Thompson, Beauvais, and Lyness 1999; Galinsky, Kim, and Bond 2001; Berg, Kalleberg, and Appelbaum 2003) can increase work-family conflict. At the same time, longer work hours have been shown to be positively related to our first measure of well-being: income (e.g., Hotchkiss and Moore 1999; Roth 2003). Thus, working long hours may exacerbate the sense of work-family conflict at the same time that it supports higher earnings. Our models of work-family conflict include indicators for the use of corporate flexibility and dependent care policies as well as measures for job characteristics such as scheduling flexibility, job volume and unpredictability, and hours worked.

Research Questions

Within the context of full-time managerial and professional work in a high-commitment financial services firm, we study two facets of employee well-being: income and work-family conflict. Which individual and workplace characteristics are associated with higher incomes? Specifically, do women and/or mothers earn less than otherwise similar men? What difference, if any, does the use of corporate dependent care or flexibility policies make?

Among parents of children younger than sixteen living at home, what factors help transform the mandated orientation of work dedication into worries that the job is draining too much time away from the children? In particular, do longer work hours, which we expect will be associated with higher salaries, also lead to a heightened sense of work-family conflict? What other factors are associated with work-family balance? Do corporate flexibility or dependent care policies seem to help?

Data and Variables

Data

In 1998, International Finance gave us permission to study work-family policies in their organization. We conducted semistructured interviews with seven key informants in 1998 and used these interviews to help us write a questionnaire that would survey managerial and professional employees on their attitudes and individual and workplace characteristics relating to work-family issues. In 1999, after first pretesting our survey at another organization, we administered it in three divisions at International Finance.[2] One division in the sample provides professional technical services to the organization, while the other two serve customers in core line functions. These divisions are not in the relatively low-paid human resources area, nor are they in the very highly paid investment banking area. We sent the U.S. survey analyzed here to all U.S.-based managerial and professional employees of two of these divisions and to a subset of the third division.[3] The total number of usable surveys completed was 519, representing 52 percent of our original survey population.[4]

The earnings analyses here are based on the completed surveys of the five hundred respondents who worked at least thirty-five hours a week (and excludes two men and one woman who worked less than thirty-five hours per week as well as respondents with missing data on the number of hours worked). We also conduct earnings analyses on the following subsamples: parents only, women only, and men only. The work-family conflict models are based on the two hundred parents of children younger than sixteen living with them.

We use ordinary least squares (OLS) regression to explore the associations of individual and workplace characteristics on two facets of employees' well-being: income and work-family conflict. Although sample sizes are relatively small, many factors expected to affect our dependent variables are already controlled for in this homogenous sample. We supplement our OLS earnings models with a decomposition analysis of the average sex difference in ln earnings.

Our cross-sectional data set prohibits us from making strict statements about causal order. The income variable reports income earned in 1998, and the data for the independent variables were collected in the summer of 1999. Yet many of these

TABLE 1

MEANS AND STANDARD DEVIATIONS FOR VARIABLES BY SEX

Variable	Men (n = 291)	Women (n = 209)
Dependent variables		
Income (from midpoints of categories; not used in models)°	$114,618 (56,605)	$83,004 (40,712)
ln income (used in models)°	11.5346	11.2289
Work-family conflict (range 1-4)	2.78 (0.78)	2.80 (0.89)
Independent variables		
Weekly hours worked°	53.67 (9.05)	50.76 (9.31)
Organizational tenure	10.17 (8.05)	11.29 (8.99)
Supervisor°	0.10	0.04
Work overwhelming in volume and predictability (range 1-4, reverse coded)	1.79 (0.46)	1.78 (0.53)
Scheduling flexibility (range 1-4)	2.52 (0.84)	2.58 (0.91)
Organizational tenure	10.17 (8.05)	11.29 (8.99)
Age	42.91 (9.05)	41.82 (0.03)
Age squared	1,922.50 (766.38)	1,830.41 (772.37)
Marriage°	0.80	0.64
Children younger than age six°	0.22	0.14
Children ages six to fifteen°	0.32	0.23
Homemaking spouse°	0.25	0
Sole or shared primary responsibility for child rearing°	0.12	0.24
Using flexibility policy	0.27	0.26
Using dependent care policy°	0.15	0.30
Controls		
White and born in United States°	0.70	0.61
Staff (vs. line) position°	0.78	0.52
In the top income category°	0.03	0.00

NOTE: Dichotomous variables coded (0, 1). Standard deviations for continuous variables shown in parentheses.
°Statistically significant differences between men and women ($p < .05$).

independent variables measure individual, family, and workplace characteristics that were initially established before the 1998 income was earned. The causal processes are likely complex and include lagged, reciprocal, and indirect effects as well as the direct effects we are able to model. Table 1 presents the means and standard deviations for all the variables in the analysis by sex.

Dependent variables

Our informants at International Finance advised us that we would have higher rates of response to the income question if we asked respondents to check off an

TABLE 2
INCOME CATEGORIES BY SEX

| | Men | | Women | |
Income Category in Dollars	n	%	n	%
1. Less than 40,000	7	2.4	13	6.5
2. 40,000-59,999	35	12.2	57	28.1
3. 60,000-79,999	49	17.0	56	27.6
4. 80,000-99,999	55	19.1	24	11.8
5. 100,000-129,000	53	18.4	28	13.8
6. 130,000-159,999	37	12.8	17	8.4
7. 160,000-189,999	16	5.6	2	1.0
8. 190,000-229,999	18	6.3	3	1.5
9. 230,000-259,999	8	2.8	3	2.2
10. More than 260,000	10	3.5	0	0
Total	288	100	203	100

income category rather than ask them to reveal their specific income. We thus traded the advantage of having a specific dollar income figure for the benefit of less missing data on this measure. Our survey question on income asked, "What was your annual salary (including bonuses) for 1998?" Respondents were then asked to circle one of ten income categories (see Table 2). Our income variable is the natural log of the midpoint dollar amount of each category for the first nine categories. Respondents in the tenth category, more than $260,000, are coded as having an income of just $260,000. As a result, variation is constrained, and our OLS model will only pick up effects that are strong enough to impact income category. Therefore, our findings on the association of our independent variables with income are biased and may be understated relative to an analysis that included actual income levels. (In our earnings models, we add a dummy variable indicating membership in the top income category as a control.)

Our indicator of work-family conflict measures one aspect of this issue: parents' concerns that their jobs interfere with sufficient time spent with family and children. From a list of six items, parents in the sample were asked to check each item that described themselves (1 = *strongly agree* to 4 = *strongly disagree*). A factor analysis of this list revealed two items that seem to tap an underlying concern about the lack of time for family. We created a scale with the mean response to these two items (alpha reliability .63): "I find enough time for my children" and "My job keeps me away from my family too much" (reverse coded). Higher values indicate higher levels of conflict.

Independent variables

Table 1 presents information, by sex, on the independent variables used in the models. All variables are either continuous (with means and standard deviations given) or dichotomous. The dichotomous variables are coded (0, 1). Most of the variables are self-explanatory, but a few require clarification.

Work characteristics that might be important in explaining work-family conflict include scheduling flexibility and an excessive volume and unpredictability of work. Our indicator for *scheduling flexibility* is the respondent's response (1 = *strongly disagree* to 4 = *strongly agree*) to this survey statement: "It is easy for me to rearrange my work schedule when I need time off for family or personal obligations." The indicator for *excessive volume and unpredictability* is the mean response (1 = *strongly agree* to 4 = *strongly disagree*) to five items, which were selected via a factor analysis from a list of ten items on job conditions. The five selected items are "I often come in to work early or stay late," "Responding to unpredictable events is a large part of my job," "Things are changing rapidly in my work unit," "My job responsibilities make it difficult for me to do some of my work at home," and "Working under tight deadlines is common in this job" (alpha reliability .65). The coding is such that *less* stressful working conditions have higher values.

Our survey asked about employees' use of several different types of corporate work-family policies that are officially available at the firm. A factor analysis revealed that respondents who took advantage of corporate work-family policies tended to use one of two categories: *family and dependent care policies* (which include child care or elder care referral services or educational materials, workers using their own paid sick time to care for a dependent, or dependent care leave of more than two weeks) or *flexibility policies* (which include flextime, flexplace/telecommuting, or compressed work week).[5] We include a binary measure of whether the respondent has used or is currently using at least one of the flexibility policies (1 = use) and a dichotomous measure of whether the respondent has used or is using at least one of the dependent care policies (1 = use). Later, we also examine the association of income with particular policies within the dependent care category. Only 2 percent of our respondents had used reduced-hours policies, so we do not include this policy category in our models.

Parents who reported that they either *took on or shared with another adult the primary responsibility for taking care of the children* in their household were coded 1. Nonparents as well as parents reporting that either their spouse or another adult cared for the children were coded 0 on this measure for sole or shared primary responsibility for child care.

Results

Earnings

First, we compare characteristics of the employees at different earnings levels. These descriptive findings foreshadow our later multivariate results. Table 2 shows that there are no women in the top salary category. For ease of interpretation, we collapsed the ten categories into five by combining categories 1 and 2, collapsing 3 and 4, and so on (results not shown here). As the salary category increases, there is a corresponding monotonic increase in the proportion of respondents who are married, who are parents of children younger than sixteen, who are male, who have a homemaking spouse, and who do not provide primary care for their children. This picture is consistent with previous research: having families is associated with higher salaries as long as one does not spend too much energy taking care of them.

Research on broad samples has documented that, net of other factors that should affect earnings, marriage and children are associated with higher incomes for men and lower incomes for women.

Parents' use of corporate work-family policies varies by earnings category and sex. There is a decrease in the proportion of fathers in each of the five salary categories who use either dependent care or flexibility policies. For example, in the lower earnings categories, up to 35 percent of fathers use dependent care and 44 percent of fathers use flexibility policies. But the proportion of policy use among fathers in the highest category is only 8 percent. Mothers have higher rates of dependent care policy use overall than fathers do but show the same monotonic decrease in policy use by salary category: 80 percent of mothers in the lowest salary use dependent care policies, and only 50 percent (two of the four mothers) in the highest category do so. In contrast, mothers in the higher salary categories are *more* likely to use flexibility polices than those earning less: only 20 percent of mothers in the lowest salary category use flexibility policies, whereas 50 percent (two women) use flexibility policies in the highest category.

Although the numbers in each cell are small, the pattern is consistent. Higher-earning fathers are less likely to use either policy type than lower-earning fathers. Higher-earning mothers are less likely to use dependent care policies than lower-earning mothers but more likely to use flexibility policies. Thus, flexibility policies may help mothers handle family caregiving responsibilities without negatively affecting their income.

We explore these patterns more systematically in the multivariate analysis. The first column of Table 3 presents the OLS earnings model for the full sample. This sample of managers and professionals in one firm has in common many of the factors that research on broad samples finds to affect wages, including organizational

TABLE 3
ORDINARY LEAST SQUARES (OLS) MODEL PREDICTING INCOME

Variable	1. Full Sample (n = 463), $B(SE)$	2. Parents (n = 187), $B(SE)$	3. Men Only (n = 275), $B(SE)$	4. Women Only (n = 189), $B(SE)$
Constant	9.086 (0.331)****	9.315 (0.781)****	9.202 (0.441)****	8.746 (0.492)****
Weekly hours worked	.015 (.002)****	.014 (.003)****	.016 (.002)****	.014 (.003)****
Supervisor	.336 (.067)****	.321 (.091)****	.345 (.076)****	.281 (.131)**
Organizational tenure	-.005 (.002)**	-.008 (.004)*	-.002 (.003)	-.006 (.004)
Age	.060 (.016)****	.058 (.037)	.049 (.022)**	.077 (.025)***
Age squared	-.055 (.000)****	-.000 (.000)	-.000 (.000)	-.001 (.000)***
Marriage	.007 (.041)	.034 (.136)	.001 (.059)	-.034 (.059)
Young children (younger than six)	.114 (.056)**	.018 (.078)	.162 (.057)***	.165 (.101)*
Children between ages six and fifteen	.159 (.041)****	—	.186 (.049)****	-.059 (.102)
Homemaking spouse	.118 (.054)**	.166 (.070)**	.084 (.052)*	—
Sole or shared primary responsibility for child care	—	—	—	.220 (.110)**
Female	-.162 (.039)****	-.145 (.088)*	—	—
Using flexibility policy	.026 (.040)	-.019 (.064)	-.038 (.048)	.100 (.069)
Using dependent care policy	-.117 (.044)***	-.064 (.067)	-.131 (.058)**	-.089 (.071)
Female × Young Children	.188 (.092)**	.160 (.118)	—	—
Controls				
White and born in United States	.117 (.036)****	.120 (.058)**	.081 (.047)	.141 (.059)**
Staff (vs. line) position	-.052 (.040)	-.197 (.067)***	-.063 (.047)	-.030 (.063)
In top income category	.525 (.125)****	.519 (.158)****	.473 (.121)****	—
Adjusted R-squared	.485	.430	.531	.310

NOTE: Income is measured as the natural log of the midpoint of one of ten income categories.
*p < .10. **p < .05. ***p < .01. ****p < .001.

size, industry, education, and occupation.[6] Within this homogeneous group, three job or worker characteristics are associated with higher earnings in the full sample: longer work hours, supervisory responsibility, and older age (column 1). We understand age to be a proxy for experience in the finance industry. In this model, organizational tenure has a negative association with earnings. Perhaps net of work hours, supervisor status, and our proxy for industry experience, those more recently recruited to the firm have used labor market competition to increase their incomes.

The presence of preschoolers and of school-aged children in the home is associated with higher incomes. Those with a homemaking spouse (all men in this sample) enjoy an additional wage premium, although the causal direction here is unclear.

The control for race-country of origin shows that white employees who were born in the United States earn more than employees of color and those born outside the United States. The control for staff (versus line) position in the organization is not statistically significant (column 1). The control for being in the top income category ($260,000 or above) is positive and statistically significant here, as it is for all the models presented in Table 3.

Net of all these characteristics (and all the workplace factors controlled for by the homogeneity of this sample), women earn significantly less than men. The use of corporate flexibility policies is not statistically significant in the full sample, but using dependent care policies is negatively associated with earnings. An interaction term of Female × Parent was not statistically significant and dropped from the model. But the interaction term of Female × Parent of Young Children is statistically significant and, rather surprisingly, shows a positive association with earnings (column 1).

The second column of Table 3 presents the findings for the subsample of parents with children younger than sixteen. The results are similar to the full sample, with the following key exceptions: age is no longer statistically significant, the negative effect of being female drops to marginal statistical significance, the interaction term of Female × Parent of Young Children is not significant here, and dependent care policy use is still negative but no longer statistically significant.

Column 3 of Table 3 shows results for male employees only. This model resembles the earlier ones, with a few variations. As we saw in the full model, work hours, supervisory responsibility, and age (interpreted as a proxy for industry experience) are associated with higher incomes. Here, reflecting previous research on broader populations, fathers earn more than other men, net of other factors. Married men do not earn significantly more than single men here, but men with a homemaking spouse do enjoy an earnings premium compared to their male coworkers (although the effect here is only marginally statistically significant). Men who use work-family policies for dependent care earn significant less than the other male respondents.

The last column (column 4) of Table 3 shows the results for female respondents only. As we saw previously, hours worked, supervisory status, and age are positively related to earnings.

Among women, having a school-aged child is not related to income. Consistent with the positive coefficient of the interaction term Female × Parent of Young Children in the full sample, column 4 of Table 3 shows that women with preschool children have marginally higher earnings than their female coworkers without preschoolers.

Since no women in the sample have a homemaking spouse, we could not measure the effects of this kind of domestic support on women's income. Instead, we included our measure of primary caregiving, which characterizes those saying they either take on alone or share with another adult the primary responsibility for caring for the children in their household. Since women tend to have more responsibility than men for all aspects of family caregiving and household management, this responsibility for primary caregiving variable helps us distinguish *among women* those with more or less intensive involvement in child rearing. For women, this measure of involved parenthood has a *positive* effect on earnings. And in contrast to men, women are not penalized for using corporate policies designed to assist with dependent care.

To better understand the apparent wage penalty for men who used dependent care policies, we disaggregated the policy types grouped in the dependent care category. In the full sample, most respondents who used policies in the dependent care category were currently using or had used either (1) child care or elder care referral services or educational materials ($n = 65$, about a third of which are men) or (2) their own paid sick time to care for a dependent ($n = 63$, again about a third are men). Only seven respondents (six women and one man) had ever used the third policy, dependent care leave of more than two weeks, which is consistent with Hochschild's (1997) findings for the firm she studied. Thus, respondents of both sexes tended to use only the less intrusive of these policies: (1) calling a 1-800 number for referrals or reading an educational brochure or (2) taking an occasional sick day. Managers and professionals in our sample are extremely unlikely to use policies such as dependent care leave that may be more visible to others at work, more intrusive of the work flow, and thereby more risky to their careers.

To determine which dependent care policy was most closely associated with lower earnings for men, we replaced the general dependent care category with a specific policy (referral service/educational materials or dependent sick time) in our models. Use of referral services or educational materials alone is not associated with income. But the use of dependent sick time is.

We substituted the dependent sick time category for the broad category of dependent care in our models and found results similar to those in Table 3. For the full sample, we found that use of dependent sick time is significantly associated with lower earnings, net of the other variables in the model ($p < .001$, results not shown). In the men-only sample, we found dependent sick time is still associated with lower earnings, although the effect is only marginally significant. In the parents model, the broad category of dependent care was not statistically significant (Table 3, column 2), but the more specific dependent sick time variable is ($p < .05$, results not shown). Whether we analyze the full sample, men only, or all parents,

TABLE 4

DECOMPOSITION ANALYSIS OF INCOME DIFFERENCES

Variable	1. Between Means	2. Due to Differences in Means	3. Between Parameters	4. Due to Differences in Returns
Weekly hours worked	2.9093	0.0487	0.0036	0.1925
Supervisor	0.0566	−0.0000	0.0004	0.0000
Organizational tenure	−1.1210	0.0005	0.0050	0.0511
Age	1.0828	0.0572	−0.0257	−1.1021
Age squared	92.09	−0.0004	0.0004	0.8275
Total: Human capital and job status		0.1055		−0.0310
Marriage	0.1350	0.0026	0.0462	0.0363
Young children (younger than six)	0.0813	0.0161	−0.0695	−0.0151
Children between ages six and fifteen	0.0890	0.0172	0.1069	0.0339
Total: Family		0.0359		0.0551
Using flexibility policy	0.0099	−0.0004	−0.1427	−0.0383
Using dependent care policy	−0.1496	0.0228	−0.0730	−0.0112
Total: Policy use		0.0224		−0.0495
White and born in United States	0.0857	0.0060	−0.0815	−0.0567
Staff (vs. line) position	0.2549	−0.0322	−0.0949	−0.0732
Total: Controls		−0.0262		−0.1299
Sum (before intercept)				−0.1552
Intercept (male-female)				0.3342
Sum		0.1381		0.1790

those who occasionally used a sick day to care for an ill child earned less than those who did not, net of other factors.

The difference between men's and women's average earnings is $31,614. Our earnings model uses units of ln dollars, and the total average difference between men's ln earnings and women's ln earnings is .306.

To further analyze this earnings gap, we decompose it into its constituent parts. We follow a standard decomposition technique that divides the logged earnings difference between women and men into the part due to differences in their mean characteristics and differences due to returns to those characteristics (U.S. General Accounting Office 2003).

We find that the portion of the .306 earnings gap attributed to men and women having different means on the independent variables is .138, or 44 percent. The remaining .179, or 56 percent, of the gap is due to differences in the returns to men's and women's characteristics.

Columns 2 and 4 in Table 4 show the contributions each set of independent variables make to the overall earnings gap. Positive values show an effect favoring men, while negative values show a female advantage. Different means for men and women on the human capital and supervisor status variables account for about one-third of the earnings gap. Most of this is due to men working slightly longer hours, on average, and having a higher likelihood of being a supervisor than women. Gender differences in the returns to human capital and job status characteristics slightly favor women, however. Overall, human capital and job status variables account for about one-quarter of the earnings gap.

Family status variables also contribute substantially to the earnings gap. Different means on the family status variables—primarily the presence of a child or children in the home younger than six or between ages six and fifteen—and differences in the returns to those characteristics explain about one-third of the gap between men's and women's earnings.

Different means on the policy use variables account for only a small portion (6 percent) of the earnings gap. Differences in the returns to these variables offset this, however; if women and men received the same returns for using work-family policies, the earnings gap would be slightly reduced. Gender differences in the means and returns to the control variables also favor women.

Gender differences in the intercept clearly favor men. Hence, while women receive a more favorable return than men on almost all variables in the analysis (with the exception of family status), these differences in the returns to particular characteristics are only half as large as the gender difference in the intercept. Men's wages are higher than women's even after considering the effects of mean differences in characteristics and differences in returns to those characteristics.

In sum, as we would expect in this high-commitment workplace, work hours are strongly associated with earnings. In this homogeneous sample, and net of several individual and job characteristics, women earn less than men. Roughly one-quarter of the gender earnings gap can be attributed to the human capital and job status variables in the model. There is also evidence of an earnings penalty for involvement in family caregiving. Men without a homemaking wife have lower incomes than others, although the causal direction is unclear. However, mothers did not suffer a wage penalty compared to nonmothers. Moreover, the mothers of young children and those most involved in child rearing seem to enjoy a wage premium relative to other female respondents. Despite these effects, overall, about one-third of the earnings gap is due to gender differences in family status variables.

Work-family conflict

Our indicator of work-family conflict measures respondents' concerns about lacking sufficient time with family due at least in part to job demands. We are primarily interested in this issue among parents, so we limit this analysis to the subsample of parents of children younger than sixteen living at home. Table 5 presents our results.

Several job characteristics are related to work-family conflict. On average, parents who work longer hours are more likely to say they experience work-family conflict, as are parents who face an excessive volume of work with unpredictability and tight deadlines. Parents who enjoy more scheduling flexibility tend to have less

TABLE 5

ORDINARY LEAST SQUARES (OLS) MODEL PREDICTING
WORK-FAMILY CONFLICT FOR PARENTS

Variable	Parents $(N = 190)$, $B(SE)$
Constant	2.525****
Weekly hours worked	.016 (.006)***
Supervisor	.241 (.160)
Work overwhelming in volume and unpredictability, reverse coded	−.350 (.105)****
Scheduling flexibility	−.220 (.064)****
Marriage	.602 (.252)**
Homemaking spouse	.058 (.126)
Female	.283 (.129)**
Using flexibility policy	−.197 (.116)*
Using dependent care policy	.158 (.125)
Adjusted R-squared	.233

*$p < .10$. **$p < .05$. ***$p < .01$. ****$p < .001$.

work-family conflict. And using corporate flexibility policies is negatively associated with conflict, although the effect is only marginally statistically significant.

Married parents report higher levels of work-family conflict than unmarried parents, perhaps in part because married respondents have yet another family relationship that jobs could potentially interfere with. Having a homemaking spouse is not statistically significant, perhaps because the work-family conflict indicator taps whether the employee himself (or herself) spends enough time with his (or her) children and family.

Even in this homogeneous sample and net of the other variables, mothers have higher levels of work-family conflict than fathers. Given the similar number of hours worked by fathers and mothers and given the control for hours worked in the model, mothers tend to count similar amounts of time away from family and children as more troubling than do fathers.

Discussion

This article has explored two dimensions of well-being among full-time managers and professionals in a financial services firm that expects and rewards long hours. With a focus on mothers, we have studied the individual and workplace factors associated with higher income (an indicator of career success) and with an enhanced sense of work-family balance.

Net of other factors, respondents working longer hours have higher incomes. And net of other factors, women earn less than men, on average. Human capital and job status variables in the model account for only one-third of the gender wage gap. The positive association of work hours with earnings and negative association of being female with earnings are consistent with Roth's (2003) study of earnings among another type of financial services professional: investment bankers in several Wall Street firms.

[W]e found that use of dependent sick time is significantly associated with lower earnings, net of the other variables in the model.

But our results on earnings are not uniformly bleak for women. Compared to other women, respondents with children younger than sixteen living at home do not suffer an earnings penalty. Surprisingly, mothers with children younger than six and mothers who have sole or shared responsibility for child care earn more than the other women in the sample. Despite the gender income gap in this sample, there is no motherhood gap; these full-time employed mothers remain on the fast track.

Consistent with other research, fathers of school-aged children earn more than other men. But there is some evidence that highly involved fathers may suffer negative career consequences. Men with a homemaking wife enjoy a marginal wage premium (although the causal direction is unclear here). Importantly, men who take advantage of the corporate policy to occasionally use sick time for caring for an ill dependent earn less than other men, and parents who use this policy earn less than other parents.

Our results for men seem to fit Acker's (1990) argument that the preferred elite worker is unencumbered by family responsibilities, while men manifesting too much devotion to family may be penalized. But Acker's argument does not fit our female respondents. We find that relative to other women in the sample, those with young children and those with primary caregiving responsibilities enjoy a modest earnings advantage.

One interpretation of these findings is that they are in part due to selection effects. Less than a third of the women in our sample have children younger than sixteen, compared to almost half of male respondents who have children in this age range. Far from being a normative status, combining motherhood with full-time professional and managerial finance careers may be seen as a challenging endeavor that not everyone will attempt.

These findings are broadly consistent with the argument that financial services firms require elite workers to manifest full-time allegiance (Blair-Loy 2003; Blair-

Loy and Wharton forthcoming). This mandate of work devotion clashes with the cultural requirement that mothers dedicate much time and energy to their children, who are understood as fragile and deserving of their care (Blair-Loy 2003; Hays 1996). Many women may decide that these cultural definitions of professionalism and motherhood are incompatible and thus chose one or the other. But women who maintain full-time careers after childbearing are likely to be highly successful and dedicated to their work at the same time they take on much of the culturally prescribed responsibility of child rearing.

Stated differently, among finance professionals who become mothers, the most professionally successful and committed may be the most likely to continue these demanding careers after childbearing. Of course, larger samples and longitudinal data are required to tease out the factors affecting the selection of certain women into motherhood and into maintaining full-time careers after motherhood in elite jobs in financial services.

Among the parents in our sample, longer work hours are associated with higher incomes and also with greater work-family conflict. Since we measure work-family conflict as the sense that one's job pulls one away from time that families and children need, it is not surprising that work-family conflict is greater among those working longer hours. Yet net of hours worked, mothers are more likely than fathers to worry about the lack of time with children and family. Fathers and mothers report similar average weekly work hours. Yet even controlling for hours worked, mothers are more likely than fathers to perceive that doing their jobs violates the cultural mandate that mothers give devoted care to their children, who are understood as vulnerable and needing that care (Blair-Loy 2003; Hays 1996; Garey 1999).

In addition to hours worked, other job characteristics affect parents' perception that their jobs are taking what should be family time. Parents who enjoy more scheduling flexibility and who take advantage of corporate flexibility policies are less likely to experience work-family conflict, while those who experience work as overwhelming in volume and fraught with tight deadlines and unpredictability are more likely to do so.

The two aspects of well-being—income and work-family balance—are partially incompatible. Reducing one's work hours to spend more time with one's children would likely reduce work-family conflict, but it could also reduce earnings and even jeopardize one's career.[7] Moreover, compared to fathers, mothers earn lower incomes and also endure greater levels of work-family conflict.

In other ways, these dimensions of well-being are orthogonal. By adding new variables to our regression models, we found that many factors associated with one dimension of well-being appear irrelevant to the other dimension. For example, supervisory responsibility is associated with higher earnings but does not significantly affect work-family conflict. Job characteristics facilitating work-family balance—the use of flexibility policies, scheduling flexibility, the use of corporate flextime policies, and lower levels of work volume and unpredictability—do not seem to affect income. Income per se has no statistically significant association with work-family conflict among parents in our sample. (Results of these additions to the models are not shown here.) Thus, opportunities appear to exist for parents to enhance one dimension of well-being at International Finance without making trade-offs on the other dimension.

Conclusion

Compared to men in the sample, mothers at International Finance are also surviving in full-time managerial and professional jobs. And compared to other women, mothers may even be thriving. Given the clashing cultural schemas of devotion to this high-commitment firm for all elite employees and of family devotion or intensive motherhood for women, it may be more challenging for women than for men to combine parenting with careers at International Finance. Certainly, it is rarer in our sample to be a mother than a father of a child younger than sixteen. But among finance professionals who become mothers, the most professionally successful and devoted to work may be the most likely to continue these demanding careers after childbearing. Further research using a more precise earnings measure and larger, ideally longitudinal samples is necessary to tease out the selection effects, articulated with societal cultural understandings of work, family, and gender that we expect are operating here. Further research is also important for understanding the extent to which these findings characterize elite workers beyond the offices at International Finance.

Our research suggests that mothers maintaining full-time careers as finance professionals are corporate treasures. They work long hours and show high levels of achievement despite their responsibilities at home. Firms like International Finance would do well to support the careers of these women. Organizing the work flow of these professionals so that they are not overwhelmed by a high volume or unpredictability and preserving their scheduling flexibility may increase work-family balance without jeopardizing productivity. Promoting the use of corporate flexibility policies may positively affect women's productivity and enhance work-family balance for parents.

Financial services firms should be concerned about the earnings penalty associated with being female found in this study and elsewhere (Roth 2003) and take steps to correct this gender earnings gap. Furthermore, our control variable for white and born in the United States had a statistically significant, positive effect on earnings, suggesting that people of color and immigrants earn less net of other factors. Further research should more fully investigate the effect of race and country of origin on earnings in elite financial services jobs.

We hope that firms will address the impotence of some of their family-friendly policies. Consistent with other research (Hochschild 1997; Jacobs and Gerson forthcoming), employees may be reluctant to use reduced-hours and dependent care leave policies because of the career penalties and lower incomes they entail.

Firms should also be concerned about the earnings penalty associated with involved caregiving for men found here, including the use of corporate policies designed to assist with the care of dependents. Even the seemingly benign and undisruptive policy of taking an occasional sick day to care for an ill dependent is associated with lower earnings at International Finance in the full sample, among parents, and among men. This practice not only hurts involved fathers, it also penalizes their career-oriented wives. If firms penalize fathers for being involved caregivers, career-oriented mothers will have to take on more responsibility at home and find it harder to stay on the fast track.

Notes

1. While our article studies the potential negative consequences of overwork, we also acknowledge the potential for positive spillover (e.g., Repetti 1994; Grzywacz and Marks 2000; Doumas, Margolin, and John 2003) or enrichment (Rothbard 2001) from work to family.

2. The sample analyzed here is a part of a larger international sample. The surveys were confidential, and they were anonymous to the extent that we knew what work group a response came from but not what individual. We conducted seven additional interviews after we collected the survey data and conducted initial analyses.

3. For the third division, the survey was sent to U.S.-based professional and managerial employees in three major geographical centers.

4. It is extremely challenging for researchers to penetrate organizations. Nevertheless, our response rate is comparable to the 52.9 percent response rate for the 1997 National Study of the Changing Workforce, a telephone survey of individuals using random-digit-dialing methods (Bond, Galinsky, and Swanberg 1998). We did extensive tests for selection bias and found no evidence that this was a problem in our data; for details, see Blair-Loy and Wharton (2002).

5. See Blair-Loy and Wharton (2002) for details on these policies and policy groupings.

6. We did not include a question on education in our survey. According to our informants at International Finance, all respondents would have at least a bachelor's degree, and many would also have MBAs or other advanced degrees.

7. As a practical matter, individual workers may be constrained from reducing work. Particular jobs require that a certain volume of work be accomplished and that time expectations from supervisors and colleagues be fulfilled. Violating those requirements and expectations may entail harsher penalties than a drop in income (or, over time, a reduction in income growth).

References

Acker, Joan. 1990. Hierarchies, jobs, bodies: A theory of gendered organizations. *Gender & Society* 4:139-58.

Bailyn, Lotte. 1993. *Breaking the mold: Women, men, and time in the new corporate world*. New York: Free Press.

Bellas, Marcia L. 1992. The effects of marital status and wives' employment on the salaries of faculty men. *Gender & Society* 64:609-22.

Berg, Peter, Arne L. Kalleberg, and Eileen Appelbaum. 2003. Balancing work and family: The role of high-commitment environments. *Industrial Relations* 42:168-88.

Blair-Loy, Mary. 2003. *Competing devotions: Career and family among executive women*. Cambridge, MA: Harvard University Press.

Blair-Loy, Mary, and Amy S. Wharton. 2002. Employees' use of work-family policies and the workplace social context. *Social Forces* 80:813-46.

———. Forthcoming. Organizational commitment and constraints on work-family policy use: Corporate flexibility policies in a global firm. *Sociological Perspectives*.

Bond, James T., Ellen Galinsky, and Jennifer E. Swanberg. 1998. *The 1997 National Study of the Changing Workforce*. New York: Families and Work Institute.

Budig, Michelle, and Paula England. 2001. The wage penalty for motherhood. *American Sociological Review* 66:204-25.

Clarkberg, Marin, and Phyllis Moen. 2001. Understanding the time-squeeze: Married couples' preferred and actual work-hour strategies. *American Behavioral Scientist* 44:1115-36.

Doumas, Diana M., Gayla Margolin, and Richard S. John. 2003. The relationship between daily marital interaction, work, and health-promoting behaviors in dual-earner couples. *Journal of Family Issues* 24:3-20.

Fraser, Jill Andresky. 2001. *White collar sweatshop: The deterioration of work and its rewards in corporate America*. New York: Norton.

Fried, Mindy. 1998. *Taking time: Parental leave policy and corporate culture*. Philadelphia: Temple University Press.

Galinsky, Ellen, James T. Bond, and Dana E. Friedman. 1996. The role of employers in addressing the needs of employed parents. *Journal of Social Issues* 52:111-36.

Galinsky, Ellen, Stacy S. Kim, and James T. Bond. 2001. *Feeling overworked: When work becomes too much*. New York: Families and Work Institute.

Garey, Anita. 1999. *Weaving work and motherhood*. Philadelphia: Temple University Press.

Glass, Jennifer L. 2002. Blessing or curse? Family responsive policies and mother's wage growth over time. Manuscript, University of Iowa, Iowa City.

Glass, Jennifer L., and Valarie Camarigg. 1992. Gender, parenthood and job-family compatibility. *American Journal of Sociology* 98:131-51.

Golden, Lonnie. 2001. Flexible work schedules: Which workers get them? *American Behavioral Scientist* 44:1157-78.

Grzywacz, Joseph G., and Nadeine F. Marks. 2000. Reconceptualizing the work-family interface: An ecological perspective on the correlates of positive and negative spillover between work and family. *Journal of Occupational Health Psychology* 5:11-126.

Hays, Sharon. 1996. *The cultural contradictions of motherhood*. New Haven, CT: Yale University Press.

Hersch, Joni, and Leslie S. Stratton. 2000. Household specialization and the male marriage wage premium. *Industrial and Labor Relations Review* 54:78-114.

Hochschild, Arlie Russell. 1997. *The time bind: When work becomes home and home becomes work*. New York: Metropolitan Books.

Hotchkiss, Julie L., and Robert E. Moore. 1999. On the evidence of a working spouse penalty in the managerial labor market. *Industrial and Labor Relations Review* 52:410-23.

Jacobs, Jerry A., and Kathleen Gerson. 2001. Overworked individuals or overworked families? Explaining trends in work, leisure, and family time. *Work and Occupations* 28:40-63.

———. 2004. *The time divide: Work, family and social policy in contemporary society*. Cambridge, MA: Harvard University Press.

Osterman, P. 1995. Work/family programs and the employment relationship. *Administrative Science Quarterly* 40:681-700.

Perlow, Leslie A. 1997. *Finding time: How corporations, individuals and families can benefit from new work practices*. Ithaca, NY: ILR Press.

Pfeffer, Jeffrey. 1997. *New directions for organization theory: Problems and prospects*. New York: Oxford University Press.

Pfeffer, Jeffrey, and Jerry Ross. 1982. The effects of marriage and a working wife on occupational and wage attainment. *Administrative Science Quarterly* 27:66-80.

Powell, Walter W. 2001. The capitalist firm in the twenty-first century: Emerging patterns in Western enterprise. In *The twenty-first-century firm: Changing economic organization in international perspective*, edited by Paul DiMaggio, 33-68. Princeton, NJ: Princeton University Press.

Repetti, Rena L. 1994. Short-term and long-term processes linking job stressors to father-child interaction. *Social Development* 3:1-15.

Roth, Louise. 2003. Selling women short: A research note on gender differences in compensation on Wall Street. Manuscript, University of Arizona, Tucson.

Rothbard, Nancy P. 2001. Enriching or depleting? The dynamics of engagement in work and family roles. *Administrative Science Quarterly* 46:655-84.

Spain, Daphne, and Suzanne M. Bianchi. 1996. *Balancing act: Motherhood and employment among American women*. New York: Russell Sage Foundation.

Thompson, Cynthia A., Laura L. Beauvais, and Karen S. Lyness. 1999. When work-family benefits are not enough: The influence of work-family culture on benefit utilization, organizational attachment, and work-family conflict. *Journal of Vocational Behavior* 54:392-415.

U.S. General Accounting Office. 2003. *Women's earnings*. Washington, DC: Government Printing Office.

Voydanoff, Patricia. 1988. Work role characteristics, Family structure demands, and work/family conflict. *Journal of Marriage and the Family* 50:749-61.

Waldfogel, Jane. 1997. The effect of children on women's wages. *American Sociological Review* 62:209-17.

The Evolution of Gender and Motherhood in Contemporary Medicine

By
ANN BOULIS

In this article, the author endeavors to clarify the shifting nature of gender and motherhood for women physicians. She examines trends in the gender gap in marriage, divorce, childbearing, work hours, and earnings. The author draws on data from the 1990 and 2000 U.S. decennial censuses and data spanning 1991 to 1997 from the Survey of the Practice Patterns of Young Physicians. Compared with women in the general population, the trends for women physicians have been favorable. Women physicians are more likely to marry and less likely to divorce than are other women. Among employed physicians, gender differences in earnings and work hours are also narrowing slightly. Nevertheless, a gap is growing between female physicians with children and childless women doctors, and a small but growing percentage of young physician mothers are electing to forgo labor force participation entirely. Thus, young physician mothers still suffer significant professional sacrifice.

Keywords: women physicians; gender gap; salary gap; work-family balance; marriage trends; family trends

Over the past several decades, women have made significant progress in the U.S. medical profession. Most notably, between 1970 and 2002, the representation of women in medical school increased from 11 to 46 percent, or by more than 300 percent, so that women now make up just less than one-half of all medical students (Association of American Medical Colleges [AAMC] 2003). According to the AAMC, in 2003, more women applied to medical school than men (Howell 2003). During the same thirty-two-year period, women's presence among practicing physicians more than doubled

Ann Boulis is a postdoctoral fellow in the sociology department at the University of Pennsylvania. She has a master's degree in public policy from Harvard University's Kennedy School of Government and a Ph.D. in medical sociology and demography from the University of Pennsylvania. Before coming to Penn, she worked in the New York State Department of Health. Her current research interests involve gender and health.

DOI: 10.1177/0002716204268923

so that women now make up just less than one-fourth of practicing doctors in the United States (Nonnemaker 2000).

In spite of this profound change, significant gender disparities remain in the medical profession. Women physicians are underrepresented in the upper echelons of medical academia and medical administration, and although women are now about 25 percent of practicing physicians, they are only 18 percent of physician researchers and 16 percent of physician administrators. Women are also concentrated in the lower-paid and lower-prestige specialties, that is, primary care, of the medical profession. According to the American Medical Association, in 1998 women were 46.5 percent of pediatricians, 28.7 percent of pathologists, and 3.4 percent of orthopedic surgeons (Pasko et al. 2000).

Adherents to [the "different voice"] perspective would expect that women who enter medicine would be more interested in providing care than seeking status or income.

Women physicians are more likely to work as employees rather than partners in a medical practice, and they work significantly fewer hours than their male colleagues. Not surprisingly, given their lower status and work effort, women physicians report significantly lower earnings than their male counterparts. Results from the nationally representative Community Tracking Study (CTS) physician survey suggest that in 1996, women physicians' annual salaries averaged only 67.8 percent of their male colleagues' salaries (ICPSR 2001).

A sizeable literature investigates the source of gender disparities within medicine, which is selectively reviewed below. There are two main schools of thought.

Some researchers suggest that gender differences in the status of physicians exist because women doctors pursue careers that enable them to assume the bulk of domestic and childrearing responsibilities. Other studies tend to emphasize the continuing role of discrimination.

While the literature on gender differences in the status of physicians is informative, it is incomplete. Most notably, little if any effort has been made to track changes in family formation among physicians over the past two decades. Furthermore, little, if any, effort has been made to understand how gender differences in earnings have changed over time for the U.S. physician population. Previous research suggests dramatic differences in marriage, divorce, and fertility for male and female physicians such that women doctors are less likely to be married, more likely to be divorced, and less likely to have children (Uhlenberg and Cooney 1990). These results are not surprising given the long period of medical training that coincides with the period of family formation and childbearing, as well as the strong career penalty that appears to be connected to family formation for women physicians. I seek to build on this analysis to see how these patterns are evolving with the entry of steadily larger cohorts of women physicians.

I also maintain that it is important to present these trends in the context of three different benchmarks: by comparing women physicians' experiences today to their counterparts a generation earlier, to their male counterparts today, and to other women in the general population. Each of these three different vantage points provides valuable insights and helps me to provide a more complete picture of what has changed, and what has not, among female physicians.

This article is organized as follows. I first turn to the issue of the gender gap in earnings among physicians. Data, results, and a discussion follow.

Gender Gap in Earnings

The gender gap in earnings among physicians is typically attributed to women's choices regarding working time and specialty choice. This perspective emphasizes the idea that women's desire to balance work and family leads them to choose different paths than do their male counterparts. For example, in a national study of physicians who finished their MDs in 1983 and 1984, Xu and colleagues (1995) found that male and female primary care physicians cited significantly different reasons for their specialty choice. While women disproportionately selected primary care because it enabled them to pursue controllable work schedules, men noted the importance of role models. Similarly, in a survey of graduating medical students at the University of Toronto, Baxter, Cohen, and McLeod (1996) found that men were more likely to cite opportunities for technical challenge, high earning potential, and prestige as key factors in their specialty choice. Female students, in contrast, were more likely to identify residency conditions, part-time work, and parental leave opportunities as factors motivating their career choice.

Research on gender differences in physician work hours yields similar conclusions. In an analysis of 1980 census data on physicians between thirty and forty-nine years of age, Uhlenberg and Cooney (1990) found a strong interaction between marriage and physicians' work habits. In 1980, female physicians living alone worked and earned more than their female colleagues living with husbands and children, while male physicians living alone worked and earned significantly less than their male colleagues.[1] Similarly, using nationally representative data on physicians working in private practice, Mitchell (1984) found that the primary factor explaining gender differences in physician work hours was the different effect of marriage on male and female physicians' work habits.

Much of the research on gender differences in physicians' incomes also highlights the role of marriage and family. In a nationally representative study of physicians younger than fifty-two during the late 1980s, Sasser (2002) found that the primary factor driving gender differences in physicians' incomes were differences in how male and female doctors responded to marriage and children. More specifically, Sasser concluded that gender differences in the incomes of physicians aged twenty-five to forty-four in 1991 stem almost entirely from the tendency for female physicians to reduce their total work time after entering marriage and becoming parents.

These studies of women physicians can be linked to a larger body of thought regarding women's roles in contemporary society. In particular, the "different voice" perspective articulated by Gilligan (1982) holds that women are generally less competitive and status conscious and more sensitive, caring, and interested in others' feelings than are men. Adherents to this perspective would expect that women who enter medicine would be more interested in providing care than seeking status or income. Consequently, a gender gap in earnings would be understandable given the different value orientations of male and female physicians.

The studies that emphasize the choices of individual women, however, often neglect to analyze the structure of medical careers in which these choices are made. Medicine is a highly demanding profession. Residency training often involves eighty or more hours of work per week and years of being on call every third or fourth night. Practicing physicians are often expected to work fifty-five or more hours per week.

This is a clear case of an occupation being designed for a full-time male breadwinner with a stay-at-home wife. As Rosabeth Moss Kanter (1977) skillfully pointed out, some careers are so demanding that they assume the availability of a stay-at-home partner to support the successful careerist. Needless to say, women physicians rarely have stay-at-home husbands, while their male counterparts often have stay-at-home wives. Blair-Loy (2003) described this type of career as requiring a quasi-religious "professional devotion." Joan Williams (2001) described individuals who pursue such career paths as the "ideal worker," namely, people with no other major time commitments who can devote the majority of their time and energy to the single-minded pursuit of the career.

As noted earlier, while the literature espousing a voluntaristic view of gender inequality among physicians is extensive, research focusing on the relationship between discrimination or structural barriers and gender differences in physicians' careers is limited. There are a few key exceptions to this trend. First, several surveys have identified gender differences in perceived discrimination, especially during graduate and undergraduate medical training (Limacher et al. 1998; Deitch et al. 1998; Field and Lennox 1996; Redman et al. 1994; Frank, Brogan, and Schiffman 1998).

Moving from schooling into the workplace, some studies suggest that academic female physicians experience discrimination (Carr et al. 1993), and official reports, editorials, and surveys often note differences in the accessibility of key resources, such as mentorship, for male and female academic physicians (Yedidia and Bickel 2001; Fried et al. 1996). Furthermore, a nationally representative random study indicated that nearly one-half of all women physicians believed that they had been discriminated against because of their gender (Frank, Brogan, and Schiffman 1998).

In light of the dramatic demographic changes in the U.S. medical workforce, and the enormous changes in the structure of the U.S. health care system, it is reasonable to wonder if this relationship between gender, family formation, work, and income has evolved for physicians. Once women physicians' individual choices are put in a historical context, many interesting questions arise.

The decline in marriage that has occurred in the general population has been less severe among women physicians.

From the point of view of individuals' choices, is the second generation of women more or less committed to full-time careers than was the first generation of female medical pioneers? Adherents to the "different voice" perspective might predict that gender differences among physicians would persist as the representation of women in medicine grows. This would occur because women would continue to pursue medical specialties that focus on caring rather than status and technological innovations and would continue to prioritize their own families over their work.

Indeed, this focus on women's choices might even be consistent with a growing gender gap. In other words, perhaps the first generation of female physicians put career first, viewing this as the only way to break down the barriers of this elite male preserve. Members of the second generation may enter medicine in a different historical context and may seek a greater balance between their careers and caring for their family. In other words, although the earliest pioneers may have had to be very talented, strong-willed, determined, and committed to blazing new paths, the women who follow them may no longer be especially unique relative to other women. This argument implies that, although the first women physicians had to survive by pursuing lives that were as close to male lives as possible, younger female physicians feel that they ought to be able to maintain a more traditional female identity. This reasoning leads to the hypotheses that over time, gender differences in income, work habits, and other aspects of physician careers should increase rather than remain stable. This question about generational shifts echoes Goldin's (2004 [this volume]) broader historical discussion of college women's plans and choices.

From the point of view of the medical profession, one may ask whether the profession is more accommodating to the special needs and concerns of female physicians. For example, are opportunities for part-time employment more plentiful than a generation ago? As women approach parity in numbers of new entrants, does the historical pattern of the exclusive career commitment persist? In other words, if the organization of the medical career of the 1950s was predicated on a male-breadwinner, stay-at-home wife family structure, is there any shift in this structure as the demographic composition of the profession changes?

Questions about gender discrimination also take on a different form when posed in a historical context. While there surely was resistance to women physicians in the years after they first entered the profession in sizable numbers (Walsh 1977), a historical vantage point allows one to ask whether there has been progress in this regard. One might expect this type of change as the presence of women in the medical profession becomes more commonplace.

An alternative possibility is the "resegregation" thesis developed by Barbara Reskin and Patricia Roos (1990). They maintained that women's entry into occupations often follows the fall in the status of that occupation. Moreover, women rarely achieve a full and effective integration of the occupation in question. In some cases, the occupation tips and switches from being predominantly male to predominantly female. In other cases, the occupation becomes increasingly internally segregated, with men monopolizing the higher-status positions and specialties while relegating women to the lower-status positions and fields. Riska (2001) has incorporated this perspective into her comparative analysis of the medical profession. Drawing on data from the United States, the former Soviet Union, and Scandinavia, she noted that the status of the profession is inversely related to women's representation in it, and she suggested that the same negative association is evident across fields and positions within medicine.

A final possibility is that the evolving structure of the U.S. health care system may be affecting the relationship between family formation, work, and gender differences among physicians. I refer to this perspective as the "structural evolution" hypothesis. In particular, as medicine has become more corporate, opportunities for controlled work schedules in large group practices and institutionalized health systems may have increased, especially for physicians in the lower-paid, primary care specialties. Thus, there may be growing inequality within the medical profession. This may contribute to a decline in the relative status of women since any group that is below the average in earnings will decline in status as a result of a growing gap between the top earnings and those at the lower echelons of the system (Blau and Kahn 2003).

On the other hand, it is possible that these structural changes have influenced the types of people who decide to pursue careers in medicine such that more physicians, regardless of gender, now prioritize balanced work schedules over income. It is equally possible that, over time, the types of people who are willing to either forgo family formation entirely or pursue the breadwinner-homemaker familial structure have become increasingly less likely to pursue careers in medicine. This would imply that there are correspondingly fewer gender differences in the work and family lives of the current generation of physicians. In this sense, changes in the composition of physicians and changes in the structure of opportunities may be related to each other.

In this article, I attempt to fill the gap in the literature by charting the changing patterns of family formation and gender disparities in medicine. I use data from the 1990 and 2000 U.S. decennial censuses and the survey of Practice Patterns of Young Physicians to examine how the relationships among gender and physician income, physician work hours, and physician family formation have changed over time. I accomplish this goal by first documenting trends in family formation, work habits, and earnings for physicians in the 1990 and 2000 U.S. decennial censuses. Then I use regression models to examine how the determinants of the gender gap in income have changed over time for physicians in the census. Finally, I expand the analysis of the determinants of the income gap with data from the 1991 and 1997 versions of the survey of the Practice Patterns of Young Physicians to examine the relationship between gender and income for a cohort of young physicians in the late 1980s and 1990s.

Data

The data for this article were drawn from the 5 percent Public-Use Microdata Sample of the 1990 United States Census and the 1 percent Public-Use Microdata Sample of the 2000 United States Census (Ruggles et al. 2004). Person records were selected for analyses based on two criteria: occupation and education. More specifically, respondents who identified themselves as a physician and as having a professional or doctoral degree were included in these analyses. The census data offer a large sample of physicians at all ages at several points in time and are thus attractive for mapping out the broad parameters of change in the profession. The limitation, however, is that the data show few details about the nature of the physicians' practice, such as specialty and practice setting.

The second data source for this article consists of the second and third rounds of the Survey of the Practice Patterns of Young Physicians (Hadley 1998, 2000). The second wave of the survey was administered in 1991. It included 6,053 physicians. The third wave of the young physicians' survey was administered in 1997. It was administered to a random sample of respondents to the 1991 survey. There were 1,549 respondents to the 1997 survey, so it is significantly smaller than the first two waves. Each version of the survey was funded by the Robert Wood Johnson Foundation.

Variables

Dependent variable

The primary outcome variable in the analysis of the census is personal earned income. It is self-reported. I eliminated all respondents who reported negative income and all respondents who were probably resident physicians from the analyses of parenting, income, and work hours. I included these individuals in the analysis of marriage and divorce so that the results would parallel those developed by Uhlenberg and Cooney (1990). The proxy for residents included anyone who was younger than fifty years of age, who reported working more than seventy-nine hours in a usual week, and who reported less than $50,000 in personal earned income. In 1990, 59 or 0.22 percent of the 27,649 respondents reported negative incomes, and 1,316 or 4.76 percent of 27,649 respondents were classified, under the proxy definition, as residents. In 2000, 0.11 percent of the 7,276 respondents defined as a physician reported negative personal earned income, and 320 or 4.4 percent of the 7,276 respondents were classified as residents.

The primary outcome variable in the analysis of the Survey of the Practice Patterns of Young Physicians is net income. It is self-reported. Residents are not included in these surveys.

Independent variables

The key covariates in the analysis of the census are hours worked in a usual week, gender, marital status, and parental status. All measures are self-reported. The hours worked in a usual week variable is capped at ninety-nine in the census. I created a dichotomous measure of whether a physician is married and a dichotomous measure of whether a physician is divorced or separated. The measure of parental status is created from a variable measuring the number of children living in the house where the respondent resides. I dichotomized this number of children variable so that it equals one if the respondent indicated that there were any children in the house and zero otherwise.

The key covariates in the analysis of the Survey of the Practice Patterns of Young Physicians are age, hours worked in a normal week, race, board certification, specialty, practice ownership, and whether a physician practices alone. In 1991, the work hours in a normal week variable is a sum of three different self-reported variables: work in a physician's primary practice, work in a physician's secondary practice, and work in a physician's tertiary practice, whenever multiple practices exist. In 1997, work hours is the sum of hours worked in a physician's primary and secondary practice whenever multiple practices exist. Practice ownership is a self-reported dichotomous variable that measures whether a physician is an owner or part owner of his or her practice. Data on gender, board certification, and specialty listed in the 1991 and 1997 surveys come from the AMA Masterfile, the sampling frame for the surveys.

Analysis

First, I examine how physician gender relates to family formation by presenting trends in marriage, divorce, and parental status for physicians by gender. Then, I assess how gender relates to physician earnings by presenting trends in personal earned income by gender.

The results are presented by age group because the impact of childbearing occurs when physicians are in their thirties and early forties and because an age breakdown will allow me to search for disparate trends. For example, narrowing differences by gender among physicians in their forties may suggest that women physicians bounce back from motherhood when their children become more independent. I expect that there may be different trends for different groups of physicians, such as married mothers and single mothers. The analysis of trends allows me to fully investigate these possibilities. It also allows me to go beyond mean differences to look for subgroups with different experiences. For example, the gender gap in earnings may be narrowing overall, but this may not fully characterize the experiences of women physicians who work part time. The last section of the results presents regression analysis, which examines the determinants of gender differences in income among employed physicians.

Results

Gender and family formation

Table 1 documents gender differences in marriage by age group for middle-aged physicians in the 1980, 1990, and 2000 censuses. Data from the 1980 census come from work by Uhlenberg and Cooney (1990). The age groups presented in Table 1 are designed to match those presented by Uhlenberg and Cooney.[2]

What is happening to marriage rates for female physicians? As can be seen for marriage, as well as for divorce and parenting, it matters what is taken as the point of comparison. I begin by examining trends over time for women physicians and then compare them to their male counterparts and to other women in the general population.

Women physicians in 2000 were less likely to be married than were women physicians twenty years earlier. For example, among women aged thirty-five to thirty-nine, 72 percent of female physicians were married in 2000, compared with 75 percent in 1980. Male physicians are more likely to be married than are their female counterparts at all ages for each of the years studied. If the percentage of married women physicians is taken as one indication of how family friendly the profession is, then medicine would seem to be even less family friendly today than it was a generation ago.

Comparing women physicians with their male counterparts, however, may serve as another useful yardstick for assessing recent trends. The data in Table 1 indicate that decline in marriage was greater among male physicians than among female physicians, so the gender gap in marriage has actually narrowed over the past twenty years. Thus, among male physicians aged thirty-five to thirty-nine, 78 percent were married in 2000, down from 87 percent in 1980. In other words, if one asks what the difference in the experiences of male and female physicians is

TABLE 1
PROPORTIONS OF GENERAL POPULATION AND OF PHYSICIANS MARRIED BY AGE AND GENDER, 1980-2000

Age	1980			1990			2000		
	Women	Men	Difference	Women	Men	Difference	Women	Men	Difference
Physicians									
30-34	.68	.80	-.12	.67	.75	-.07	.63	.72	-.09
35-39	.75	.87	-.12	.73	.85	-.12	.72	.78	-.06
40-49	.74	.90	-.16	.73	.88	-.14	.71	.87	-.16
30-50				.71	.84	.13	.69	.82	.13
General population									
30-34	.78	.76	.02	.69	.61	.08	.62	.55	.07
35-39	.81	.83	-.01	.70	.70	.00	.65	.62	.03
40-49	.84	.86	-.02	.71	.76	-.05	.69	.67	.02
30-50									

SOURCE: 1990 and 2000 numbers were calculated from the 5 percent 1990 and the 1 percent 2000 Public-Use Microdata Samples (Ruggles et al. 2004). 1980 numbers come from Uhlenberg and Cooney (1990).

today, the answer is that the gender gap in marriage rates has become somewhat attenuated.

A final point of evaluation involves comparing women physicians with other women. Here is yet another perspective from which to understand the experiences of women physicians. The data indicate that the decline in marriage among women in the general population was much sharper than was the case for women physicians. Continuing with the thirty-five to thirty-nine age group, 65 percent were married in 2000, down from 81 percent in 1980. As a result, whereas female physicians trailed other women in marriage in 1980, they have eliminated this differential and are now at least slightly more likely than other women to be married at all ages.

Thus, professional success for women physicians is associated with a lower likelihood of being married for women than for men. While not all women seek marriage, the lower marriage rates of women physicians suggest that marriage continues to mean different things for male and female physicians and that it remains harder for women to combine these roles than it is for men. On the other hand, careers in medicine now no longer pose a greater obstacle to marriage than do other jobs. The decline in marriage that has occurred in the general population has been less severe among women physicians. Thus, while combining marriage and career is not more likely for women physicians today than it was in 1980, the gap between women physicians and other women in marriage rates has been eliminated, and now women physicians are approximately at parity and may even have a small advantage.

The relative improvement in the marriage rates of female physicians is consistent with a recent improvement in the marriage projects of educated women (Goldstein and Kenney 2001).

Table 2 documents the proportions of men and women who are divorced or separated. Cross-sectional data on divorce need to be treated cautiously because it is not possible to separate incidence and persistence. In other words, if women are more likely to be divorced, it may be due to a higher divorce rate or it may be due to divorced women remarrying at a lower rate than their male counterparts and therefore remaining divorced for a longer period of time.

Divorce has declined among female physicians younger than forty but has roughly stood still among those older than forty. At the same time, divorce has declined for male physicians. As a result, the gender gap in divorce among physicians has actually increased between 1980 and 2000 (13 percent for women versus 6 percent for men in 2000 among those aged forty to forty-nine).

Sorting out among possible alternative explanations for the decline in divorce among physicians is not possible given the limitations of these data. One explanation is that male physicians are marrying later and thus reducing their chances of divorce by choosing more carefully or waiting until they can spend more time on their marriage. An alternative possibility is that because male physicians marry later, their years of risk of divorce have decreased. Regardless of the reason, this trend causes the relative odds of female divorce among forty- to fifty-year-olds to increase from 1.63 or (.13/.08) to 2.17 or (.13/.06) in 2000.

TABLE 2
PROPORTIONS OF GENERAL POPULATION AND OF PHYSICIANS DIVORCED OR SEPARATED BY AGE AND GENDER, 1980-2000

Age	1980			1990			2000		
	Women	Men	Difference	Women	Men	Difference	Women	Men	Difference
Physicians									
30-34	.08	.06	.02	.04	.04	.00	.03	.05	-.02
35-39	.08	.07	.01	.09	.05	.04	.07	.05	.02
40-49	.13	.08	.05	.13	.07	.06	.13	.06	.07
General population									
30-34	.11	.09	.03	.15	.11	.04	.14	.10	.04
35-39	.12	.09	.03	.17	.13	.04	.17	.13	.04
40-49	.11	.08	.03	.19	.14	.05	.20	.16	.04

SOURCE: 1990 and 2000 numbers were calculated from the 5 percent 1990 and the 1 percent 2000 Public-Use Microdata Samples (Ruggles et al. 2004). 1980 numbers come from Uhlenberg and Cooney (1990).

183

On the other hand, female physicians are now markedly less likely to be divorced than are women in the general population. For example, in 1980, women physicians aged forty to forty-nine were 2 percentage points more likely than other women their age to be divorced. By 2000, women physicians aged forty to forty-nine were actually 7 percentage points less likely than other women their age to be divorced.

The trends in both marriage and divorce highlight the importance of putting the experiences of women physicians in the broader context of trends occurring in American society. In both cases, focusing on trends in the experiences of women physicians would not suggest major changes have occurred during this period. The results in Tables 1 and 2 suggest that, relative to their male colleagues, women who enter medicine continue to marry at significantly lower rates and divorce at higher rates. Comparing women in medicine to women in other pursuits, however, suggests an improvement in the relative position of medicine in terms of the compatibility of work and family.

Table 3 documents trends in the frequency with which married and unmarried physicians and the general population report having at least one child younger than eighteen in the house by age for the 1990 and 2000 censuses. Fertility rates (as reflected in the presence of children at home) for female physicians increased slightly between 1990 and 2000. Overall, 65 percent of female physicians between ages thirty and fifty have children at home in 2000, compared with 63 percent in 1990. It is difficult to detect a "second generation" pattern for female physicians from these parenting data. In other words, female physicians today are only slightly more likely to become mothers than were their counterparts a generation earlier. There is no evidence of a wholesale departure from the profession and a return to family among female physicians. (This issue is revisited below in the discussion of exits from the profession.)

Male physicians were more likely to have children at home than were female physicians throughout this period. Again, combining this demanding career with having a family remains easier for men than for women physicians. Fertility did not increase as quickly for the families of male physicians between 1990 and 2000, however, and so the gender gap in parenting narrowed for physicians during this period. While this trend certainly signals increasing gender equality in fertility among younger physicians, it does not necessarily imply increasing equality in total fertility. The recent tendency for male physicians to delay marriage may have also caused male physicians to delay becoming fathers, and it is possible that the ultimate fertility of male physicians will deviate little from the past.[3]

Comparing women physicians to other women in terms of childbearing is less informative because other women are more likely to have their children at younger ages than women physicians. Nonetheless, the gap between the fertility of female physicians and women in the general population narrowed between 1990 and 2000. In 1990, women physicians were 8 percentage points less likely to report a child in the house than women in the general population in this age group. By 2000, that difference had declined to 3 percentage points.

TABLE 3

THE FREQUENCY OF REPORTING A CHILD IN THE HOUSE BY AGE, GENDER, AND MARITAL STATUS FOR NONRESIDENT PHYSICIANS AND THE GENERAL POPULATION, 1990 AND 2000

Age	1990			2000			Male Growth	Female Growth
	Male	Female	Ratio, Female-Male	Male	Female	Ratio, Female-Male		
Physicians								
30-34								
Total	0.55	0.48	0.87	0.52	0.51	0.98	-0.06	0.06
Married	0.72	0.64	0.90	0.69	0.71	1.04	-0.04	0.11
Unmarried	0.03	0.09	3.51	0.17	0.40	2.36	5.53	3.38
35-39								
Total	0.76	0.68	0.89	0.70	0.65	0.93	-0.07	-0.03
Married	0.88	0.84	0.96	0.88	0.83	0.94	0.00	-0.02
Unmarried	0.06	0.19	3.14	0.06	0.19	3.10	0.02	0.01
40-50								
Total	0.80	0.71	0.89	0.80	0.71	0.89	0.00	0.00
Married	0.89	0.83	0.94	0.89	0.84	0.94	0.01	0.01
Unmarried	0.17	0.38	2.23	0.03	0.10	3.68	-0.83	-0.73
30-50								
Total	0.73	0.63	0.86	0.73	0.65	0.89	-0.01	0.03
Married	0.85	0.78	0.92	0.86	0.81	0.94	0.01	0.03
Unmarried	0.09	0.22	2.44	0.10	0.27	2.59	0.14	0.21

(continued)

TABLE 3 (continued)

Age	1990			2000			Male Growth	Female Growth
	Male	Female	Ratio, Female-Male	Male	Female	Ratio, Female-Male		
General population								
30-34								
Total	0.53	0.71	1.33	0.48	0.67	1.39	-0.09	-0.05
Married	0.80	0.84	1.04	0.78	0.82	1.05	-0.03	-0.02
Unmarried	0.08	0.45	5.61	0.10	0.42	4.21	0.26	-0.06
35-39								
Total	0.63	0.76	1.21	0.58	0.74	1.28	-0.08	-0.03
Married	0.86	0.87	1.01	0.85	0.87	1.02	-0.01	0.00
Unmarried	0.12	0.52	4.37	0.13	0.49	3.67	0.14	-0.04
40-50								
Total	0.65	0.67	1.04	0.58	0.64	1.10	-0.10	-0.05
Married	0.80	0.75	0.93	0.79	0.74	0.93	-0.02	-0.01
Unmarried	0.16	0.50	3.02	0.16	0.45	2.89	-0.05	-0.09
30-50								
Total	0.61	0.71	1.16	0.56	0.67	1.21	-0.09	-0.05
Married	0.82	0.81	0.98	0.80	0.79	0.99	-0.02	-0.02
Unmarried	0.12	0.49	4.03	0.13	0.45	3.38	0.11	-0.07

SOURCE: 1990 and 2000 numbers were calculated from the 5 percent 1990 and the 1 percent 2000 Public-Use Microdata Samples (Ruggles et al. 2004).

The trends in marriage, divorce, and fertility present a mixed picture with respect to gender inequality among physicians. Male and female physicians have become closer to one another in terms of marriage and parenting, but the gap in terms of divorce has grown.

In contrast, comparisons between female physicians and the general population of women yield a clear conclusion; over time, women physicians are becoming relatively more likely to combine work and family. Female physicians are less likely to be married today than they were thirty years ago, but this decline is significantly less than the corresponding decline in the general population. Similarly, female physicians' odds of divorce have actually declined relative to the corresponding odds for women in the general population. Finally, our data suggest that the odds of becoming a parent are increasing for female physicians and that female physicians are coming to more closely resemble women in the general population.

Gender and the earnings of physicians

Table 4 documents trends in income among employed nonresident physicians between 1990 and 2000. This table allows me to assess the recent earnings of female physicians against two points of comparison, male physicians and female physicians ten years ago.

Between 1990 and 2000, female physicians experienced marked increases in real mean income in all age groups except those aged sixty-five and older. Overall, the mean adjusted personal earnings of female physicians increased 21 percent, while the median increased by 9 percent.

This notable difference in the trends for mean and median income reflects a growing inequality in earnings among physicians. Increases in real earnings were significantly better for female physicians than for their male colleagues. Men's mean earnings increased by 16 percent, yet the median earnings remarkably did not change at all, after adjusting for inflation. And men's median earning actually declined among younger physicians, a point that is discussed in more detail below. Women's progress caused the gender difference in earnings to narrow slightly between 1990 and 2000. In particular, in 1990, women physicians earned an average of 60 percent of what male physicians earned. By 2000, this ratio had increased by 5 percentage points. These data still show, however, a substantial gender gap in earnings for physicians in 2000, and the two groups are not likely to converge any time soon.

These data also reveal the growth of income inequality among nonresident physicians. This trend is evident overall and within each of the age and gender groups examined in Table 4 except men 30 to 34. Most notably, between 1990 and 2000, the ratio of the 90th percentile earner to the 10th percentile earner increases from 7.24 to 10.00 for men and from 8.03 to 15.22 for women.

Growing inequality is typically bad news for the groups at the bottom of the heap. Thus, the growth of inequality in the U.S. labor market has presented a challenge to women and minorities, who have to "swim upstream" to overcome this structural change in the labor market (Morris and Western 1999). As noted above,

TABLE 4
TRENDS IN ADJUSTED PERSONAL EARNED INCOME BY AGE AND GENDER FOR EMPLOYED PHYSICIANS, 1990 AND 2000

Age	Median Income			Mean Income			90th Percentile			10th Percentile		
	Men	Women	Ratio, Female-Male	Men	Women	Ratio, Female-Male	Men	Women	Ratio, Female-Male	Men	Women	Ratio, Female-Male
2000												
30-34	50,000	42,000	0.84	82,771	63,224	0.76	155,500	120,000	0.77	33,000	17,100	0.52
35-44	150,000	100,000	0.67	184,691	120,093	0.65	330,000	312,500	0.95	41,200	30,000	0.73
45-54	173,000	100,000	0.58	205,347	130,788	0.64	330,000	320,000	0.97	52,000	28,000	0.54
55-64	150,000	100,000	0.67	186,474	127,956	0.69	330,000	322,000	0.98	36,000	25,000	0.69
65+	70,000	30,700	0.44	104,122	60,663	0.58	317,000	150,000	0.47	8,000	3,200	0.40
Overall	133,000	80,000	0.60	170,235	107,449	0.63	330,000	309,000	0.94	33,000	20,300	0.62
1990												
30-34	63,990	43,855	0.69	85,291	59,325	0.70	171,273	109,797	0.64	26,579	17,276	0.65
35-44	159,472	90,368	0.57	164,226	103,536	0.63	259,830	180,482	0.69	59,802	30,150	0.50
45-54	169,492	99,670	0.59	183,264	111,373	0.61	260,306	235,219	0.90	77,678	31,281	0.40
55-64	153,099	93,026	0.61	160,788	103,183	0.64	259,854	193,287	0.74	57,144	21,263	0.37
65+	73,092	45,620	0.62	94,313	58,729	0.62	224,590	125,983	0.56	7,974	4,784	0.60
Overall	132,894	73,092	0.55	147,133	88,405	0.60	259,828	170,738	0.66	35,881	21,263	0.59

SOURCE: 1990 and 2000 numbers were calculated from the 5 percent 1990 and the 1 percent 2000 Public-Use Microdata Samples (Ruggles et al. 2004).

however, female physicians narrowed the gap in earnings relative to their male counterparts.

The increase in overall income inequality suggests an increasing bifurcation in the medical profession. Possible explanations for increases in income inequality among physicians include, but are not limited to, increasing differences in the earnings of physicians in different medical specialties and increasing differences in the work effort of physicians.[4]

Gender and work-family connections

Parenting and income

Table 5 presents trends in median income for employed nonresident physicians for 1990 and 2000 by household composition. This table allows me to compare female physicians in three ways: (1) across family statuses, (2) over time, and (3) to male physicians.

When comparing physician mothers to other women, I find that marriage and maternity are not as significant a barrier as might be hypothesized but that the gap between mothers and other female physicians appears to be growing. First, it appears that, in general, marriage by itself does not result in reduced earnings; indeed, marriage is accompanied by a small earnings advantage among same-age female physicians. For example, in 2000, the median earning of married childless women between ages thirty and fifty exceeded that of single childless women ($90,000 vs. $75,000), although the earnings trajectory was steepest for single childless women.

Second, although employed female physicians with children ultimately earn less than either employed married women without children or unmarried women without children, the earnings differences are limited. When nonresident physician mothers are compared to other women, the maternity disadvantage never exceeds 10 percent, and it is not consistent until the thirty-five to forty age group. In 1990, married nonresident mothers in the youngest age group actually report higher median income than single nonmothers.

Third, these data indicate that between 1990 and 2000, the status of employed physician mothers declined relative to employed female physicians without children in all categories except the 30 to 34 age group, and even in the youngest age category, the ratio of physician mother earnings to married childless female physicians declined. It is only when compared to young, single, childless women that physician mothers' earnings remain stable. Thus, between 1990 and 2000, the earnings of physician mothers did not keep pace with the earnings of other female physicians. While these results differ from those reported by Sasser (2002),[5] my findings are broadly consistent with those reported by Uhlenberg and Cooney (1990) with respect to working and nonworking physicians in the 1980 census. These authors find that the median income of married mothers aged forty to fifty was 98 percent of the median income of married nonmothers. The comparable figure for the 2000 census was 95 percent.

TABLE 5
GENDER, HOUSEHOLD COMPOSITION, AND ADJUSTED MEDIAN NET INCOME FOR EMPLOYED PHYSICIANS BY AGE: 1990 AND 2000, RESIDENTS EXCLUDED

Age	1990 Male	1990 Female	1990 Ratio, Female-Male	2000 Male	2000 Female	2000 Ratio, Female-Male	1990 Ratio, Fathers	2000 Ratio, Fathers	1990 Ratio, Mothers	2000 Ratio, Mothers	Male Growth	Female Growth
30-34												
Total	79,736	57,144	0.72	63,000	55,000	0.87					-0.21	-0.04
No spouse/ no children	59,802	52,360	0.88	49,000	50,000	1.02	1.13	1.02	1.03	1.24	-0.18	-0.05
Spouse/ no children	67,829	53,900	0.79	50,000	62,000	1.24	1.56	1.73	1.16	1.16	-0.26	0.15
Spouse/ children	93,026	60,865	0.65	85,000	58,000	0.68	1.37	1.70	1.13	0.94	-0.09	-0.05
No spouse/ children	132,894	43,855	0.33	320,000	37,200	0.12						
35-39												
Total	146,183	86,381	0.59	130,000	97,000	0.75					-0.11	0.12
No spouse/ no children	118,275	79,736	0.67	104,000	97,500	0.94	1.11	1.08	1.21	1.18	-0.12	0.22
Spouse/ no children	131,565	96,348	0.73	112,000	115,000	1.03	1.33	1.39	1.08	0.98	-0.15	0.19
Spouse/ children	156,815	86,381	0.55	145,000	96,000	0.66	1.19	1.29	0.90	0.83	-0.08	0.11
No spouse/ children	120,811	96,348	0.80	298,500	90,000	0.30						

40-50													
Total	168,231	97,212	0.58	160,000	95,000	0.59						-0.05	-0.02
No spouse/no children	132,894	95,683	0.72	125,000	100,000	0.80	1.25	1.15	1.08	1.00		-0.06	0.05
Spouse/no children	166,205	103,657	0.62	144,000	100,000	0.69	1.28	1.39	1.00	0.90		-0.13	-0.04
Spouse/children	170,738	95,683	0.56	174,000	90,000	0.52	1.03	1.21	0.92	0.90		0.02	-0.06
No spouse/children	162,564	104,986	0.65	130,000	90,000	0.69							
30-50													
Total	146,183	79,736	0.55	138,000	85,000	0.62						-0.06	0.07
No spouse/no children	104,986	70,682	0.67	100,000	75,000	0.75	1.14	1.02	1.09	1.20		-0.05	0.06
Spouse/no children	119,604	76,746	0.64	102,000	90,000	0.88	1.52	1.50	1.13	1.14		-0.15	0.17
Spouse/children	159,472	79,736	0.50	150,000	85,500	0.57	1.33	1.47	1.04	0.95		-0.06	0.07
No spouse/children	159,472	95,683	0.60	142,000	76,000	0.54							

SOURCE: 1990 and 2000 numbers were calculated from the 5 percent 1990 and the 1 percent 2000 Public-Use Microdata Samples (Ruggles et al. 2004).

For men, married physicians, especially fathers, tend to earn the most. While our findings for women were surprising, the relationships for men are consistent with those found throughout the labor force (Gorman 1999). That is, married fathers enjoy a striking earnings advantage over married and unmarried childless male physicians, and married childless male physicians earn more than single childless male physicians. Among employed physicians aged forty to fifty, for example, married fathers earned between 3 and 21 percent more than married men without children and between 28 and 39 percent more than unmarried men without children.

When female physicians are compared to their male colleagues, increasing equality for women as a group can be seen. The implications of this trend remain unclear, however, especially for physician mothers. On the positive side, women experienced real growth in median income across household compositions and significant growth in their earnings when compared to men. On the other hand, the growth in women's relative earnings stems as much from declines in male income as from increases in female income.

Furthermore, although the relative earnings of female physicians are improving over time, in 2000, the relative earnings of women in all household compositions declined with age. For example, in 2000, the relative earnings of forty- to fifty-year-old single childless women are lower than the relative earnings of thirty-five- to thirty-nine-year-old single childless women, and the relative earnings of thirty-five- to thirty-nine-year-old single childless women are lower than the relative earnings of thirty- to thirty-four-year-old single childless women. The increasing difference between male and female earnings over the life course suggests that the disadvantages endured by women accumulate over time regardless of their household composition.

The story for physician mothers is even less rosy. Most notably, the disadvantage suffered by female parents relative to male parents remains significantly larger than the corresponding disadvantages suffered by married and unmarried childless women. For example, in 2000, among women aged forty to fifty, mothers' median earnings were 57 percent of what fathers earned, while married women without children earned 88 percent of what men in comparable situations earned, and unmarried women without children earned 75 percent of what their male peers earned.

Parenting and work hours

Table 6 presents mean weekly work hours by gender, household composition, and age for employed nonresident physicians in the 1990 and 2000 censuses. Table 6 reveals further evidence of increasing equality for women as a group relative to men. Most notably, over time, the work effort of female physicians is coming to more closely resemble the work effort of men who share their household composition. This trend is most pronounced for single physicians without children but is evident for married childless women and physician mothers. It is worth noting, however, that the declining gender difference is due in part to slight declines in the weekly work hours for employed nonresident male physicians.

TABLE 6
GENDER, HOUSEHOLD COMPOSITION, AND ADJUSTED MEAN WORK HOURS FOR EMPLOYED PHYSICIANS BY AGE: 1990 AND 2000, RESIDENTS EXCLUDED

Age	1990 Male	1990 Female	1990 Ratio, Female-Male	2000 Male	2000 Female	2000 Ratio, Female-Male	1990 Ratio, Fathers	2000 Ratio, Fathers	1990 Ratio, Mothers	2000 Ratio, Mothers	Male Growth	Female Growth
30-34												
Total	55	48	0.87	56	49	0.87						
No spouse/no children	54	50	0.94	51	55	1.08	1.02	1.11	1.04	0.98	-0.06	0.09
Spouse/no children	55	52	0.95	56	54	0.95	1.05	1.17	0.91	0.80	0.03	0.03
Spouse/children	56	45	0.81	59	44	0.74	1.03	1.05	0.88	0.82	0.05	-0.04
No spouse/children	62	50	0.81	58	46	0.78						
35-39												
Total	56	46	0.82	56	48	0.86						
No Spouse/no children	53	50	0.94	55	54	0.99	1.03	0.96	1.04	1.00	0.03	0.08
Spouse/no children	55	52	0.96	53	54	1.03	1.07	1.05	0.86	0.83	-0.04	0.04
Spouse/children	57	43	0.76	57	45	0.78	1.04	1.09	0.83	0.83	0.01	0.04
No spouse/children	55	49	0.88	54	47	0.88						
40-50												
Total	55	46	0.83	55	46	0.84						
No spouse/no children	48	51	1.06	51	50	0.98	1.14	1.02	0.94	1.01	0.06	-0.03
Spouse/no children	55	48	0.88	52	50	0.96	1.15	1.09	0.85	0.89	-0.05	0.04
Spouse/children	56	44	0.79	56	45	0.80	1.01	1.07	0.91	0.88	0.01	0.01
No spouse/children	54	48	0.89	50	47	0.94						

(continued)

TABLE 6 (continued)

Age	1990 Male	1990 Female	1990 Ratio, Female-Male	2000 Male	2000 Female	2000 Ratio, Female-Male	1990 Ratio, Fathers	2000 Ratio, Fathers	1990 Ratio, Mothers	2000 Ratio, Mothers	Male Growth	Female Growth
30-50												
Total	55	47	0.84	55	48	0.86						
No spouse/no children	53	50	0.94	52	53	1.01	1.04	1.03	1.03	1.00	-0.01	0.06
Spouse/no children	55	51	0.93	54	52	0.98	1.06	1.09	0.86	0.84	-0.02	0.03
Spouse/children	56	43	0.77	57	45	0.79	1.02	1.05	0.84	0.85	0.02	0.04
No spouse/children	55	48	0.88	51	47	0.92						
30-34												
% long week	0.51	0.33	0.66	0.70	0.53	0.76						
% short week	0.04	0.12	3.16	0.03	0.14	4.78						
% regular week	0.45	0.55	1.20	0.27	0.33	1.22						
35-39												
% long week	0.51	0.26	0.50	0.74	0.53	0.71						
% short week	0.03	0.17	5.31	0.02	0.16	8.04						
% regular week	0.46	0.57	1.26	0.24	0.31	1.31						
40-50												
% long week	0.47	0.23	0.49	0.70	0.48	0.69						
% short week	0.03	0.15	5.17	0.03	0.19	5.93						
% regular week	0.50	0.62	1.22	0.27	0.33	1.21						
30-50												
% long week	0.49	0.27	0.55	0.71	0.51	0.71						
% short week	0.03	0.15	4.62	0.03	0.17	5.92						
% regular week	0.48	0.58	1.21	0.26	0.32	1.23						

SOURCE: 1990 and 2000 numbers were calculated from the 5 percent 1990 and the 1 percent 2000 Public-Use Microdata Samples (Ruggles et al. 2004).

NOTE: Long and short weeks are more than fifty-five hours and less than thirty-five hours on average, respectively. Regular weeks are all other weeks.

As in the case of income, however, that status of physician mothers is more questionable. First, although the work hours of physician mothers as a group increased during the 1990s, this overall trend masks a decline in work effort for the youngest mothers. This trend is not surprising since mothers in this age group are most likely to have the youngest and most dependent children. Second, physician mothers report significantly lower average workweeks than either childless female physicians or male physicians. In an average week, physician mothers in 2000 worked between 74 and 80 percent of what physician fathers work and between 80 and 89 percent of what childless female physicians work. Third, although physician mothers are gaining ground with respect to their male colleagues, there is increasing inequality in work effort between physician mothers and other female physicians. The one exception to this occurs between physician mothers and married childless women between ages forty and fifty. These trends do not support the emergence of a second generation of female physicians who are reducing their work hours to better balance work and family. While there may be an inclination to do so, the data presented here on work patterns do not provide evidence that women physicians are able to put any such proclivities into practice.

In 2000, female physicians who were married
with children living at home earned . . .
37 percent less than their male counterparts.

Part-time employment (thirty-five hours per week or less) remains very much the exception for physicians younger than age fifty. Women are much more likely to be employed part-time than are men before age fifty, and there is a barely discernable increase in part-time employment for women (from 15 to 17 percent). An intriguing pattern is that part-time employment for women does not peak during the childbearing years but increases with age. This is evident in both 1990 and 2000 and is evident for men as well as women. At the other end of the hours spectrum, women are increasingly likely to work long hours and have narrowed the gap among most age groups compared to men. The chances of working more than fifty-five hours per week for women, compared to men, jumped from 55 to 71 percent during this decade. There is thus a modest trend toward bifurcation in working time among physicians that resembles a similar trend in the labor force (Jacobs and Gerson 2004).

Although the work effort of employed female physicians came to more closely resemble the effort of their male colleagues during the 1990s, the implications of this trend for life satisfaction are unclear. Physicians work significantly longer hours than the general population. In 2000, for example, employed male physicians reported an average workweek of 55.5 hours, compared with 45.0 for other employed men of the same age. Similarly, in 2000, employed female physicians between ages thirty and fifty reported an average of 48.0 hours per week. This compares with 38.0 hours for employed women of the same age in the general population. Thus, increases in work effort may signal increasing pressures on female physicians with regard to their lives outside of work. Trends in work effort are especially interesting in light of trends in marriage and family discussed earlier. Women physicians appear to be faced with a decision between parenting and reduced work and earning schedules on one hand and childlessness and work and earnings schedules that are more closely aligned with those of male physicians on the other.

Although the work effort of employed male and female physicians is becoming more equal, in analyses not shown, I find that trends in employment are slowly drifting in the opposite direction. As in the case of earnings and weekly work hours, inequality is most pronounced for physician mothers. In fact, between 1990 and 2000, employment rates declined 7 percent for physician mothers in the thirty to thirty-four group and 5 percent for physicians in the thirty-five to forty group. Since employment rates for men in the comparable age and household composition categories remained constant during the 1990s, the employment rates for physician mothers went from 98 percent of employment rates for physician fathers in 1990 to 95 percent of physician fathers in 2000. This pattern may suggest that some female physicians find that medical practice is unable to accommodate their desire to work part-time and is resulting in their departure (at least temporarily) from medical practice. This would be consistent with the data reported by Stone and Lovejoy (2004 [this volume]) on women who drop out of fast-track careers.

In spite of these trends, it is worth emphasizing that employment rates for physicians of all ages and household compositions are extremely high. Over time, employment never goes below 90 percent for female physicians regardless of their age or status as mothers and below 96 percent for male physicians regardless of age or household composition status. These trends compare to 79.2 percent and 91.0 percent for women and men of the same age in the general population. Thus, the exits of female physicians from medical practice should not be overstated.

Explaining gender differences in income and work

In this section, I examine the role of marriage, parenting, hours worked, specialty, and practice setting in contributing to the gender difference in income for physicians. I draw on two complementary data sources. First, I conduct a regression analysis of the gender gap in earning using the census data for 1990 and 2000. The central feature of this analysis is that it is conducted separately by marital and parental status. The census data have enough cases to allow for a separate analysis of these groups. This analysis allows me to assess the role of working time owing to parental and marital demands for women in each of the different marital and parental statuses. Then, a series of parallel analyses are presented that assess the determinants of income for physicians in the 1990 and 1996 Survey of the Practice

Patterns of Young Physicians. This analysis extends the analysis of the census by assessing the extent of the gender gap in earnings that is attributable to gender differences in specialization and practice environment.

Table 7 presents ordinary least squares regression models with the natural log of personal earned income as the dependent variable. The analysis is restricted to physicians who are no longer residents, using the proxy definition of residents described earlier. I restrict the analysis to physicians between ages thirty and fifty because I am primarily interested in the effect of parenting on income. Since the odds that children have left the home increases dramatically after age fifty, any lingering effect of earlier parenting would be hard to identify. I present three nested models that examine the unadusted gender effect (model 1) with a second model that controls for age and age squared and a third model that adds the effect of weekly working time.

The unadjusted earnings gap—presented in model 1—parallels the findings presented in Table 5. (Note that the precise figures are slightly different because the analysis presented in Table 7 is based on the log of earnings whereas Table 5 was based on median earnings.) The evidence presented in Table 7 indicates that women physicians continue to trail their male counterparts in each marital and parental category.

How much of the gender gap is due to differences in working time? I begin with the case of married parents. This is the group with the largest unadjusted gender gap in earnings. In 2000, female physicians who were married with children living at home earned 62 percent less than their male counterparts before adjusting for age and working time. After these adjustments, working mothers earn 37 percent less than their male counterparts. This evidence makes it clear that physicians who are working mothers on average pay a substantial price in terms of professional success, as captured by the basic indicator of putting in fewer hours per week. But the evidence just as clearly indicates that there is a large gender gap even after working time is controlled for. Whether this residual gap is due to specialty, practice setting, or other factors will be analyzed in Table 8.

On a more optimistic note, the unexplained gap among married parents is smaller in 2000 than was the case in 1990 (37 percent difference vs. 46 percent in 1990). This evidence is clearly consistent with a slowly declining gender gap in earnings.

Compared to the large gender gap among working parents, the size of the gap among married physicians without children at home is much narrower. Among this group, a 22 percent unadjusted gap is reduced to a 17 percent gap once age and working time are controlled. Compared to married parents, for couples with no children at home, the original gender gap is smaller, working time explains less of the gap since male and female work schedules are more similar, and the residual gender gap is smaller. The trend over time again is positive, with the adjusted gap being smaller in 2000 than was the case in 1990 (17 vs. 26 percent).

Physicians who are single parents may have arrived at this status as a result of divorce rather than premarital births. However they arrived in this status, how are

TABLE 7

THE DETERMINANTS OF LOGGED PERSONAL EARNED INCOME FOR
MARRIED PARENTS AND NONPARENTS IN THE 1990 AND 2000 CENSUSES

1990 Married Parents

	Model 1 B	Model 1 Standard Error	Model 2 B	Model 2 Standard Error	Model 3 B	Model 3 Standard Error
Intercept	11.54	0.01***	3.88	0.41***	3.43	0.41
Female	-0.64	0.02***	-0.57	0.02***	-0.46	0.02*
Age			0.35	0.02***	0.35	0.02***
Age squared			-0.39	0.03***	-0.38	0.03**
Weekly work hours					0.01	0.00**
R^2	.092		.172		.201	
n	10,633		10,633		10,633	

2000 Married Parents

	Model 1 B	Model 1 Standard Error	Model 2 B	Model 2 Standard Error	Model 3 B	Model 3 Standard Error
Intercept	11.90	0.02**	3.07	1.06**	2.04	1.02**
Female	-0.62	0.04***	-0.57	0.04***	-0.37	0.04***
Age			0.41	0.05***	0.41	0.05***
Age squared			-0.47	0.07***	-0.46	0.06***
Weekly work hours					0.02	0.00***
R^2	.085		.1368		.1917	
n	2,408		2,408		2,408	

1990 Nonmarried Parents

	Model 1 B	Model 1 Standard Error	Model 2 B	Model 2 Standard Error	Model 3 B	Model 3 Standard Error
Intercept	11.53	0.06***	2.73	2.50	2.24	2.32
Female	-0.52	0.08***	-0.47	0.08***	-0.33	0.08*
Age			0.41	0.13**	0.37	0.12***
Age squared/100			-0.47	0.15**	-0.42	0.14**
Weekly work hours					0.02	0.00**
R^2	.0913		.1410		.2562	
n	365		365		365	

2000 Nonmarried Parents

	Model 1 B	Model 1 Standard Error	Model 2 B	Model 2 Standard Error	Model 3 B	Model 3 Standard Error
Intercept	11.69	0.16***	4.75	5.66	4.64	5.56
Female	-0.55	0.19**	-0.53	0.19**	-0.46	0.19*
Age			0.34	0.28	0.30	0.28***
Age squared			-0.41	0.34	-0.35	0.34**
Weekly work hours					0.02	0.01**
R^2	.0517		.0482		.07	
n	129		129		129	

1990 Married Nonparents

Intercept	11.27	0.02***	3.40	0.83	2.68	0.81
Female	−0.40	0.04**	−0.31	0.04**	−0.26	0.04*
Age			0.36	0.04**	0.37	0.04***
Age squared/100			−0.40	0.05**	−0.40	0.05**
Weekly work hours					0.01	0.00**
R^2	.043		.197		.2297	
n	2,056		2,056		2,056	

2000 Married Nonparents

Intercept	11.48	0.05***	1.25	2.04	0.63	2.01
Female	−0.22	0.09*	−0.19	0.09*	−0.17	0.09*
Age			0.48	0.11***	0.48	0.10***
Age squared			−0.55	0.13***	−0.55	0.13**
Weekly work hours					0.01	0.00**
R^2	.011		.1421		.1689	
n	439		439		439	

1990 Nonmarried Nonparents

Intercept	11.14	0.02***	2.69	0.83***	2.32	0.81***
Female	−0.33	0.04***	−0.30	0.04***	−0.26	0.03***
Age			0.40	0.04***	0.38	0.04***
Age squared			−0.45	0.06***	−0.43	0.05***
Weekly work hours					0.01	0.00***
R^2	.032		.153		.198	
n	2,375		2,375		2,375	

2000 Nonmarried Nonparents

Intercept	11.42	0.05***	3.27	1.78	2.98	1.74
Female	−0.23	0.08**	−0.19	0.07**	−0.20	0.07**
Age			0.38	0.09**	0.36	0.09***
Age squared			−0.44	0.12**	−0.41	0.12**
Weekly work hours					0.01	0.00**
R^2	.013		.0903		.10	
n	622		622		622	

SOURCE: 1990 and 2000 numbers were calculated from the 5 percent 1990 and the 1 percent 2000 Public-Use Microdata Samples (Ruggles et al. 2004).

*$p < .05$. **$p < .01$. ***$p < .001$.

they fairing earnings-wise? The gender gap is smaller among this group than among married parents. This reflects the fact that single mothers put in more hours of work per week than do married mothers, while single dads work substantially less than married dads. The unadjusted gap narrowed from a 33 percent gap in 1990 to a 23 percent gap in 2000, and the adjusted gap narrowed from 26 to 20 percent.

Last, the gap among single physicians is quite large and has relatively little to do with gender differences in working time. Single women actually reported working about the same number of hours as their male counterparts in 2000. Not surprisingly, the gender gap does not narrow substantially as a result of age and working time among this group. (The unadjusted gap is 23 percent and the adjusted gap is 20 percent. The adjusted gap declined from 26 to 20 percent between 1990 and 2000.)

In general, then, age and weekly work hours explain a large portion of the gender gap in earnings but do not explain all of it. The contribution of working time to the gender gap in earnings is largest for married parents and smallest for single, childless physicians.

Between 1990 and 2000, the unadjusted gender difference in earnings remained stable for parents but declined for childless physicians. This trend occurred for both married and unmarried physicians. It suggests that there is greater equality in earnings for childless physicians now than there was in 1990. The data in Table 7 also make it clear that the percentage of the gender gap attributable to age and weekly work hours depends on marital and parental status.

I replicated the analysis in the census with the Survey of the Practice Patterns of Young Physicians. These data provide a check on the census data and also allow for an analysis of the contribution of specialty and practice setting to the gender gap in earnings. Table 8 presents these results for employed nonresident physicians in the 1990 and 1996 versions of the Survey of the Practice Patterns of Young Physicians.

A key finding from Table 8 is that controlling for physician specialty and practice environment explains a relatively modest additional portion of the gender gap in earnings but does not explain the entire gender gap. For example, among married parents in 1997, the gender gap declines from a 35 percent gap to a 32 percent gap when board certification and specialty are added to the analysis. Even the addition of practice structure and size (owning one's practice versus working for other physicians, working in a solo practice or not) lowers the gap in this case only slightly, from 32 to 30 percent. Thus, the yawning gender gaps observed in the census data do not quickly vanish with the addition of specialty and practice setting. This sizable residual gap is consistent with various forms of discrimination.

With respect to marital and parental status, the Young Physicians data track those I obtained with the census data in a number of important respects. As in the census, I find a significant unadjusted gender difference in earnings for physicians in the Survey of Young Physicians. (I do not report results for unmarried parents because of the low number of observations.) I also find that, like the results from the census, the gender difference in earnings is most pronounced for married par-

TABLE 8

EFFECT OF GENDER ON PERSONAL EARNED INCOME
FOR EMPLOYED PHYSICIANS AGED THIRTY TO FIFTY,
CONTROLLING FOR VARIOUS CHARACTERISTICS:
1990 AND 1996 IN THE SURVEY OF YOUNG PHYSICIANS

	1991		1997	
Married parents	B	Standard Error	B	Standard Error
No controls	−.49	.02°°°	−.45	.05°°°
Adding age	−.46	.02°°°	−.45	.05°°°
Adding weekly work hours	−.37	.02°°°	−.35	.05°°°
Adding race	−.37	.02°°°	−.35	.05°°°
Adding board certification and specialty	−.33	.02°°°	−.32	.05°°°
Adding practice structure	−.30	.02°°°	−.30	.05°°°
R^2		.3638		.2042
n		4,132		1,007
Married nonparents				
No controls	−.24	.04°°°	−.31	.05°°°
Adding age	−.24	.04°°°	−.32	.12°°°
Adding weekly work hours	−.22	.04°°°	−.27	.12°°°
Adding race	−.22	.04°°°	−.25	.13°
Adding board certification and specialty	−.17	.04°°°	−.21	.12
Adding practice structure	−.13	.04°°°	−.20	.11
R^2		.2744		.2086
n		695		83
Single, childless physicians				
No controls	−.28	.04°°°	−.26	.10°
Adding age	−.27	.04°°°	−.28	.10°°
Adding weekly work hours	−.26	.04°°°	−.31	.10°°
Adding race	−.25	.04°°°	−.31	.10°°
Adding board certification and specialty	−.25	.04°°°	−.26	.10°
Adding practice structure	−.24	.04°°°	−.25	.10°
R^2		.2026		.2086
n		758		113

°$p < .05$. °°$p < .01$. °°°$p < .001$.

ents, followed by single childless individuals, followed by those who are married without children.

In the census, the most recent adjusted gender gap in earnings is just more than twice as big (37 vs. 17 percent, or 2.2 times as large) for married parents as for married childless physicians. In the Survey of the Practice Patterns of Young Physicians, the gender gap is twice as large (28 vs. 14 percent) for married parents as for married childless physicians.

As in the census, the unadjusted gender gap in earnings remains relatively constant for married parents in the Young Physicians' Survey. However, one of the few key differences in results involves trends in the unadjusted gender gap in earnings among childless physicians in the Survey of Young Physicians and comparable trends from the census. While the unadjusted gender gap in earnings declines over time for childless physicians in the census, it increases and remains stagnant for physicians in the Young Physicians Survey. One possible explanation for this difference involves the fact that the gender gap in earning grows with age, and the Young Physicians data are following a group into the period in life where the earnings between male and female physicians diverge. It is probably the case that this aging experience offsets the modest period trend toward a narrowing gender gap observed in the census data.

Together these results indicate that the status of women physicians, with respect to earned income, is slowly improving regardless of their household composition. Nevertheless, the pace of this improvement depends greatly on whether a woman is married and has children. Furthermore, these analyses indicate that the gender difference in earnings is not entirely due to choices regarding work effort.

Conclusions

This article suggests that the significant influx of women into medicine has been accompanied by a modest but notable decline in the gender gap among physicians in a variety of areas. This is evident in data on marriage, parenthood, and income. As a whole, these trends do not support the pessimistic view that the gender gap grows as women increasingly are trapped in a low-paid female ghetto within the medical profession.

Nor do the data indicate that a second generation of female physicians has entered medicine with different values and behaviors than the first generation of female pioneers. The evidence does indicate that male and female physicians are more likely than their peers in the general population to be married and that completed fertility of male and female physicians is increasing, relative to the rest of the population. However, this family focus has not changed the structure of work patterns. On the contrary, I find that more women are working fifty-five hours per week or more and that there is only a slight increase in the proportion working part-time.

The data clearly support the proposition that inequality is growing within medicine. Male median income declined for those younger than fifty, while men's mean income increased. This could only happen with a divergence in the earnings experiences of the top echelon of physicians. And indeed, the ratio of the top earners to the bottom earners in medicine grew during the 1990s. Inequality in earnings increased for both male and female physicians over the 1990s.

Women narrowed the gap compared to men somewhat by becoming more like men in how they practice medicine.

It is notable that women managed to make a modest degree of progress despite these unfavorable trends in the structure of earnings. Groups at the bottom have to "swim upstream" in the face of growing inequality, and women physicians were able to make small gains despite these structural shifts.

However, physicians who are also mothers continue to trail their male counterparts by a large margin and increasingly are falling behind other women physicians. The relative work effort of mothers between ages thirty and fifty increased slightly. This trend masks age-specific phenomena, however. In fact, the ratio of maternal work hours to male work hours and the ratio of maternal work hours to childless women work hours for the thirty to thirty-four age group actually declined between 1990 and 2000. Furthermore, the average workweek of physician mothers remained significantly below that of either childless women or men in 2000 in spite of the slight increases in work.

In spite of the continued disparity in work effort, the relative earnings of physician mothers, with respect to physician fathers, increased from .50 to .57 between 1990 and 2000. This improvement was slight, however, and was due in part to declines in the median incomes of physician fathers. The real improvement in mothers' earnings may be due to increasing tolerance of working women with children in the medical profession or to their increasing work hours.

The findings presented in this article indicate that there are substantial improvements in the gender gap in earnings among employed physicians. It indicates that the gender gap in income for younger employed physicians is declining in part because more young mothers have opted not to work and because those women who remain in the workforce and remain childless are maintaining work habits that more closely parallel those of men.

Thus, women narrowed the gap compared to men somewhat by becoming more like men in how they practice medicine. Increasing numbers of women in medicine are adopting the male career model. The medical career, which emerged during a period of male breadwinners and stay-at-home wives, is alive and well despite the massive influx of women into the profession.

The profession as a whole, however, has taken limited steps to change to better accommodate the sharp increase in women in the profession. Part-time employment remains quite limited. And the small but growing number of women leaving medicine suggests that the profession may not be offering women the flexibility they want and need.

The large unexplained gaps in earnings for men and women in the same marital and parental status is consistent with persisting discrimination. While the narrowing of the earnings gap may be viewed as progress, the remaining, unexplained differentials—even when controls for specialty and practice type are included in the analysis—suggest that women are paid less for similar types of work.

Women are becoming increasingly incorporated into the medical profession, but on what terms? They are not becoming incorporated with men on fully equal terms, either in terms of their earnings prospects or their chances to become married and have a family. So full equality within medicine remains elusive. On the other hand, there is little evidence of a marked deterioration in women's status. Women are not increasingly ghettoized within the profession. On the contrary, they have been taking some modest but notable positive steps—in the areas of marriage, divorce, parenting, and earnings. The fact that there has been progress on all of these fronts speaks clearly against an overly pessimistic assessment of recent trends.

How should the status of women be characterized at the present time? I would offer the term *incomplete incorporation*. By this I mean that the structure of medical careers continues to represent a major challenge to physicians who want to marry and raise a family without a stay-at-home partner. Since women physicians rarely have stay-at-home partners, the intense demands of a medical career tend to pose difficult dilemmas for women physicians. They experience delayed marriage and childbearing, have small families, and face significant chances of divorce, even while their earnings and professional status continue to trail those of their male counterparts. The challenge of restructuring medical careers in such a way that involved parents can succeed as physicians as well as in their family lives is one that remains for the medical profession, and it will become increasingly salient as women physicians' numbers continue to grow.

Notes

1. Uhlenberg and Cooney (1990) also found that that in 1980, only 7 percent of married male physicians had wives who worked as many hours per week as they did, and 64.3 percent of married male doctors had wives who were not in the labor force. On the other hand, the authors found that all married female physicians had husbands pursuing professional careers.

2. Marriage rates in 1990 and 2000 are similar to 1991 and 1997 marriages rates in the Survey of the Practice Patterns of Young Physicians for similar age groups. The census data are presented here because it is a much larger data set, which allows for comparisons across cohorts.

3. Results from the Survey of the Practice Patterns of Young Physicians suggest that, while fertility is increasing among physicians of both genders who are at least forty years old, gender inequality is declining in this age group.

4. I find that these trends probably contribute to increasing income inequality among women but not men. Data from the Survey of the Practice Patterns of Young Physicians suggest that, between 1990 and 1996, the second and third rounds of the survey, the ratio of primary care net income to specialist net income decreased from .68 to .65 for female physicians and from .69 to .68 for male physicians. Thus, it appears that

an increasing gap in the incomes of specialists and primary care physicians is playing a role in increasing income inequality overall. Data from the 1990 and 2000 censuses indicate that the percentage of women reporting at least fifty-five hours in a normal workweek increased 4 percent and that the percentage of women reporting thirty-five or fewer hours in a normal workweek increased 1 percent. At the same time, the percentage of men working at least fifty-five hours a week increased 1 percent, and the percentage of men working thirty-five or fewer hours per week remained stable. Additional possible explanations for income inequality include changes in the racial makeup of male and female physicians and changes in the geographic distribution of male and female physicians. Data from the Survey of Young Physicians suggests that the disparity between white and nonwhite male physician salaries increased 3 percent between 1990 and 1996. Thus, if the representation of racial minorities increased, inequality would also increase. Unfortunately, exploration of these potential relationships is beyond the scope of this article.

5. These findings contrast with those of Sasser (2002), whose analysis of the first and second rounds of the Survey of the Practice Patterns of Young Physicians suggests that women physicians receive an annual earnings penalty of 13 percent for marriage, of 14 percent for having one child, and of 22 percent for having more than one child. It is possible that my findings differ from those of Sasser because her analysis focuses on physicians younger than forty-four in 1991 who have finished their residency training. My analysis includes physicians between thirty and fifty years of age. Sasser also limits her analysis to women working more than twenty hours a week. I include women reporting more than one hour a week, which should allow for even greater impact of motherhood by including those working very short workweeks.

References

Association of American Medical Colleges. 2003. *AAMC data book*. Washington DC: Association of American Medical Colleges.

Baxter, N., R. Cohen, and R. McLeod. 1996. The impact of gender on the choice of surgery as a career. *American Journal of Surgery* 172 (4): 373-76.

Blair-Loy, Mary. 2003. *Competing devotions: Career and family among women executives*. Cambridge, MA: Harvard University Press.

Blau, F. D., and L. M. Kahn. 2003. Understanding international differences in the gender pay gap. *Journal of Labor Economics* 21 (1): 106-44.

Carr, P., J. Noble, R. H. Friedman, B. Starfield, and C. Black. 1993. Choices of training programs and career paths by women in internal medicine. *Academic Medicine* 68 (3): 219-23.

Center for Studying Health System Change. 2001. Community tracking study physician survey, 1996-1997: [United States] [Computer file]. 2nd ICPSR version. Washington, DC: Author [producer], 2001. Ann Arbor, MI: Inter-university Consortium for Political and Social Research [distributor], 2001.

Deitch, C. H., J. H. Sunshine, W. C. Chan, and K. A. Shaffer Deitch. 1998. Women in the radiology profession: Data from a 1995 national survey. *American Journal of Roentgenology* 170 (2): 263-70.

Field, D., and A. Lennox. 1996. Gender in medicine: The views of first- and fifth-year medical students. *Medical Education* 30 (246): 52.

Frank, E., D. Brogan, and M. Schiffman. 1998. Prevalence and correlates of harassment among US women physicians. *Archives of Internal Medicine* 158 (4): 352-58.

Fried, L. P., C. A. Francomano, S. M. MacDonald, E. M. Wagner, E. J. Stokes, K. M. Carbone, W. B. Bias, M. M. Newman, and J. D. Stobo. 1996. Career development for women in academic medicine: Multiple interventions in a department of medicine. *JAMA* 276 (11): 898-905.

Gilligan, C. 1982. *In a different voice: Psychological theory and women's development*. Cambridge, MA: Harvard University Press.

Goldin, Claudia. 2004. The long road to the fast track: Career and family. *Annals of the American Academy of Political and Social Science* 596:19-35.

Goldstein, J. R., and C. T. Kenney. 2001. Marriage delayed or marriage forgone? New cohort forecasts of first marriage for U.S. women. *American Sociological Review* 66 (4): 506-19.

Gorman, E. H. 1999. Bringing home the bacon: Marital allocation of income-earning responsibility, job shifts, and men's wages. *Journal of Marriage and the Family* 61 (1): 110-12.

Hadley, Jack. 1998. Practice patterns of young physicians, 1991: [United States] [Computer file]. ICPSR version. Washington, DC: Georgetown University, Center for Health Policy Studies [producer], 1993. Ann Arbor, MI: Inter-University Consortium for Political and Social Research [distributor], 1998.

———. 2000. Practice patterns of young physicians, 1997: [75 largest metropolitan statistical areas in the United States] [Computer file]. ICPSR version. Washington, DC: Jack Hadley, Georgetown University, Center for Health Policy Studies [producer], 1999. Ann Arbor, MI: Inter-University Consortium for Political and Social Research [distributor], 2000.

Howell, W. L. J. 2003. Medical school applications increase. *Association of American Medical Colleges Reporter*, December.

Jacobs, J. A., and K. Gerson. 2004. *The time divide: Work, family, and gender inequality*. Cambridge, MA: Harvard University Press.

Kanter, Rosabeth Moss. 1977. *Men and women of the corporation*. New York: Basic Books.

Keil, L. 1998. *Community Tracking Study Physician Survey: Round 1, General Distribution Survey methodology report*. Technical Publication 9. Washington, DC: Center for Studying Health System Change.

Limacher, Marian C., Carol A. Zaher, Mary N. Walsh, Wendy J. Wolf, Pamela S. Douglas, Janice B. Schwartz, Janet S. Wright, and David P. Bodycombe. 1998. The ACC professional life survey: Career decisions of women and men in cardiology. *Journal of the American College of Cardiology* 32 (3): 827-35.

Mitchell, J. 1984. Why do women physicians work fewer hours than men physicians? *Inquiry* 21 (4): 361-68.

Morris, M., and B. Western. 1999. Inequality in earnings at the close of the twentieth century. *Annual Review of Sociology* 25:623-57.

Nonnemaker, L. 2000. Women physicians in academic medicine: New insights from cohort studies. *New England Journal of Medicine* 642 (6): 399-405.

Pasko, T., B. Seidman, and S. Birkhead. 2000. *Physician characteristics and distribution in the US 2000-2001 edition*. Chicago: American Medical Association.

Redman, S., D. Saltman, J. Straton, B. Young, and C. Paul. 1994. Determinants of career choices among women and men medical students and interns. *Medical Education* 28 (5): 361-71.

Reskin, Barbara F., and Patricia Roos. 1990. *Job queues, gender queues: Explaining women's inroads into male occupations*. Philadelphia: Temple University Press.

Riska, E. 2001. *Medical careers and feminist agendas*. New York: Alldine De Gruyter.

Ruggles, Steven Matthew Sobek, Trent Alexander, Catherine A. Fitch, Ronald Goeken, Patricia Kelly Hall, Miriam King, and Chad Ronnander. 2004. Integrated Public Use Microdata Series: Version 3.0 [Machine-readable database]. Minneapolis, MN: Minnesota Population Center [producer and distributor].

Sasser, Alicia. 2002. Gender differences in physician pay: Tradeoffs between career and family. Manuscript.

Stone, Pamela, and Meg Lovejoy. 2004. Fast-track women and the "choice" to stay home. *Annals of the American Academy of Political and Social Science* 596:62-83.

Uhlenberg, P., and T. Cooney. 1990. Male and female physicians: Family and career comparisons. *Social Science & Medicine* 30 (3): 373-78.

Walsh, M. R. 1977. *Doctors wanted, no women need apply: Sexual barriers in the medical profession, 1835-1975*. New Haven, CT: Yale University Press.

Williams, Joan. 2001. *Unbending gender: Why family and work conflict and what to do about it*. New York: Oxford University Press.

Xu, G., S. L. Rattner, J. J. Veloski, M. Hojat, S. K. Fields, and B. Barzansky. 1995. A national study of the factors influencing men and women physicians' choices of primary care specialties. *Academic Medicine* 70 (5): 398-404.

Yedidia, M. J., and J. Bickel. 2001. Why aren't there more women leaders in academic medicine? The views of clinical department chairs. *Academic Medicine* 76 (5): 453-65.

SECTION THREE

Comments and
Other Contexts

COMMENT

Mommies and Daddies on the Fast Track in Other Wealthy Nations

By
GWEN MOORE

Social and cultural contexts, as well as public policies, shape the experiences of women and men in demanding occupations. This article compares work-family themes in the conference papers to research outside of the United States, especially to a mid-1990s survey of twelve hundred women and men holding the highest positions in elected politics and business in twenty-seven capitalist democracies, the Comparative Leadership Study. Analyses show that most leaders in the comparative study have married and are parents. Family responsibilities fall disproportionately on the women in top leadership positions. Marriage and parenthood impinge on women's careers to a far larger extent than they do on similarly situated men's. An international perspective on work-family conflicts highlights ways in which the United States is similar to and different from comparable countries. In many ways, the United States differs little. Yet the Nordic countries appear more successful in lessening work-family conflicts, even for top leaders.

Keywords: elites; leaders; gender; work-family; comparative; business; politics

S ocial and cultural contexts, as well as public policies, shape the experiences of women and men in demanding occupations. Women's employment in influential positions in the public and private sectors varies cross-nationally. Taking politics as an example, in the 2003 Swedish election, more than 45 percent of the parliamentarians who were elected are women. This contrasts sharply with the United States, where women hold just 14 percent of congressional seats, a smaller proportion than in fifty-nine other nations (InterParliamentary Union Web site, www.ipu.org, accessed January 16, 2004). Still, men hold nearly all top economic posts in

Gwen Moore is an associate professor of sociology and a former director of the Institute for Research on Women at the State University of New York at Albany. With Mino Vianello, she edited Gendering Elites: Economic and Political Leadership in 27 Industrialised Societies *(2000) and* Women and Men in World Elites *(2004). Her research focuses on comparative elite studies; analyses of gender and authority; and investigations of personal, community, and national network structures.*

DOI: 10.1177/0002716204268753

all countries throughout the world (Adler and Izraeli 1994; Wirth 2001). These variations across countries and sectors demonstrate the importance of placing the articles in this volume in an international perspective.

In this comment, I will compare some of the work-family themes of the conference papers to research outside of the United States, especially to the findings of a mid-1990s survey of approximately twelve hundred women and men who held the highest positions in elected politics and private business in twenty-seven capitalist industrial nations, including twenty-one European nations, Australia, New Zealand, and others in North America and Asia (Vianello and Moore 2000).[1] This collaborative project—the Comparative Leadership Study—gathered information on the leaders' backgrounds and careers, experiences in office, and gender and career attitudes as well as current family characteristics (Vianello and Moore 2000).

Consistent with the conference papers' findings on lawyers, professors, scientists, and finance managers, the majority of the women and men in the Comparative Leadership Study were or had been married or cohabiting. Marriage was more common for the men leaders than for their women counterparts, as has been found in previous research. Eighteen percent of the women and 8 percent of the men had never married. Virtually all of the men (94 percent) and most (75 percent) of the women leaders were currently married or cohabiting (Neale 2000, 158-59).

Most leaders of both sexes in the international study were also parents. Just over one-fourth of the women and less than 10 percent of the men had no children (Kuusipalo, Kauppinen, and Nuutinen 2000, Table 15.1). Among parents, women more often had just one child (Neale 2000, 158-59). The vast majority of men (88 percent) and three-fifths of women were living with both a partner and at least one child at the time of the survey (Kuusipalo, Kauppinen, and Nuutinen 2000, Table 15.1).

Most top business and political leaders in the comparative study, as well as those in professional and managerial positions in the United States, marry and have at least one child. These leaders face the dilemma of combining a demanding career and family life.

How do they manage this work-family conflict? Rarely by cutting back on working time. Even in countries with relatively shorter workweeks and longer vacations than the United States, the national leaders in our study reported far longer working hours than the general workforce in their country (Woodward and Lyon 2000; also see Jacobs and Winslow 2004 [this volume]). Politicians average more than sixty-five hours per week and business leaders about ten hours fewer, with little gender difference (Woodward and Lyon 2000, Table 8.1). In addition, few female leaders and almost none of their male colleagues had worked part-time or interrupted their careers for care work (Neale 2000; also see Epstein et al. 1998). Especially among managerial elites, the typical career proceeds without interruption from its beginning (Blair-Loy 2003).

In dual-career families, both partners work hard and long in paid employment. Taking time from paid work for child care or household labor is difficult. Some leaders—mostly men—have spouses who were not in paid employment, worked part-time, or had less demanding occupations. Dual-career families—with both partners in senior positions in the labor force—were far more common for the women leaders in our study than for the men (see Boulis 2004 [this volume] for similar patterns among physicians). More than 70 percent of the men—and just more than one-third of the women—had partners who were not in paid employment or who worked in nonprofessional jobs with no supervisory responsibilities (Kuusipalo, Kauppinen, and Nuutinen 2000, Table 15.2; see Stone and Lovejoy 2004 [this volume]).

Child care responsibilities clearly fell disproportionately on women, even for those holding top economic and political positions.

Most leaders earn high enough salaries to pay others to perform some of the household labor and child care. Yet most women in our research did some of these tasks themselves in spite of their long workweeks. The amounts done differ considerably between men and women. Well more than half of the men and none of the women reported that their spouse had cared for their children when they were preschoolers (Kuusipalo, Kauppinen, and Nuutinen 2000, Table 15.4). Likewise, one in five women (nearly all politicians) and no men had cared for their preschool children themselves (Neale 2000, Tables 13.1 and 13.2; Kuusipalo, Kauppinen, and Nuutinen 2000, Table 15.4). Child care responsibilities clearly fell disproportionately on women, even for those holding top economic and political positions.

In response to a question about the division of household labor, few women (9 percent) and about a quarter of the men reported doing none (Kuusipalo, Kauppinen, and Nuutinen 2000, Table 15.2). Nearly a third of the women business and political leaders said they did more than half of the household labor themselves, including 13 percent of the women business leaders who reported doing all the housework (Neale 2000, 164-65; Kuusipalo, Kauppinen, and Nuutinen 2000, Table 15.2; Esseveld and Andersson 2000, Table 16.2).

Family responsibilities, including care of young children and completion of household labor, fall disproportionately on women, even among those in top leadership positions in the professions, management, and politics. Marriage and, even more, parenthood impinge on women's careers to a far larger extent than they do on similarly situated men's. Compared to women, fast-track men are more frequently married and parents. And men also more often have wives who are not in a demanding career and are thus more available for child care, housework, and involvement in building his career (see Stone and Lovejoy 2004). Women are frequently married to highly placed men who have as many time constraints as they do and thus are less available for sharing family labor and focusing on advancing the woman's career.

Research beyond the United States generally paints a similar picture to that portrayed in these conference papers. But this broad picture obscures variations in patterns within regions or countries. When one looks more closely at work-family conflicts in European and other industrialized countries, variations appear. National cultural norms and social policies provide contexts for the employment and family lives of workers in demanding occupations (see Wax 2004 [this volume]).

The Nordic countries stand out as models of (relatively) woman- and family-friendly societies. Gender equality norms are widespread, government policies support women's equal participation in public life, and women's rates of paid employment are high. According to Kuusipalo, Kauppinen, and Nuutinen (2000), the Nordic countries have replaced the male breadwinner model with the dual-earner model. They wrote, "Parental leave, flexible working hours and state childcare support women's right to work and men's right to fatherhood" (p. 178). Data from the Nordic countries in the Comparative Leadership Study (Denmark, Finland, Norway, and Sweden) do show fewer gender differences in family status and duties than are seen in other areas of Europe, North America, Asia, Australia, and New Zealand (Vianello and Moore 2000, pt. III).

Public child care is widely available in the Nordic countries, and about 30 percent of leaders placed their preschool children in it. Nordic male leaders were more involved in household labor than men in the other regions: 20 percent reported doing at least half of the housework themselves. Nordic men's higher rate of household labor may be partly due to Nordic norms against employing private household workers.

Despite men's greater participation in family care in the Nordic countries, women do even more. Twice as many women leaders reported caring for their preschool children (26 percent of women vs. 14 percent of men), and nearly two-thirds of women reported doing at least half of the housework (Esseveld and Andersson 2000). Primarily mothers, not fathers, apparently use the generous parental leave policies available in the Nordic countries.

Career pathways and occupational settings also affect work-family conflicts, as noted by several conference participants (Blair-Loy, Fox, Jacobs and Winslow, Mason and Goulden, Noonan and Corcoran). Careers in management and science, for instance, require an early and steady commitment from aspirants, often beginning in high school. Dropping in and out or beginning a career later in life is hardly an option for these fields. In the Comparative Leadership Study, business-women had the lowest rates of marriage and childbearing (Vianello and Moore 2000). By contrast, some top careers are more flexible and more easily entered at an older age. Elected politicians, for example, often enter politics in their late twenties or even thirties. Politics, then, is not closed to women who have reared children or begun in other careers. Some strategies to improve the work-family balance for women and men in demanding careers seem unrealistic for those in senior leadership positions. Jerry Jacobs (forthcoming) has called for institutions to clearly state that tenure-track faculty are expected to work no more than fifty hours per week to create a "family-compatible workstyle." Reduced working hours for national leaders in politics, business, or voluntary associations is not a workable solution. Top leaders in key institutions are expected to show total devotion to their work (e.g., Kanter 1977; Blair-Loy 2003). Possibly more feasible is Phyllis Moen's (2004) advocacy of social expectations that careers include "second acts" and "time-outs" allowing men and women to develop integrated career and family lives. For those aspiring to national elite positions, a time-out early in their career to have and rear children—as taken by many women politicians—could facilitate a more compatible career and family life.

Nordic men's higher rate of household labor may be partly due to Nordic norms against employing private household workers.

An international perspective on the work-family conflicts discussed in the conference helps to show in what ways the United States is similar to and different from other countries. In many ways, the United States differs little, as I have shown above. Yet the Nordic countries appear more successful in lessening work-family conflicts, even for women and men in top positions. These countries have made extraordinary progress in opening political decision–making positions to women. Women are prominent among prime ministers, cabinet members, and members of parliament in Denmark, Finland, Norway, and Sweden. Women constitute a critical mass in their parliaments, erasing their token status and normalizing the image of politics as a woman's game as well as a man's game (Kanter 1977; Epstein 1988). Scholars and policy makers would benefit from a closer examination of these models promoting gender equality.

Note

1. For details on the research design of the Comparative Leadership Project, see Sansonetti et al. (2000). The nations included are Austria, Australia, Belgium, Canada, the Czech Republic, Denmark, Finland, France, Germany, Greece, Hungary, Ireland, Israel, Italy, Japan, the Netherlands, New Zealand, Norway, Poland, Portugal, Russia, Slovenia, Spain, Sweden, Switzerland, United Kingdom, and the United States.

References

Adler, Nancy J., and Dafna N. Izraeli, eds. 1994. *Competitive frontiers: Women managers in a global economy*. Cambridge, MA: Blackwell.

Blair-Loy, Mary. 2003. *Competing devotions: Career and family among women executives*. Cambridge, MA: Harvard University Press.

Boulis, Ann. 2004. The evolution of gender and motherhood in contemporary medicine. *Annals of the American Academy of Political and Social Science* 596:172-206.

Epstein, Cynthia Fuchs. 1988. *Deceptive distinctions: Sex, gender and the social order*. New Haven, CT: Yale University Press.

Epstein, Cynthia Fuchs, Carroll Seron, Bonnie Oglensky, and Robert Saute. 1998. *The part-time paradox: Time norms, professional lives, family, and gender*. New York: Routledge.

Esseveld, Johanna, and Gunnar Andersson. 2000. Career life-forms. In *Gendering elites: Economic and political leadership in 27 industrialised societies*, edited by M. Vianello and G. Moore, 189-204. London: Macmillan.

Jacobs, Jerry A. Forthcoming. The faculty time divide. *Sociological Forum*.

Jacobs, Jerry A., and Sarah E. Winslow. 2004. Overworked faculty: Job stresses and family demands. *Annals of the American Academy of Political and Social Science* 596:104-129.

Kanter, Rosabeth. 1977. *Men and women of the corporation*. New York: Basic Books.

Kuusipal0, Jaana, Kaisa Kauppinen, and Iira Nuutinen. 2000. Life and career in north and south Europe. In *Gendering elites: Economic and political leadership in 27 industrialised societies*, edited by M. Vianello and G. Moore, 177-88. London: Macmillan.

Moen, Phyllis. 2004. Integrative careers: Time in, time out, and second acts. Presidential Address, Eastern Sociological Society meetings, February 20.

Neale, Jenny. 2000. Family characteristics. In *Gendering elites: Economic and political leadership in 27 industrialised societies*, ed. M. Vianello and G. Moore, 157-68. London: Macmillan.

Sansonetti, Silvia, Dawn Lyon, Gwen Moore, Jenny Neale, and Michal Palgi. 2000. Methodology. In *Gendering elites: Economic and political leadership in 27 industrialised societies*, edited M. Vianello and G. Moore, 11-16. London: Macmillan.

Stone, Pamela, and Meg Lovejoy. 2004. Fast-track women and the "choice" to stay home. *Annals of the American Academy of Political and Social Science* 596:62-83.

Vianello, Mino, and Gwen Moore, eds. 2000. *Gendering elites: Economic and political leadership in 27 industrialised societies*. London: Macmillan.

Wax, Amy L. 2004. Family-friendly workplace reform: Prospects for change. *Annals of the American Academy of Political and Social Science* 596:36-61.

Wirth, Linda. 2001. *Breaking through the glass ceiling: Women in management*. Geneva, Switzerland: International Labour Office.

Woodward, Alison, and Dawn Lyon. 2000. Gendered time and women's access to power. In *Gendering elites: Economic and political leadership in 27 industrialised societies*, edited by M. Vianello and G. Moore, 91-103. London: Macmillan.

COMMENT

Elite Careers and Family Commitment: It's (Still) about Gender

By
SCOTT COLTRANE

Men and women are increasingly likely to pursue careers in elite professions, but gendered expectations about homemaking and breadwinning continue to shape opportunities for professional advancement and individual decisions to marry, have children, regulate employment hours, or use "family-friendly" programs. This article describes how the Victorian ideology of separate spheres and other gendered beliefs and practices have spawned a modern-day "career advancement double standard" in which professional women who marry or have children are considered less serious about their careers, whereas professional men who marry or become fathers are considered more likely candidates for promotion. Trends in the general population toward more gender equality in labor force attachment and family labor sharing are compared to slower changes among elite professionals such as doctors, lawyers, and bankers.

Keywords: family; fathers; housework; parenting; gender; elite professions; dual-career couples; work-family

When academic researchers first began studying work-family trade-offs in the 1970s, they turned their attention toward high-status dual-career professional couples. According to conventional wisdom, doctors, lawyers, scientists, and professors were most likely to overcome the sexist stereotyping and the gender discrimination that discouraged men and women from sharing breadwinning and family caregiving. More than a quarter-century later, men and women in high-status professional careers are likely to share breadwinning, but the accommodation of those careers to family concerns is limited by nostalgic family ideals and

Scott Coltrane is a professor of sociology and associate director of the Center for Family Studies at the University of California, Riverside (UCR). He is past president of the Pacific Sociological Association, recipient of the UCR Distinguished Teaching Award, and principal investigator on NIH-funded longitudinal studies of Mexican American and European American families. His books include Family Man, Gender and Families *and* Families and Society.

DOI: 10.1177/0002716204268776

gender stereotypes. Despite uneven progress in women's professional advancement, the basic assumption that family caregiving is the exclusive responsibility of women remains. As the articles in this volume attest, more women have entered elite professions, but they face difficult choices and are more likely than men in these professions to delay or forgo marriage or childbirth. In fact, I suspect that achieving work-family balance is now easier in middle- and working-class occupations than it is in the elite professions.

Even recent federal efforts at welfare reform and child support selectively reinforce [a Victorian] ideal, insofar as they are designed to collect money from absent fathers and to encourage mothers to marry.

The elite professions have been slow to accommodate changing family situations or to embrace fully the concept that family caregiving demands should allow a person to work part-time at various stages of the life course. These professions could do a much better job of providing flexibility and family-friendly options to those who receive training to be doctors, lawyers, bankers, scientists, or researchers. The articles presented here show some improvement but also continuing inequities in specializations, earnings, benefits, and promotions between women and men. Although much has changed since the 1970s, the ideal professional worker is still a man with a stay-at-home wife who fulfills *his* family obligations through being a breadwinner. To move through the professional ranks (e.g., receive promotions, become a partner, get tenure), one is still expected to devote huge amounts of time and emotional energy to the profession, an expectation that renders career advancement and raising a family virtually incompatible—at least for women.

Why is the work-family juggling act *not* a major issue for men in these professions? When men become husbands and fathers, coworkers and superiors perceive them as being more serious and more deserving of career advancement than their single or childless counterparts. "Family men" are seen as partner "material" and are assumed to possess the mature leadership qualities that qualify one to be a manager or CEO. Curiously, the opposite reasoning is applied to women. When they become wives and mothers, it is expected that family obligations will inevitably intrude on their ability to commit themselves to their demanding careers. Whereas previously they might have been on the "fast track," the act of getting married or having children subtly renders these women "less qualified" for advancement. This career advancement double standard, reflected as much in informal interactions, workplace cultures, and personal beliefs as in official policies, comes out of Victorian-era cultural ideals that also brought us the sexual double standard (only men should have sexual affairs), exclusionary hiring practices (only men are worthy of employment), and differential wage rates (men should be paid more than women because they need a "family wage"). The career advancement double standard represents a last vestige of separate-spheres ideology, in which husbands are assumed to be breadwinners and wives are assumed to be homemakers (Coltrane 1998; Coontz 1992). Even recent federal efforts at welfare reform and child support selectively reinforce this ideal, insofar as they are designed to collect money from absent fathers and to encourage mothers to marry.

In *The Cultural Contradictions of Motherhood* (1996), Sharon Hays showed how separate-spheres ideology shapes personal as well as institutional expectations about women being more kind, caring, and nurturing than men. Women *do* provide more family care and emotional support than men, but Hays demonstrates that conventional expectations for "intensive mothering" are socially constructed and subject to historical change. New mothers often hope that a subliminal "maternal instinct" will show them how to parent but ultimately find that they must develop their parenting skills by reading books, talking to other mothers, and interacting with their children. Conversely, Nicholas Townsend (2002) described how separate-spheres ideology urges men to define their family contributions by their work commitments. Townsend showed that men embrace a "package deal" of marriage, work, fatherhood, and homeownership and strive to maintain a division of labor based on symbolic "father breadwinners" and "mother homemakers." Even men whose wives are employed tend to define their family obligation as earning money, justifying their limited role in everyday family life by invoking the belief that children should be cared for by their mothers. Townsend showed how men's parenting is mediated by wives who schedule and manage family life, as mothers and fathers collude in a gendered system of parenting that keeps fathers on the sidelines as helpers, playmates, and occasional disciplinarians.

What's wrong with this picture? Such patterns contradict popular ideals about "new" fathers who participate in the details of raising children, but historical analyses show that fathering ideals and practices are not necessarily congruent (Coltrane 1996; Griswold 1993; LaRossa 1997; Mintz 1998). More to the point, the continued symbolic significance of intensive mothers and breadwinner fathers serves to reproduce unequal gender relations at a time when gender equality is gaining acceptance in education and in the workplace (Coontz 1992). Elsewhere, I have argued that nostalgic family policies based on breadwinner fathers and mothers who marry and avoid divorce "for the sake of the children" are predicated on false assumptions about the causes and consequences of changes in family structure (Coltrane 2001; Coltrane and Adams 2003). In contrast to jeremiads about family breakdown, the institution of marriage is not in danger of disappearing, and marriage promotion is unlikely to lift significant numbers of children out of poverty. The real problem is continued acceptance of separate-spheres ideology and the failure of social institutions to accept gender equality in the home and in the workplace.

In the past several decades, Americans have witnessed huge changes in both the work and the family sides of the work-family equation. Women's labor force participation has risen dramatically, as have the educational achievement and occupational training of women. Women are now more likely to attend college than men (though their career trajectories and earnings continue to lag behind those of men). On the family side, dual-earner couples have become the norm. In 1960, there were more than twice as many breadwinner-father/homemaker-mother families as dual-earner families, but in 2000, there were more than twice as many dual-earner families as breadwinner-father/homemaker-mother families. And the number of other family types, including single-mother and single-father families, has grown even faster. Although patterns differ across subgroups of the population, American couples are having fewer children later in their lives. And women are increasingly able to have children outside of marriage, with the largest change coming for women older than thirty (see Coltrane and Collins 2001).

[W]hen men perform more of the routine housework, employed women feel that the division of labor is fairer, are less depressed, and enjoy higher levels of marital satisfaction.

Changes in the division of family labor between spouses have been relatively slow, and few couples report equal sharing. Nevertheless, men have increased their contributions significantly, especially on weekends (Coltrane 2000; Pleck and Masciadrelli 2003). Based on national time-diary studies, Robinson and Godbey (1997) reported that American women's time spent on housework declined by one-third from the 1960s to the late 1980s and men's relative contributions doubled, increasing from about 15 to 33 percent of the total. Even more change has occurred in American men's performance of child care. From the 1960s to early 1980s, fathers interacted with their children about a third as much as mothers and were available about half as much as mothers (Lamb et al. 1987). During the mid-1980s to early 1990s, the average coresident father interacted about two-fifths as much as the mother and was available to his children almost two-thirds as much (Pleck 1997). In the late 1990s, he was available to his children about three-fourths as much as the mother, interacting on weekdays about two-thirds as often but more than four-fifths as much on weekends (Pleck and Masciadrelli 2003; Yueng et al.

2001). At the same time, however, in most families, fathers and mothers share much less of the responsibility for the planning, scheduling, emotional management, and other behind-the-scenes activities associated with raising children (Coltrane 2004; Deutsch 1999).

Because the average woman still does about twice the amount of routine housework as the average man, and because findings of greater proportionate sharing among married couples are driven more by women's time adjustments than men's, researchers have focused on the continuing importance of gender in the allocation of domestic work (Coltrane 2000; Thompson and Walker 1989). Most researchers find that married men create as much (or more) demand for household labor than they perform, whereas women tend to perform domestic labor to meet the demands necessitated by the presence of children and husbands. We do know that when men perform more of the routine housework, employed women feel that the division of labor is fairer, are less depressed, and enjoy higher levels of marital satisfaction. We also know that the allocation of household tasks is associated with variation in the employment hours of both men and women, their relative earnings, their beliefs about gender and family, and their living arrangements. Family size, age, life stage, ethnicity, presence and contribution of children, and a host of other factors also enter into the household labor allocation process, but in general we can say that the person with less power and fewer resources does more of it (Coltrane 2000).

Unfortunately, most researchers study *either* housework *or* child care, so we have an incomplete picture of how they fit together. We do know that when men feel responsible for child development, they tend to share more of the daily parenting, including supervising, driving, helping with homework, and interacting. These patterns are also associated with more sharing of the cooking, meal cleanup, shopping, housecleaning, and laundry. In other words, when men participate in the more nurturing and supportive activities that serve children, they are also more likely to share in child and home maintenance activities. In contrast, when men participate in parenting as symbolic household heads, coaches, or playmates, they are somewhat less likely to share domestic work with their wives (Coltrane 2004; Coltrane and Adams 2001).

Changes in attitudes toward work and family opportunities and obligations for men and women have arguably changed more rapidly than actual behaviors. Most American men now say they value home and family over work. Young men and women now expect to share breadwinning, and most even say that housework and child care should be shared equally when both spouses are employed. Young men tend to expect that the workplace and family sharing they endorse will occur with little thought or effort, whereas most young women worry about the details. Young women anticipate that balancing career and family obligations, as well as negotiating fair sharing arrangements for housework and child care, will be difficult (Coltrane 1998, 2000, 2004). We can thus see that accommodations to new attitudes of sharing are partial and incomplete, with many women and their employers still assuming that women will specialize in family work and cut back on work hours after marrying or having children. These patterns help explain why women in elite professions delay getting married or having children.

The forces driving changes in fathers' involvement in working- and middle-class families should continue. Women share more family work with their male partners when they are employed more hours, earn more money, have more education, and believe in sharing. All these trends are likely to continue for the foreseeable future. Similarly, men share more family work when they are employed fewer hours and believe in sharing and when their wives earn more. Whether these trends will exert enough pressure on men in dual-career professional couples to do more at home remains to be seen, but early indications are that change in the elite professions may be lagging behind change in the working class. It should also be noted that when women in elite professions hire working-class and immigrant women to provide domestic family services, it reduces their own hours of family labor but does little to challenge the privileged position of husbands in families and often contributes to perpetuating race, class, and gender hierarchies in the larger labor market. Thus, maintaining separate-spheres ideology has repercussions beyond the marriage and family patterns of the relatively privileged men and women who become doctors, lawyers, scientists, professors, and bankers.

Most American men now say they value home and family over work.

In summary, belief in separate gender spheres continues to shape socialization into elite professions and the gendered organization of work and family life for individuals in these positions. Categorical distinctions between mothering and fathering perpetuate expectations that women will raise children and men will do little direct family work. These symbolic distinctions are theoretically linked to the maintenance of male dominance throughout the society (Coltrane 1996; Coltrane and Adams 2001; Connell 1987; Osmond and Thorne 1993). To counter such inequities, we should stop assuming that women should provide domestic services and emotional support to husbands, children, and other family members. We should also stop assuming that men are incapable of nurturing children and doing housework. In the long run, such a shift would promote earnings equity for women and lead to more work flexibility for elite professionals as well as for other workers. Only by focusing on the gender stereotypes inherent in our expectations for professionals will we be able to transcend them in the future.

References

Coltrane, Scott. 1996. *Family man: Fatherhood, housework, and gender equity*. New York: Oxford University Press.

———. 1998. *Gender and families*. Thousand Oaks, CA: Pine Forge Press.

———. 2000. Research on household labor: Modeling and measuring the social embeddedness of routine family work. *Journal of Marriage and the Family* 62:1209-33.

———. 2001. Marketing the marriage "solution": Misplaced simplicity in the politics of fatherhood. *Sociological Perspectives* 44:387-422.

———. 2004. Fathering: Paradoxes, contradictions, and dilemmas. In *Handbook of contemporary families: Considering the past, contemplating the future*, edited by Marilyn Coleman and Lawrence Ganong. Thousand Oaks, CA: Sage.

Coltrane, Scott, and Michele Adams. 2001. Men's family work: Child-centered fathering and the sharing of domestic labor." In *Working families: The transformation of the American home*, edited by R. Hertz and N. Marshall, 72-99. Berkeley: University of California Press.

———. 2003. The social construction of the divorce "problem": Morality, child victims, and the politics of gender. *Family Relations* 52:21-30.

Coltrane, Scott, and Randall Collins. 2001. *Sociology of marriage and the family*. 5th ed. Belmont, CA: Wadsworth.

Connell, Robert W. 1987. *Gender and power*. Stanford, CA: Stanford University Press.

Coontz, Stephanie. 1992. *The way we never were*. New York: Basic Books.

Deutsch, Francine. 1999. *Halving it all*. Cambridge, MA: Harvard University Press.

Griswold, Robert. 1993. *Fatherhood in America: A history*. New York: Basic Books.

Hays, Sharon. 1996. *The cultural contradictions of motherhood*. New Haven, CT: Yale University Press.

Lamb, Michael E., Joseph Pleck, Eric Charnov, and James Levine. 1987. A biosocial perspective on parental behavior and involvement. In *Parenting across the lifespan*, edited by Jane B. Lancaster, J. Altman, and Alice S. Rossi, 11-42. New York: Academic Press.

LaRossa, Ralph. 1997. *The modernization of fatherhood: A social and political history*. Chicago: University of Chicago Press.

Mintz, Steven. 1998. From patriarchy to androgyny and other myths: Placing men's family roles in historical perspective. In *Men in families*, edited by Alan Booth and Ann C. Crouter, 3-30. Mahwah, NJ: Lawrence Erlbaum.

Osmond, Marie W., and Barrie Thorne. 1993. Feminist theories: The social construction of gender in families and society. In *Sourcebook of family theories and methods*, edited by Pauline G. Boss, William J. Doherty, Ralph LaRossa, Walter R. Shumm, and Susan K. Steinmetz, 591-623. New York: Plenum.

Pleck, Joseph H. 1997. Paternal involvement: Levels, sources, and consequences. In *The role of the father in child development*, 3rd ed., edited by M. E. Lamb, 66-103. New York: John Wiley.

Pleck, Joseph H., and Brian P. Masciadrelli. 2003. Paternal involvement: Levels, sources, and consequences. In *The role of the father in child development*, 4th ed., edited by Michael E. Lamb. New York: John Wiley.

Robinson, John P., and Geoffrey Godbey. 1997. *Time for life: The surprising ways that Americans use time*. University Park: Pennsylvania State University Press.

Thompson, L., and A. J. Walker. 1989. Gender in families: Women and men in marriage, work, and parenthood. *Journal of Marriage and the Family* 51: 845-71.

Townsend, Nicholas W. 2002. *The package deal: Marriage, work and fatherhood in men's lives*. Philadelphia: Temple University Press.

Yueng, W. Jean, John F. Sandberg, Pamela E. Davis-Kean, and Sandra L. Hofferth. 2001. Children's time with fathers in intact families. *Journal of Marriage and Family* 63:136-54.

COMMENT

This article offers an overview of and commentary on the articles in the volume, ponders some of the issues they raise, and recommends further research possibilities.

Keywords: work-family balance; leave policies; gender and social roles

Where We Are Now and Future Possibilities

By
JOYCE P. JACOBSEN

I want to make three types of comments, the first set regarding the conference's papers, the second set regarding future research, and the third set regarding the link between the papers and the policy suggestions made by various participators in the conference.

Taken as a group, the papers given at this conference present an interesting set of case studies of different high-powered, relatively gender-integrated professions. Several patterns appear consistently in the studies. First, marriage and even children do not appear to hold back some women from having career success; although given that they are high achievers, they might make even more money and be promoted even faster without their family ties. Second, who you marry—and perhaps also what kind of children you have, in terms of their level of need for parental time and attention—may matter for your career. Third, marriage and children do not hinder—and may help—men in their careers.

The studies bring up a number of causality issues but do not attempt to resolve them. For example, several of the presentations referred in passing to the question of whether having a wife who is a full-time "homemaker" is a big career advantage for men, as measured by such men having higher earnings than otherwise-comparable married men. A series of papers,

Joyce P. Jacobsen is Andrews Professor of Economics at Wesleyan University. She is the author, with Gil Skillman, of Labor Markets and Employment Relationships *(Blackwell, 2004). She has also published* The Economics of Gender *(Blackwell, 2nd ed., 1998), along with a number of articles on sex segregation, labor force participation, and determinants of earnings.*

DOI: 10.1177/0002716204268815

including my own (Jacobsen and Rayack 1996), consider alternative explanations for the observed pattern that such men have higher earnings than other married men, namely, that potential high earners are more likely to marry women who work in the home (a marriage market matching effect) and that women whose husbands make high earnings are able to reduce their paid work hours because of their higher household income (reverse causality). We test these two arguments separately, using a fixed effects model on panel data to consider the marriage market matching effect and instrumental variable controls for the endogenous nature of the wife's labor supply decision on cross-sectional data to consider the reverse causality effect. Subsequent papers (Blackaby, Carlin, and Murphy 1998; Hotchkiss and Moore 1999; Chun and Lee 2001) have also considered one or both of these alternative explanations, using alternative data sources. All of these papers find that much of the correlation between husband's earnings and wife's work hours is due to these alternative causes. Another such question that arises from the studies is why having three or more children has a measurably larger negative effect on earnings. But which people have a third or higher-order child these days, both among men and women, and for what reasons? Such births may occur for a very different set of reasons than the first one or two, and these couples may have different observed and unobservable earnings-related characteristics than those with fewer children.

This leads me to wonder what further research would complement existing studies. It is great to have this round of papers focusing on particular professions, but it would be even greater to see a follow-up round of papers all using panel data so we could see what happens to members of these professions over time. Panel data would allow for better addressing of questions of the type I just mentioned regarding causal direction. But even repeated independent samples would allow for synthetic cohort analysis to see if the possible trends suggested by these papers hold up over time.

I am also motivated, in part on a personal level, to find out the answer to the question, If you are married, have young kids, and work full-time, what must you sacrifice? It would be interesting to use time diary data to answer this question. Once enough data accretes from the newly operating American Time Use Survey, researchers would be able to relate the time use information to these labor force survey results. Until that occurs, here are my hypotheses regarding what goes: (1) time spent with one's extended family (this may be relatively easy for many high achievers because they may often not live near their family); (2) time with nonworkplace friends (again, may be easy for many high achievers—if you move around, your friends are scattered, and you do not expect to see them often anyway); (3) time spent socializing at work (or maybe this is actually high; anecdotal evidence on Japan when it was in its long-hours phase was that much time spent at work was not actually productive); (4) high-quality labor-intensive housework—substitution occurs, both of capital for labor and low-cost labor for high-cost labor—cooking and sewing exist for many high achievers only as rarely pursued hobbies rather than as daily activities. There may be limits to how much you can reduce housework, but if you hire a yard service and never invite people over for dinner, no one need know how bad your house looks inside. So time diary data—as well as consumption pattern data—would be key for understanding how work patterns and earnings fit into the whole picture of how living patterns vary by family type.

If you are married, have young kids, and work full-time, what must you sacrifice?

Assuming the papers portray an accurate depiction of the way things are for the people in high-powered professions, what do we want to change, if anything? In general, the papers tended to be better at laying out the work-family patterns than at making a clear link between the work-family patterns and what workplace or social policies they lead one to advocate. Even if you agree that the patterns laid out in the conference of very long work hours in the United States (both in an absolute sense and compared to other countries) in a number of high-earning professions, and continuing barriers to advancement for women in occupations that essentially require long hours and continuous labor force attachment to achieve promotion are problematic and require some form of policy intervention, it is nonetheless clearly quite hard to come up with a "fix." Altering many of the existing patterns would require significant coordination across businesses and employees or significant government intervention to change work hour norms and prevailing opinions regarding the relative desirability of leave takers as employees. Significant questions remain unanswered regarding how men, women, and employers would react to various types of initiatives.

However, the papers do offer some clues as to what types of strategies might be more likely to work. In particular, in comparing the effects of formal versus informal personnel structures, both in evaluation and in family friendliness, the papers offer some intriguing leads.

A high degree of formality, in the form of up-or-out gateway points, makes it harder for women to move up, to stay in the profession, and to avoid the drop-off in earnings that can accompany an extended leave from work. The Noonan and Corcoran article, "The Mommy Track and Partnership," describes a big drain of women out of law firms with partnership decisions; and the Mason and Goulden article, "Marriage and Baby Blues," describes a similar drain out of academic positions involving tenure decisions. Those women who stay in such professions disproportionately fall into the lower-paying tracks within them (e.g., non-tenure-track positions for academics; nonprofits, smaller law firms, and non-partner-track positions for lawyers). Conversely, more flexibility in career track and more openness to career sequencing assists women in maintaining professional positions. The Boulis article, "The Evolution of Gender and Motherhood in Contemporary Medicine," notes relatively small drop-offs in earnings for physicians following extended leaves (usually parenting related); and the Blair-Loy and Wharton article, "Mothers in Finance," demonstrates that later entry into the occupation is possible for brokers.

Both men and women want to avoid gaps and part-time stints in their work record . . .

On the other hand, a high degree of informality, namely, creating ways of shifting or reducing work time that do not go "on the record," appears to be more family friendly. Both men and women want to avoid gaps and part-time stints in their work record and also want to avoid having to deal with a bureaucrat to arrange child care. Thus, one can see how academia can be family friendly: You can tell colleagues that you have decided to stay at home to get some work done—and then also be available to take care of a sick child. Or you can work less hard on your research for some months while taking care of family matters and make up the time later—you may have one fewer publication, but you do not have a gap in your work record. This line of thinking implies that full-leave programs, even if mandated, would be relatively less attractive to parents and caregivers than flexible work-time programs that allow for altered hours, working at home one or more days a week, or use of personal days.

This type of "mandated flexibility" is distinct from situations where people have to negotiate with bosses regarding special arrangements; people need sufficient autonomy to be able to take advantage of these opportunities without having to negotiate each case as a special deal. Hence, automatic leave policies (i.e., non-optional paid leave) can be one way to break this, but it is a hard sell to employers and employees alike if it is not mandated to exist across all employers (otherwise, you might still have trouble getting a new job if you leave the current employer), and it may affect the probability of hiring on the front end if some groups (i.e., women) appear more likely to be users of mandated leave—whether or not that is actually the case.

In addition, policy suggestions need to take into account how social norms regarding how we should spend our time away from work affect our productivity at work. If you are filling the role of the family scheduler and thus make sure the car pool is covered and the brownies are baked for the school bake sale, those details may or may not be manageable during true slack time at work. The hypothetical work-home divide does not exist, in fact, for many of us. This is not necessarily a bad thing: I generally think it is a good thing that I can do home-related chores while at work and vice versa. Many work and home tasks require follow-up and being on call rather than being easily compartmentalized into distinct time periods that are known in advance. Thus, another way in which jobs can be flexible is to make this blending of home and work obligations possible but not required.

This brings me to my last policy-related point: we need to think about the structure of off-work time and space. The sum of work time *plus* commuting time makes careers even more burdensome. The central city and suburban ring structure, which already may have been less than optimal for integrating work and family life, has given way to an extended exurban structure in many areas in which you rarely work in the city where you live and do not choose your residential location based on your current job—partly because you will likely not be at that job five years from now. My husband describes Connecticut as a state in which everyone wakes up in his or her small town and gets in the car and drives to a different small town for work. This problem is exacerbated for the two-career couple, who must choose a location that is at least minimally acceptable to both parties, but who nonetheless often lock at least one member into an absurdly long commute. Consider this in the context of the Jacobs and Winslow paper, "Overworked Faculty," which found long hours *everywhere* in academe; this phenomenon may be related in part to two-career academic marriages. How many two-academic couples have commuting marriages in which they work like crazy during the week and then alternate being in one or the other location on weekends? More generally, it would be interesting to discover how hours worked vary by day of the week or by weekday versus weekend day; this is another thing we will be able to learn more about once more time diary data become available in the near future.

In closing, let me underscore a point that occurred either implicitly or explicitly in many of the papers: men as well as women are subject to both work norms and social norms. Thus, the difficulty in reconciling work norms and social norms cannot be characterized as either a woman's issue or a family-related issue. It is part of a broader discussion of gender and social roles in society and the rigidity of those roles.

References

Blackaby, D. H., P. S. Carlin, and P. D. Murphy. 1998. What a difference a wife makes: The effect of women's hours of work on husbands' hourly earnings. *Bulletin of Economic Research* 50 (1): 1-18.

Chun, Hyunbae, and Injae Lee. 2001. Why do married men earn more: Productivity or marriage selection? *Economic Inquiry* 39 (2): 307-19.

Hotchkiss, Julie L., and Robert E. Moore. 1999. On the evidence of a working spouse penalty in the managerial labor market. *Industrial & Labor Relations Review* 52 (3): 410-23.

Jacobsen, Joyce P., and Wendy L. Rayack. 1996. Do men whose wives work really earn less? *American Economic Review* 86 (2): 268-73.

COMMENT

Policy Alternatives for Solving Work-Family Conflict

HEIDI HARTMANN

The failure of highly educated women to stay in the labor market represents a wasted societal investment. Despite publicity suggesting that educated mothers are increasingly staying home, the long-term trend is toward greater work effort by all mothers, especially highly educated ones. Policy measures can address the reasons some women do drop out by making it more possible for professionals, as well as other workers, to combine work and family. In addition, the double standard in parenting needs to be attacked so that, eventually, men are just as likely as women to take care of children at the same level of intensity and women's and men's labor force participation patterns will look even more similar than they do today.

Keywords: employment; family and work policies; family-friendly workplace

T he failure of highly educated women to stay in the labor market represents a wasted societal investment. Despite the recent spate of publicity suggesting that educated mothers are increasingly staying home (Belkin 2003; Wallis 2004), the long-term trend is toward greater work effort by all mothers, including especially

Heidi Hartmann is the president of the Washington-based Institute for Women's Policy Research (IWPR), a scientific research organization that she founded in 1987 to meet the need for women-centered, policy-oriented research. She is also a research professor at George Washington University. She is a coauthor of Unnecessary Losses: Costs to Americans of the Lack of Family and Medical Leave, Equal Pay for Working Families, *and* Survival at the Bottom: The Income Packages of Low-Income Families with Children. *She has published numerous articles in journals and books, and her work has been translated into more than a dozen languages. She lectures widely on women, economics, and public policy; frequently testifies before the U.S. Congress; and is often cited as an authority in various media outlets. Prior to founding IWPR, she was on the faculties of Rutgers University and the New School for Social Research and worked at the National Research Council/ National Academy of Sciences. In 1994, she was the recipient of a MacArthur Fellowship Award for her work in the field of women and economics. She is vice-chair of the National Council of Women's Organizations.*

DOI: 10.1177/0002716204269626

226
ANNALS, *AAPSS*, 596, November 2004

highly educated ones. Using fifteen years of data from the Panel Study of Income Dynamics, Stephen Rose and I found that about 30 percent of prime age women workers (women aged twenty-six to forty-four in 1983 who had at least one year with earnings between 1983 and 1998) were out of the labor force four or more years during the fifteen-year study period (Rose and Hartmann 2004). About half the women had earnings every year. The proportion with substantial time out of the labor market is significant, but it is a falling proportion. In the prior fifteen years, the proportions were reversed. About 50 percent of working women spent four or more years out of the labor force, while about 30 percent worked every year. Another data source, the Current Population Survey, has shown dramatic increases in the labor force participation of mothers. For example, between 1976 and 2002, women aged fifteen to forty-four who had a child in the prior twelve months increased their labor force participation from 31 to 55 percent. While the rate peaked in 1998 at 58.7 percent, and has fallen slightly since, the long-term trend is clearly one of increase (U.S. Census Bureau 2003). It is possible that the recent dip is due primarily to the end of the long economic boom, the subsequent recession, and the relatively jobless recovery. Married women with a youngest child under six years of age increased their labor force participation from 11.9 percent in 1950 to 62.8 percent in 2000, while married women with older children (children between the ages of six and seventeen) increased their labor force participation from 28.3 percent in 1950 to 77.2 percent in 2000 (U.S. Census Bureau 1976, 2002).

Overall, women are increasing their labor force participation, and more educated women work more than other women. Yet despite the huge increases in mothers' labor force participation, taking time out of the labor market is not an uncommon experience for women.

Stone and Lovejoy (2004 [this volume]) identified five reasons women in their study decided to stay home. Two relate primarily to the work world, in which huge work demands were accompanied either by workplace inflexibility or economic restructuring. Two relate primarily to family demands—the perception on the part of the mothers that older children needed them more and, for a few, a strong commitment to traditional family values. A fifth reason is related to both the work and family spheres and is labeled "husband career spillover"—some of the husbands earn much more than their wives in very demanding jobs and do not help with family care. Several alternative labels might be considered for this phenomenon: husband exemption, husband inflexibility, husband power, male power, patriarchy.

The reason I find most puzzling is the presence of older children and the increased intensity that parenting teenagers is perceived to require. In general, much research finds that the older the children, the more time fathers spend with them, so if older children need more parental care, it seems that at least sometimes it might be the fathers and not the mothers who would take time off from work to spend with them. Also, since a substantial minority of married women outearn their husbands, it would be economically rational for fathers to become at-home parents in at least some families. For example, Rose and Hartmann (2004) found that approximately 15 percent of women who were continuously married and employed for fifteen years earned more than their husbands over that period.

Is the tendency of some highly privileged women to stay home with teenagers just another example of increased cultural support for ever rising standards of ever more intensive parenting? Or does it simply correspond to the time in the mother's career when she faces challenges at work and realizes she will either have to find a new job if she wants to move ahead or stay where she is and stagnate, the typical midcareer challenge? When faced with blocked careers, men seem to change their hairstyles, buy sports cars, and have affairs and/or look for a new job. Do women at a similar career stage stay home with their teenagers? Is staying at home a socially sanctioned alternative to forging ahead at work or coming to terms with work—for high-achieving women? Is it an alternative that is especially convenient for the continued dominance of men in leadership positions in society?

Overall, women are increasing their labor force participation, and more educated women work more than other women.

In terms of policy solutions, our society could go several different ways in attempting to solve work-family challenges. First, of course, is always the status quo or no change. This alternative seems the least likely to me, simply because women are voting with their feet, toward more work in the labor market. They are investing in themselves by increasing their educational attainment; they are generally marrying later and having fewer children. They seem to be seeking economic autonomy and economic security through their own employment as well as through marriage and family formation.

Second, women could become more like men. This is the course we have been following. In their economic behavior, women have become more like men. Women have increased their labor force participation dramatically, along with their educational preparation. Now the pattern of women's labor force participation over the life cycle looks quite similar to men's. It peaks in the prime earning years, and in the aggregate, we no longer observe a dip in women's labor force participation during the childbearing years. Married women with children have also increased their hours of work substantially—from 869 hours in 1979 (that is, less than a half-time job) to 1,255 hours annually on average in 2000, an increase that is equivalent to working ten additional weeks at full-time hours (Mishel, Bernstein, and Boushey 2003). The more intense labor force participation by women is no doubt increasing the demand for more family-friendly workplaces. I expect this trend, for women's economic behavior to increasingly resemble men's, to continue.

Third, men could become more like women. While in some ways men's behavior is becoming more like women's, changes in this direction have been far more limited. Between 1950 and 2000, men's labor force participation fell more than 15 percentage points (from 86 percent in 1950 to 71 percent in 2000), while during the same period women's rose nearly 25 percentage points (from 34 percent in 1950 to 58 percent in 2000). Thus, men's and women's labor force participation is converging—once more than 50 percentage points distant, there are now less than 15 percentage points separating them (Jacobs 2004). As men work less, are they doing more housework? To some extent, yes. Pointing out that married men are the only group of adults who increased their time spent on housework between 1978 and 1988, Francine Blau (1998) argued that this change represents the better bargain that working women are able to strike with their husbands. Subsequent to the passage of the Family and Medical Leave Act in 1993, a slightly larger proportion of men than women report taking advantage of its provisions to care for a newborn, newly adopted, or foster child (Commission on Family and Medical Leave 2000). I also expect this trend, of men changing their behavior to spend more time out of the labor market and in family care, to continue, albeit slowly.

Fourth, women's economic behavior could remain different from men's and society could compensate women better for their time spent in child rearing and family care. Currently, most women are able to work fewer hours than men and devote more time to family care on average than men do because they marry higher-earning men and rely on them financially. As a society, we in the United States rely on individual men to compensate women for their lost working time, a mechanism that due to nonmarriage and divorce is imperfect at best. Our social provisions for single mothers are penurious, and we have even fewer subsidies for middle-class women who provide family care full-time. The amount of social compensation that would be necessary to make women whole were they not relying on individual men would be quite large, so this societal choice seems very unlikely to me, though there are many potential ways of providing partial redress that could be helpful (such as providing caregiver credits in the Social Security System; see Hartmann and Hill 2000).

Fifth, we could adjust our social and economic institutions to be more compatible with caring by both men and women. Stone and Lovejoy (2004) emphasized this alternative in their policy recommendations. They stressed the need for more good part-time jobs—part-time jobs that would pay well per hour, provide fringe benefits, and lead to career growth. Unfortunately, such part-time jobs are all too rare, even in professions that require a high level of educational preparation. In a study on part-time work among professionals and managers, Hartmann, Yoon, and Zuckerman (2000) found that only a few occupations offered part-time jobs at all comparable to full-time jobs—the best were held by nurses (in the public and private sector), scientists (including engineers, mathematicians, and computer and natural scientists) in large private firms, and special education teachers. While the development of better part-time jobs could create a part-time ghetto for women, I am less concerned about such a development than I once was. I think men would increasingly opt for reduced hours if the quality of jobs were better. Substantial shares of both men and women work part-time under age twenty-five and over age sixty-one. Currently, however, in the child-rearing years, men's part-time work falls while women's increases. Men are probably working more hours during these years than they would prefer, at least partly to compensate for women's reduced hours. Better reduced-hours employment opportunities would make this a more attractive option for both genders. Other working-hour policies that could improve gender equity include reducing the normal work week for all, below the forty hours where it has been stuck since 1938 when the Fair Labor Standards Act was passed; protecting workers from mandatory overtime; increasing the premiums paid for overtime work; and including professional workers in the overtime provisions.

The more intense labor force participation by women is no doubt increasing the demand for more family-friendly workplaces.

In my view, one important strategy for bringing about a more equitable division of labor between the sexes is to develop a multifaceted campaign against the double standard in parenting. Currently, society accepts a double standard in which mothers do much more of the parenting work than fathers. Mothers invest more of their time in caring for their children personally, take more time off from work to do so, and impose higher standards on the quality of their own care of children than men do. They seem to feel more guilt than men do when they work long hours. Indeed, there seems to be an ideology of intensive motherhood developing that threatens not only to rein women in and get them back in the home but also to destroy the progress our society has made in getting men more invested in their children (Hays 1996). It undermines gender equity as well. It also threatens to set up the conditions for another male critique of women who mother too much and ruin their children's lives, similar to what occurred in reaction to the domesticity of the 1950s. To prevent this predictable scenario, we need to mount a serious attack on this growing ideology in the popular media, stressing the importance of women's career development to women's self-fulfillment (a happy mother is a good mother) and the value of good-quality group child care and preschool to the healthy development of children. We also need to generate a flood of studies showing how critical men's involvement is to their children's healthy development and to be sure these findings also permeate public opinion. We need to support women who want to put career first and men who want to put family first. And most of all, we need to develop and support norms of sharing caring labor. This struggle is too important to allow a conservative ideology to blanket the airwaves and the opinion space and push us back to a 1950s feminine mystique.

References

Belkin, Lisa. 2003. The opt-out revolution. *The New York Times Magazine*, October 26, p. 42.

Blau, Francine D. 1998. Trends in the well-being of American women, 1970-1995. *Journal of Economic Literature* 36 (1): 112-65.

Commission on Family and Medical Leave. 2000. *Balancing the needs of families and employers*. Washington, DC: U.S. Department of Labor, Employment Standards Administration.

Hartmann, Heidi, and Catherine Hill. 2000. *Strengthening social security for women: A report from the working conference on women and social security*. Washington, DC: Institute for Women's Policy Research.

Hartmann, Heidi, Young-Hee Yoon, and Diana Zuckerman. 2000. *Part-time opportunities for professionals and managers: Where are they, who uses them and why?* Washington, DC: Institute for Women's Policy Research.

Hays, Sharon. 1996. *The cultural contradictions of motherhood*. New Haven, CT: Yale University Press.

Jacobs, Eva E. 2004. *Handbook of U.S. labor statistics*. Lanham, MD: Bernan.

Mishel, Lawrence, Jared Bernstein, and Heather Boushey. 2003. *The state of working America 2002/2003*. An Economic Policy Institute Book. Ithaca, NY: ILR Press.

Rose, Stephen J., and Heidi I. Hartmann. 2004. *Still a man's labor market: The long-term earnings gap*. Washington, DC: Institute for Women's Policy Research.

Stone, Pamela, and Meg Lovejoy. 2004. Fast-track women and the "choice" to stay home. *Annals of the American Academy of Political and Social Science* 596:62-83.

U.S. Census Bureau. 1976. *Statistical abstract of the United States: 1976*. Washington, DC: Government Printing Office.

———. 2002. *Statistical abstract of the United States: 2002*. Washington, DC: National Technical Information Service.

———. 2003. *Fertility of American women: June 2002*. Report P20-548. Washington, DC: U.S. Department of Commerce.

Wallis, Claudia. 2004. The case for staying at home. *Time* 163 (12, March): 50.

BOOK REVIEW ESSAY

Mary Blair-Loy. 2003. *Competing Devotions: Career and Family among Women Executives.* Cambridge, MA: Harvard University Press. 269 pp. ISBN 0-674-01089-2.

Phyllis Moen, ed. 2003. *It's about Time: Couples and Careers.* Ithaca, NY: Cornell University Press. 436 pp. ISBN 0-8014-4080-7.

The Contemporary Myth of Choice

Harriet B. Presser. 2003. *Working in a 24/7 Economy: Challenges for American Families.* New York: Russell Sage Foundation. 254 pp. ISBN 0-87154-670-1.

Janet C. Gornick and Marcia K. Meyers. 2003. *Families that Work: Policies for Reconciling Parenthood and Employment.* New York: Russell Sage Foundation. 392 pp. ISBN 0-87154-356-7.

By
ROSANNA HERTZ

*M*ona Lisa Smile, a fictional account of Wellesley College in the 1950s, centers on the powerful pressures on women to find a husband, settle down, and have a family. Although "choice" is a subtheme in the movie, it is historically out of place. Education was an accessory that women brought to marriage. The idea that those Wellesley women had a choice to use their educations in the workplace or to enter graduate school and a career is a feminist idea that did not take hold until twenty years after the time in which the movie was set.

Fifty years later, undergraduate women's studies and sociology majors at Wellesley College are convinced they have a choice. Today's Wellesley graduates rarely sport engagement rings; instead they are likely to go to graduate school immediately (or after a brief work stint).

Rosanna Hertz is the Luella LaMer Professor of Sociology and Women's Studies at Wellesley College, where she has taught for the past twenty years. Presently she chairs the Women's Studies Department. She is the author of the widely acclaimed More Equal than Others: Women and Men in Dual-Career Marriages *(University of California Press).*

DOI: 10.1177/0002716204270000

Choices between continued employment and family are not made until almost a decade after college graduation. Similarly, throughout the United States—and regardless of sex, race, or social class—marriage and the birth of a first child are being postponed until a later age. For most Americans, then, the dilemmas of work-family occur once men and women are entrenched in the labor force.

At the beginning of the twenty-first century, women have become full-time and continuous participants in the labor force. Even though the gender composition of the workforce has changed, the demands and structure of careers and jobs within firms have remained relatively static. The hegemonic culture of the workplace both assumes and depends upon an infrastructure in which individuals sequence their lives according to jobs and career demands. Ideas about work success continue unabated by the changing labor force (see Moen and Blair-Loy). Individuals are expected to sacrifice excessive individualism to be "team players." The corporate emphasis on contributing to the achievement of organizational goals directly diminishes the possibility of placing individual (or family) needs first (see Hertz 1986, 19). Part-time employees threaten the team metaphor and the ideology of the collective (i.e., organizational) good.

Recently published books address new work-family concerns. The rise of dual-earner couples and the rise in single mothers (who were either once married or never married) have created greater family diversity. Phyllis Moen and her colleagues in *It's about Time* and Harriet B. Presser in *Working in a 24/7 Economy* address the challenges diverse families face by exploring the "time frames" (Moen, p. 5) that are embedded in every aspect of our culture, including jobs and career paths and life cycle events. Moen et al. analyze the "time famine" (p. 37) couples face as they deal with a complicated arithmetic of how many hours two-earners can work outside the home and still have a family life. The mismatch between an intransigent work world that presumes a neotraditional family and the realities of dual-earner families is a major focus of this book.

As the "night has become the new frontier" (Melbin 1978), the challenges of a nonstandard work schedule have also arisen for families. The interaction between growth in women's labor force participation and the expansion of the service sector has led to jobs around the clock. The rise in nonstandard work schedules has led to even greater family complexity, demonstrated by Presser's book.

"Choice" is reserved for the educational (and top corporate) elites Mary Blair-Loy analyzes in *Competing Devotions*. Because they can financially afford it, many of these women return to the breadwinner/homemaker template. However, employment has not translated into gender equality in the home for women executives. They are painfully aware that this struggle is part of the cultural war over motherhood. In her book, Blair-Loy raises the question of how much agency even these elite women have in choosing family over work or vise versa.

Gornick and Meyers, in *Families that Work: Policies for Reconciling Parenthood and Employment*, call for a new and expanded government role to address the inability of families and workplaces to resolve these problems. Their solutions promote both caregiving and social equality. They locate the U.S. work-family issues within the context of other industrialized countries and show just how far the

United States lags behind other nations. They offer a vision of the United States that will give families back time (for instance, setting standard workweeks at less than forty hours and limits on nonstandard hours), that will allow parents more paid time at home with young infants and toddlers and a system of subsidized child care that will ensure proper standards of quality for early childhood education. Gender specialization would dissolve once women and men were freed from employment-related constraints, enhancing the likelihood of gender equality.

Key findings from the these books deserve particular attention.[1]

The Time Famine: Competing Demands of Work and Family

Moen and her colleagues' ambitious volume relies upon a large database of middle-class dual-earner couples in the United States that they collected. The focus of this important research is on the reality of two jobs in one family and how couples strategize to meet the demands of the workplace and family. *It's about Time* exposes the numerous ways in which the outdated infrastructure of time embedded in jobs and occupational paths constrain workers and families alike throughout the life course. By focusing on the couple as the unit of analysis—not the individual—Moen creates a theoretical model in which the employee and his or her spousal work-family arrangements interlock with workplace constraints.

Moen views work hours as a result of strategic decisions made by couples, which may be different for husbands and wives. These arrangements are neither static nor linear, and they may vary over the life cycle and by historical period. Depending upon children's ages, career stage, and moves toward retirement, work-hour arrangements may have different implications for an individual's quality of life. Young dual-earner couples without children find it easier to meet expectations of working long hours than do couples at other life stages. This study finds that there is no prevailing work-hour strategy among these dual-earner couples. Instead, there is a range of work-hour strategies that varies across the life cycle. Two in five are neotraditional, one in five couples have both partners working long hours, and dual-earner couples that work regular day hour schedules are scarce (Presser's book presents a similar finding). Couples that have "inverted" gender norms are also rare; for instance, wives work longer hours than husbands.

The authors report a substantial gap between the number of hours husbands and wives in dual-earner couples say they would like to work and the number of hours they actually do work. It is startling that for both men and women and at every life stage, three-quarters are working more than they prefer. They work those hours because those are the hours built into the kind of work they do. (Presser's findings from a national data set concur.) To a lesser, though important, extent, they do so because of financial concerns.

Judging from the accounts of families in this study, there is never a "right" time to have children. Professionals delay and then settle for fewer children because they hope to have them during a transition career point. The difficulty of juggling work and family is a greater problem for women than men. Wives do more child care than husbands, and they have less leisure time than either husbands or women without children.

If two careers are to be nourished, they must also be constrained—usually by a set of rules about how competing demands are to be resolved and how the home-making or reproductive activities of marriage are to be organized. Couples in ear-lier periods were more likely to have a strategy where husbands' job opportunities received priority. In almost two-thirds of these couples, however, one or both spouses report that in major decisions, their two careers have been prioritized equally or the wife's career came first. Still, men are more likely to take advantage of such an opportunity than women.

Moen and her colleagues also find that there are no longer single career paths. Women are still more likely to move in and out of the labor force than men, but roughly half of all respondents have a career centered on a "norm of instability." Men are as likely as women today to select job changes over continuous employ-ment because of intrinsic rewards over economic ones. Having two earners in the same family may allow for these varying paths. Feeling successful at family life or work life predicts perceptions of success in the other domain. There is a synergy across domains. Similar to Presser's study, couples in which both spouses work day hours report greater life success.

Work-family integration also appears to explain whether women or men want to gradually retire. As couples move toward retirement, some spouses would prefer gradual retirement by reducing work. Employers, also part of the data collected, rarely offer such programs. Various retirement benefits are also structured for full retirement, reducing hours gradually may decrease certain pension plans, and so on. The lack of gradual retirement plans is another example of outmoded assump-tions about the necessity of full-time employment, even if employers might benefit from such a transition plan.

Shifting More Workers to the New Frontier: Families Pushed to Their Limit

Historically, families have proven remarkably adaptable in responding to the transformation of economic systems. *Working in a 24/7 Economy* expands the dis-cussion of time as it reports which hours individuals work and the impact of those hours on their families, their health, and their overall well-being. Two-fifths of all employed Americans work mostly during evenings, nights, and weekends or on rotating shifts. Presser finds that people cite job constraints—not personal-familial considerations—as their main reason for working the shifts they do. Interestingly, only a minority of mothers and even fewer fathers say they work nonstandard hours because these hours facilitate child care.

These new frontier workers are not producing services for the global economy. Instead, the top ten occupations in the United States that employ workers in nonstandard hours are those that service local communities in low-paying service occupations like cashiers, sales workers, janitors, and nurses. They are not paid much differently from their fixed-day counterparts; that is, there is no compensation differential to provide extra pay in exchange for less desirable hours.

[F]or both men and women and at every life stage, three-quarters are working more than they prefer.

"Split-shift" couples, in which spouses work very different schedules, characterize one-fourth of dual-earner couples. This ratio increases to one-third when couples have children younger than five, and almost one-half of couples include a spouse who works weekends. Couples are more likely to work different shifts the younger the age of the spouses, the lower their education, and the larger the number of children. The ratio is higher among blacks than whites. Split-shift couples are more prevalent among the working poor. This translates into days and nights in which spouses are often not home together, and parents are often not home at such times with their children.

A very real feature of shift work is that the physical space in which the family resides remains fixed, but the temporal and social patterns that define it change dramatically from day patterns of family life. Couples were more likely to express greater marital dissatisfaction when either husband or wife worked a shift than when both spouses worked days, even though couples without children appear to cope better with nonstandard work schedules. Working nights and rotating shifts increase the odds of separation and divorce for couples with children. When mothers worked these shift schedules, especially rotating shifts, the risk of divorce is even higher. To have a clearer picture of how shift work exacerbates marital discord, Presser calls for more in-depth analysis of the reasons for certain shift-work schedules and how they change over time, taking into account gender differences in working nonstandard hours and duration of marriage. In short, the psychological and physiological stresses associated with an individual working nights and rotating shifts dramatically affect family life.

Rarely does center-based child care operate 24/7. When women work standard hours, they usually have *day* care options. However, when women work nonstandard hours, about half of all family types (dual-earner and single mothers)

SAGE Publications • 2455 Teller Road, Thousand Oaks, CA 91320 U.S.A. • Telephone: (800) 818-7243 (U.S.) / (805) 499-7774 (Outside of U.S.)
FAX: (800) 583-2665 (U.S.) / (805) 499-0871 (Outside of U.S.) • E-mail: journals@sagepub.com • Website: www.sagepub.com

CALL: 800-818-7243   FAX: 800-583-2665   E-MAIL: journals@sagepub.com   WEBSITE: www.sagepub.com

H01190

THE ANNALS OF THE AMERICAN ACADEMY OF POLITICAL AND SOCIAL SCIENCE – PAPERBOUND   *Frequency: 6 Times/Year*

☐ Please start my subscription to The ANNALS of the American Academy of Political and Social Science – Paperbound (J295)
ISSN: 0002-7162

Prices	U.S.	Outside of U.S.
Individuals	☐ $75	☐ $99
Institutions	☐ $490	☐ $514

PAYMENT

☐ Check enclosed. (Payable to SAGE)   ☐ Bill me.
☐ Charge my: ☐ MasterCard ☐ VISA ☐ AmEx ☐ Discover   (Phone number required)

Card #   Expiration Date

Signature

Name

Address

City/State/Zip Code/Country

Phone   E-mail

☐ Sign me up for SAGE CONTENTS ALERT (please include your e-mail address).

Subscriptions will begin with current issue unless otherwise specified. Prices quoted in U.S. funds and subject to change. Prices outside U.S. include shipping via air-speeded delivery.
*Canadian customers please include appropriate GST and other provincial taxes.

SAGE Publications · 2455 Teller Road, Thousand Oaks, CA 91320 U.S.A. · Telephone: (800) 818-7243 (U.S.) / / (805) 499-9774 (Outside of U.S.)
FAX: (800) 583-2665 (U.S.) / / (805) 499-0871 (Outside of U.S.) · E-mail: journals@sagepub.com · Website: www.sagepub.com

NO POSTAGE
NECESSARY
IF MAILED
IN THE
UNITED STATES

BUSINESS REPLY MAIL

FIRST-CLASS MAIL   PERMIT NO. 90   THOUSAND OAKS, CA

POSTAGE WILL BE PAID BY ADDRESSEE

SAGE PUBLICATIONS
PO BOX 5084
THOUSAND OAKS CA 91359-9707

rely *solely* on family members. Depending upon which shift mothers worked, fathers may be available to care for children; this is particularly the case when mothers work fixed evenings or nights. When women work rotating schedules (most likely their husbands are not rotators), grandparents are likely to supplement father care.

Single mothers are more likely than married mothers to work a nonstandard shift. Moreover, they are more likely to work weekends. Nonstandard hours and weekends was highest among single mothers with children younger than five years of age. Single mothers also earn less than married women and therefore find that making time for family is even more problematic. Presser finds that nonmarried mothers are likely to split child care with their mothers (the children's grandmothers), who are also likely to be employed but on different hours. Live-in partners may also provide child care, which we need to know more about. Weekend work involves having family members who are available to care for children. These families use a patchwork of care arrangements.

Mothers are concerned about the care of their children when they work. Married mothers with children younger than five are more likely to report they work nonstandard hours because of child care. By comparison, single mothers, who are often younger and have less education than married women, are less employable, and their lack of work opportunities is a major parameter of constraint in their lives. Finding employment (nonstandard hours and weekends) is a first-order concern for these women, and it dictates how they organize their children's care. For each family type, Presser finds that mother's work schedule is clearly linked to whether she relies on multiple child care arrangements, even if "job-related reasons" is the primary reason women give for working nonstandard hours.

All hours in the day are not equal. The routines of everyday life and critical institutions that families attend (such as schools) continue to presume a fixed-day schedule of work hours. Work during nonstandard hours imposes on family life in many ways, particularly when families have children. Even though Presser finds that working certain shifts may make it easier for parent-child interactions (eating meals together or helping with homework) and may lead to men doing more of the housework, nonstandard work schedules produce a great deal of stress. Fathers may care for young children more often when their wives work certain shifts over others, but it is unclear from this data what that care entails. Moreover, these data sets cannot tell us whether families move activities to other time frames (for instance, eating dinner at 3 p.m.) or whether women and children live on schedules separate from their husbands.

Most chilling are the challenges faced by single mothers and their families. They are the most likely to work nonstandard work schedules and to receive the lowest pay. As women move from welfare to work, Presser cogently argues, they are the ones most likely to encounter a misfit between child care arrangements and work hours. She calls for more research to understand the nuances of the increasing number of shift workers. Most pressing are child care arrangements that better fit the needs of the poorest families in our nation.

Motherhood Unresolved: The Hegemony
of the Gendered Division of Labor

Mary Blair-Loy frames her study, *Competing Devotions*, in terms of "schemas of devotion," which she defines as "cognitive maps that help define and organize our thoughts and assumptions" (p. 5). The work devotion and family devotion schemas are ideal types that reflect a traditional division of labor between spouses. The former schema demands a high level of work commitment and loyalty, devotion of the "good breadwinner." The family devotion schema assigns women responsibility for the home and family and is predicated on the belief that intensive mothering is crucial to raising children. Blair-Loy studied the career paths of elite women with high-powered careers in finance that ultimately slide into one of these two schemas. However, each group contains a subgroup of "innovators" who strive to recast each cultural system by combining demanding careers with motherhood.

She analyzes how women conceptualize their workforce participation in relation to their home lives, their experiences of what Hertz (1991) has termed the "test of manhood" in male-dominated professions, the effects of combining demanding "male careers" with motherhood, and their husband's participation in child care. She argues that work and family contingencies are viewed through the lens of the devotion schemas. Often "turning points," usually a family crisis, become pivotal for explaining women's return to the home. Without workplace support for childrearing, women's response to inadequate child care (including high turnover of nannies) is to reduce hours or resign. Regardless, some women are ardent believers that they made the "right" decisions for themselves and their families. Other women wish they did not have to make such drastic choices that either precluded children or high-powered careers.

Among the executives working in financial services, Blair-Loy found that thirty-six of the fifty-six women remained childless, upholding the work devotion schema. Not only are they reifying the masculine idea of work as a "test of manhood," but also childlessness is a response, she argues, to the inability to reconcile demands of loyalty to both work and family. Therefore, these women, who are the oldest in her study, implicitly uphold the family devotion schema of motherhood as a primary alliance that does not mesh well with career mobility.

The youngest women in this study, who are more likely to have established and experienced career success after the mid-1970s, marry later. Work experience, income, and status before marriage give these women resources that allow them to craft a different life course, including an egalitarian marriage. They buck the cultural schema of family devotion. Some refashion the meaning of wife and mother. They are comfortable delegating household work and child care to paid providers who are key to this life path. Similar to their spouses, these women express their care of family by being "good providers." Ironically, their nannies—women who often lack choices and work out of economic necessity—also demonstrate that they are "good mothers" to their children by sending home a paycheck while caring for other women's children. The linkage between women and broader stratification of families domestically or globally is not taken up in this book. (See Hertz [1986] for an early argument about domestic stratification of families. See also Collins [1990], Chang [1994], Wrigley [1995], Hondagneu-Sotelo [2001].) Furthermore, these professional women view their children as resilient and autonomous, not in need of intensive mothering. These women are challenging intensive motherhood, not work cultures.

Historically, families have proven remarkably adaptable in responding to the transformation of economic systems.

A second group in this study (twenty-five women) relinquishes singular devotion to full-time careers to make the family devotion schema primary. They, like the childless women in this study, believe children are fragile and need continuous mother-nurturing. Motherhood is a calling, and therefore, these full-time mothers regard full-time executives with children as selfish careerists, even when motherhood is not completely fulfilling. They are able to financially afford to stay home because they are married to men who are also high-powered earners. However, ten of these twenty-five women work part-time. Their employment takes a backseat to the family devotion schema. The family devotion schema allows men to continue to excel at careers and absolves them from equal, or even much, family responsibility. In short, the lack of workplace transformation leaves women with limited options; therefore, divergent views of motherhood pit women against one another.

Blair-Loy argues that part-time women in the family-committed group are challenging the work devotion schema of unrelenting loyalty to one's career. They ask to be treated like "elite workers," wanting to remain in high-status positions while also believing in the family devotion schema. Bosses and coworkers often define them as uncommitted, and job advancement is slower or curtailed. Blair-Loy argues that they use their education and high status to transform part-time jobs into viable work environments for elite employees. This does not, however, create a trickle-down effect, that is, either more part-time employees in lower-level positions or new beliefs about work commitments of part-timers. In effect, elites may change their own position, but this individual model does not expand and include any collective good.

One of the more interesting contributions of *Competing Devotions* is Mary Blair-Loy's discussion of agency. In my opinion, sociologists do not address often enough whether individuals have agency and, if so, how much, in their decision making. Are we all pawns of deeply rooted belief systems and social structure, or do we have agency to determine our lives? Devotion schemas, Blair-Loy (p. 177) argues, "help *create* those individual desires, induce appropriate emotions, and thus powerfully reinforce interactional and institutional patterns." This means that we have limited agency. The ability to resist only appears as futile chipping away at ideologies that are powerful enforcers of the broader social system. This study begins a long overdue dialogue about individual agency that work-family research should fruitfully and more fully explore.

Expanding the Government Role: Toward an Earner-Carer Society

Children become pivotal as work-family concerns are intensified by a crisis in caregiving/care work. Families are having fewer children, with more families choosing to have only one child and a rising number of women remaining childless. While there may be individual economic benefits to declining fertility, social costs of less children may have long-term economic effects on families and the larger society. An overall fertility decline may prove a problematic social and economic solution to the pressures of work-family conflicts. Therefore, policies that focus more on caregiving are essential.

Families that Work: Policies for Reconciling Parenthood and Employment offers up a new model for solving numerous problems raised by the other books discussed in this review. The authors, Janet C. Gornick and Marcia K. Meyers, start with a bipartisan issue: the crisis in care, particularly the concern about the well-being of America's children. Their goal is to move the conversation beyond fragments that treat child well-being, the conflict between work and family life, and gender inequality as separate issues *and* that treat child care as a wholly private concern (p. 5).

Gornick and Meyers demonstrate the myriad ways that U.S. women's labor force participation has not created gender equality but has instead exacerbated a stalled revolution in the home. Men, for the most part, have not become equal caregivers in the family. Ironically, women's child care and home responsibilities have become commodified, not in the state-organized way that U.S. socialist-feminists had envisioned, but rather via the market (see Hertz 1986, chap. 5: "Childcare Arrangements: Helping Hands"; Garey et al. 2002). As socialist-feminist voices in the United States quieted, those in Europe spoke loudly and contributed to the policy designs of other industrialized countries. While the United States has resisted redistributing the costs of childrearing, the authors have selected eleven comparison countries that share principles of social welfare entitlement and relatively homogeneous outcomes to examine how alternative family policies have altered employment and caregiving and in the process created greater gender equality. In other countries that industrialized at the same time as the United States, the authors point out, these transformations have been accompanied by the development of welfare state programs and collective-bargaining arrangements that shift a portion of the cost of caregiving from families to the government. While the vast majority of U.S. employees receive benefits through employment, entire programs are primarily public, including health insurance, sickness pay, and maternity benefits. The United States continues a limited role for the government and therefore greater reliance on employer-employee provisions.

All hours in the day are not equal. . . .
[N]onstandard work schedules produce
a great deal of stress.

There is no quick fix to the crisis in the United States. However, the authors call for an expansion of government policies to realize a new social order in which earner and carer are equally valued, resulting in a "dual-earner-dual-carer" society, a label first used by the British sociologist Rosemary Crompton. The authors state, "This is a society that recognizes the rights and obligations of women and men to engage in both market and carework and one that values children's needs for intensive care and nurturance during their earliest years" (p. 12). This model moves child care away from private market exchanges to public responsibility where parents reallocate their daily time use to make the care of young children a priority. The authors are also keenly aware of the implications of this new order for the significant number of single mothers. They recommend the addition of a combination of benefits to ensure both economic security and social inclusion.

What would it take to become a dual-earner-dual-carer society? The authors argue that three important transformations need to occur. First, the gendered division of labor needs to be dissolved. Gender inequalities in the labor market are intimately tied to gender inequalities in the home because the time women spend in unpaid work—particularly child care—reduces their availability for employment. To meet in the middle, men need to shift substantial portions of their time back home, while women (on average) need to increase modestly the number of hours they are employed to contribute more earnings. Men and women, then, would more equally share in the child care and household work, which would end full-time stay-at-home moms (and a gendered division of labor). Fathers are more likely to spend more time in routine and nonroutine household work and in child care than those fathers in the comparison countries. The United States lags behind in equal wages, in institutional supports for part-time work, and in affordable child care. Furthermore, U.S. labor force participants are more likely to work nonstandard hours and to work a higher number of workweeks with less vacation time. Without expanded workplace supports and public programs, it is unclear that couples will choose egalitarian divisions of labor.

Second, workplaces must change to allow parents to care for young children without penalizing individuals in wages, benefits, or job advancement for taking time off. Workplaces might also reward productivity, not hours at work, or emphasize products over face time as a way to transform the work culture. Third, the government needs to be involved to support caregiving work and redistribute the costs of raising children to the entire society. Government intervention, similar to other comparative countries in this book, needs to secure workplace changes through labor market regulations—from reducing standard working hours to granting temporary leave for family reasons.

Gornick and Meyers's specific policy recommends starting with maternity leaves in the United States that are inadequate (in duration and compensation) in comparison to other countries. The authors recommend that new mothers should have several months of paid leave with a benefit structure that would be progressive (e.g., benefits capped for high-earning mothers). Wage replacement in an earner-carer framework would reduce the costs of child care for mothers, provide short-term economic support for families, and make leave available to low- as well as high-earning families. To ensure gender equality, the authors also recommend that parents (fathers or mothers) should have the option between them to spend one full year at home, inclusive of the period of maternity leave. Throughout a child's life, parents would be allowed additional emergency leave, for instance, in the case of a sick child. Children would have access to parents as a priority in this model.

Education and care in early childhood *and* school schedules for older children constitute another critical policy domain for an earner-carer society. Other countries care for young children following parental leaves through a system of extensive publicly supported child care and preschool programs as well as after-school programs. For women not to be the parent that drops out of the labor force when a "crisis in care" occurs (such as in the case of the women Mary Blair-Loy studied), we need to revamp the present U.S. patchwork system of education and design quality care arrangements while parents are employed. Growing numbers of children, especially white children and affluent children, are left to care for themselves (see Casper and Smith 2002).

To implement the earner-carer model, the United States would have to rethink children and claim them as "public goods," and we would also have to acknowledge that the present market-based system of child care is inadequate to meet the well-being of children. The authors make a strong argument for the benefits to families and the United States as a whole if this new model is embraced.

Conclusion

Feminism may have helped accelerate the transformation of women's employment in the labor force; however, inequalities remain. Attempts to reduce those inequities in the labor market have proven so far to be futile. Unless something drastic changes, the more difficult battle for gender equality will be fought not in the nation's factories and corporate high-rises but in its private homes.

A family life squeezed for time, with parents often working round the clock and where dual-earners and single mothers worry about how they will raise the next generation while caring for their own parents, ought to be a central concern to policy makers in the United States. We are at a major impasse that needs creative solutions. As the books above argue empirically, market-based solutions have only escalated the problems families face. When women reallocate their time from family and caregiving to paid employment, they move from traditionally nonmonetized activities into monetized activities. The value of nonmarket work such as caring for children is not simply about replacement costs (for instance, hiring the cheapest body from a Third World country) or increasing the pay or ratio of workers to children. Foregrounding care needs within the context of families means more than just increasing the wages of paid caregivers and the flexibility of unpaid caregivers. Even though these are important changes, they just target the same bodies that are already doing the caregiving (Garey et al. 2003, 711-12). On one hand, we need to create a different social, political, and economic accounting system. On the other hand, we need to reassess how to locate caregiving, perhaps similar to volunteerism in communities or internships in organizations, so that it is an essential to the broader cultural. This would lead to investment of resources (including parental time and quality care) in raising children. Instead of unequal childhoods, the U.S. government needs to share the cost of caregiving. Without government involvement, private investments in children will fall below levels needed to produce economically and socially optimal outcomes, as Gornick and Meyers argue. Children's well-being is at stake, which can no longer be side-stepped, as the stress to families continues to increase as more individuals work nonstandard schedules. While dual-earners are the key family structure mostly addressed in these books, as the percentage of single mothers increases, a partner is no longer a safety net, and for these families, the question of sharing between partners is an academic exercise.

The federal government's involvement in family life can move us to more or less inequality. Without policy support, women, as shown in all of these books, are the ones who lose out the most. There has been a stalemate in the ways in which the federal government has been involved in work-family policies. The growing crises the authors in these books discuss are serious and threaten to undermine families; collectively, these books ought to be used by federal officials as policy blueprints.

Note

1. Moen's data come from the Cornell Couples and Career Study, which include three primary data sources: a series of focus-group interviews and one-on-one in-depth interviews, a telephone survey of working couples, and interviews with human resource personnel at participating companies collected primarily in 1998 and 1999. Presser's data come from the May 1997 Current Population Survey and the National Survey of Families and Households (two waves: 1987-88 and 1992-94). Blair-Loy conducted in-depth interviews with

two groups of women that were theoretically selected in 1994 and 1995. The first group is executive women in finance-related fields ($n = 56$) whom she located through a professional networking organization. The second group is women who left full-time business careers when they had children ($n = 25$). She used a snowball sample to find them.

References

Casper, Lynn M., and Kristin E. Smith. 2002. Self-care, class and race. *Journal of Family Issues* 23 (6): 716-27.

Chang, Grace. 1994. Undocumented Latinas: The new "employable mothers." In *Mothering: Ideology, experience and agency*, edited by Evenlyn Nakano Glenn, Grace Chang, and Linda Rennie Forcey, 259-86. New York: Routledge.

Collins, Patricia Hill. 1990. *Black feminist thought: Knowledge, consciousness and the politics of employment.* Boston: Unwin Hyman.

Garey, Anita Ilta, Karen V. Hansen, Rosanna Hertz, and Cameron Macdonald. 2002. Care and kinship: An introduction. Special issue: "Care and Kinship, Part 1," *Journal of Family Issues* 23 (6): 703-15.

Hertz, Rosanna. 1986. *More equal than others: Women and men in dual-career marriages.* Berkeley: University of California Press.

———. 1991. Dual-career couples and the American dream: Self-sufficiency and achievement. *Journal of Comparative Family Studies* 22 (2): 247-63.

Hondagneu-Sotelo, Pierrette. 2001. *Domestica.* Berkeley: University of California Press.

Melbin, Murray. 1978. *Night as frontier: Colonizing the world after dark.* New York: Free Press.

Wrigley, Julia. 1995. *Other people's children.* New York: Basic Books.

SECTION FOUR

Quick Read Synopsis

Q
R
S

Mommies and Daddies on the Fast Track: Success of Parents in Demanding Professions

Special Editors: JERRY A. JACOBS and
JANICE FANNING MADDEN
University of Pennsylvania

Volume 596, November 2004

Prepared by Herb Fayer (Consultant)

SECTION ONE: OVERVIEWS

The Long Road to the Fast Track: Career and Family

Claudia Goldin, Harvard University

Background College women graduates across the past century fall into one of five distinct cohorts (by college graduation year) related to work and family.
- 1900-19: Given the constraints they faced, these women chose either family *or* career.
  - More than 50 percent of the entire cohort did not have children, the highest by far of any cohort.
  - Similarly, a relatively high proportion (more than 30 percent) did not marry.
  - At age forty-five, only 20 percent of those who married were working.
- 1920-45: They were more likely to enter the labor force and later start a family.
  - About 25 percent of those currently married were in the labor force at age thirty.
  - About 80 percent had married by age fifty.
- 1946-65: These women had families first and then went to work.
  - About 90 percent married, about 90 percent of them having children.
  - Only 17 percent of the entire cohort was childless.
  - Half married by age twenty-three (a historically young pattern), probably to someone they met at college.

- About 75 percent were working at age forty-five (much more than the previous cohort).
  - But they became increasingly discontented with jobs available to women.
- 1966-79: They aspired to have a career first; family would follow.
  - Median age at first marriage increased to more than twenty-five.
  - Although many deferred marriage somewhat, 88 percent had married by their midforties. But about 19 percent of these women were childless at age forty, as was 28 percent of the entire cohort.
  - About 65 percent of those currently married were working at age thirty-five and about 80 percent at age forty-five, much higher than previous cohorts.
  - The dominant employment shifted from teaching to a variety of professions, and from 13 to 18 percent attained family and career.
- 1980-90: These women wanted to have a career and family at the same time.
  - They deferred marriage as did cohort four.
  - Eighty percent of the young and married worked.
  - Higher proportions than any preceding cohort—between 21 and 28 percent—had both career and family by age forty.

The achievements of each cohort build on both the accomplishments and frustrations of the previous one.

Reasons for the Changes

The main factors that led college graduate women to pursue career and family were

- increasing opportunities to work in fulfilling careers with the growth of white collar jobs,
- the rise of more varied educational experiences for women,
- contraceptive technologies than helped women control their fertility and better plan for career and family, and
- labor market changes that served to loosen social constraints and lowered barriers in various fields of endeavor.

Family-Friendly WorkplaceReform: Prospects for Change

Amy L. Wax, University of Pennsylvania Law School

Background

A number of people have called for workplaces that are more welcoming to employees with family responsibilities. Such proposals include some combination of

- shorter, more predictable, and more flexible work hours;
- new part-time and work-sharing options;
- time off for emergencies and child care;
- guaranteed leave with job security for childbearing and child rearing;
- child care subsidies and tax breaks; and
- on-site day care options.

NOTE: In addition, proponents of reform advocate deep-seated structural changes in compensation and benefit practices and relations of power and responsibility within the workplace. They push for the abolition of the so-called mommy track that relegates second-class status and diminished opportunities to those workers who adopt patterns of work more amenable to family life.

Pathways to Change

Two principal approaches can be used to achieve reform:
- One stresses the importance of action from within organizations, with emphasis on private, internal, local initiatives to alter workplace norms, conventions, and practices.
- The other calls for government-mandated interventions designed to facilitate proper care for children with less sacrifice of parents' job opportunities, advancement, or compensation.

Neoclassical Economic Explanations and Prescriptions

Neoclassical economic theory provides both an explanation for why family-friendly reforms have failed to proliferate and normative arguments for why they *should* not.
- Proposed reforms, these theories argue, are not economically feasible, viable, fair, or efficient and thus do not increase net social welfare.
- They may actually disadvantage the groups whom reforms are intended to help as employers feel compelled to hire fewer workers from protected categories (e.g., women or mothers), to lower wages of the benefited group, or to shunt benefited workers into segregated job categories. Of course, these actions can be offset by laws regarding equal pay and discrimination if both are effectively enforced, but the "if" is problematic.
- These theories question whether family-friendly reforms are compatible with a diversity of patterns of work, especially when mandated changes tend to legislate uniform practices of one track for all.
- Furthermore, regulatory measures generally impose out-of-pocket costs or losses on firms. Firms that fail to offset these costs (by, e.g., passing them along to consumers) may lose in the competition with other firms.
- Unfortunately, there is no reliable way to determine in advance if the benefits to family-friendly practices will exceed their costs or whether benefits can be generated in ways that can be used to compensate those who bear the burden of those costs.

Game Theory

Game-theoretic approaches challenge the assumptions of neoclassical economics and suggest that many existing work practices are actually dysfunctional, suboptimal, and not as efficient as believed. Game theories offer alternative explanations for why organizations tend not to adopt family-friendly work practices. They also proffer more optimistic analyses of the conditions under which reforms are possible, if difficult to sustain.
- Game theories incorporate more realistic dynamics into their models.
  - Workers and managers do not work in isolation but rather interact over periods of time. Moreover, workers can agree to cooperate or compete with each other.
  - Individuals often feel compelled to work very long hours to avoid being placed at a competitive disadvantage relative to peers in hierarchical organizations that rank performance relative to one's peers.
  - "Face time," making sure you are always seen at work, increases an employee's hours on the job and may be encouraged by employers who limit part-time and flexible options while rewarding workers who "win the race."
  - Because of the need to evaluate, and the difficulty of evaluating, worker performance, firms tend to favor reward structures that create incentives for workers jockeying for advantage vis-à-vis coworkers.

- Game theories explain resistance to adopting family-friendly practices, in the face of evidence that many employees in prestigious law firms and other professions want them, via several mechanisms:
  - Employers want to see gains in return for their costs, yet eliminating current incentive structures will introduce disruption and uncertainty and likely introduce large initial costs that are difficult to offset.
    - Nonmonetary benefits will have to be revalued.
    - Legal obstacles will have to be overcome.
    - Handling employees' reluctance to change can be difficult.
    - Employers will be tempted to assign the costs of change to those who take advantage of the family-friendly features.
    - A self-serving bias can lead workers to underestimate the value they place on family-friendly reforms.
    - A lack of reliable information can lead to mistrust and second-guessing.
  - Workers themselves may resist reform from the fear that they will be undercompensated in the long run.
    - Workers will want assurances of opportunities for advancement and other nonmonetary benefits, which may not be possible in some cases.
    - They may balk at reduced pay associated with shorter hours.
    - Employers may hold back too much compensation to pay for reforms.
    - Even those who really want family-friendly features may see the cost as undesirable.

Prisoner's Dilemma Game Theories
This variation of game-theoretic models demonstrates how certain payoffs to working in a rat race versus a family-friendly environment tend to drive players in such games toward a rat-race dynamic. Although these models tend to ignore the role of a "third party," employers will tend to favor the rat-race paradigm as well except under conditions that are hard to realize (although important to recognize).

"Stag Hunt" or Coordination Game Theories
These models provide another framework for understanding modern workplace dynamics. Unlike the prisoner's dilemma, they are structured such that individually optimal strategies are also the most efficient overall strategy. Under these conditions, work dynamics tend to reach a steady state of either rat-race or family-friendly dynamics, but these models also show that a small number of individuals who violate these norms can tip the equilibrium to the opposite pattern. Moreover, it is easier to tip the equilibrium toward the rat race than toward family-friendly practices. Family-friendly conditions are best achieved when organizations consist of like-minded employees who share and openly communicate these values with each other (and who are successful in recruiting birds of the same feather in the long run). Enforcing these norms can be difficult, and they create conditions that are ripe for freeloaders, who tend to destabilize the norm.

A Realistic Optimism
Many economists and legal scholars have criticized proposed and existing legislated mandates, such as family leave and job protection for parents, as inefficient and counterproductive. Much of this criticism, however, rests on a foundation of neoclassical economic theory that employs unrealistic assumptions and fails to explain important workplace practices. Game-theoretical approaches employ more realistic assumptions about workplace dynamics. Although they too demonstrate how difficult it is to achieve and sustain family-friendly practices, they offer a portrait of how such practices can actually be more efficient than current ones and the conditions under which family-friendly practices are most likely to take hold. Given that much of the criticism

of these reforms centers on an argument concerning the inefficiencies that
they breed, there is value in demonstrating the conditions under which they
may actually create more efficient outcomes.

Fast-Track Women and the "Choice" to Stay Home

Pamela Stone, Hunter College, CUNY;
and Meg Lovejoy, Brandeis University

Background

The phenomenon of women who leave professional careers to become stay-at-home moms has been little studied.
- When these women quit work, it may signal to supervisors and colleagues that women are not committed to work, and this may lead to discrimination against women workers in general.
- The portrayal of women's decisions about work and family has been described as part of a broad backlash against feminism and gender egalitarianism.
- Women with professional degrees are out of the labor force at a rate about three times that of their male counterparts, and they overwhelmingly cite family responsibilities as the reason.
- To get at the actual reasons, we need an understanding of their actions and the complex decision making leading up to them.

Research

The findings by Stone and Lovejoy contradict the view that women's decisions are an expression of their unfettered preferences for home over career.
- Women have a high degree of ambivalence about leaving their jobs to be at home.
- They found it hard to leave their jobs because they took pride in their professional accomplishments and derived intrinsic pleasure from their work.
- Only 16 percent of those studied made an unrestrained choice to be stay-at-home mothers.
  - They had always planned to be full-time mothers.
  - They and their husbands place high value on at-home mothering.
  - They do not see child care as an acceptable option.

Work-Related Factors

Work-related factors were the most frequently mentioned reason for quitting, cited by 86 percent of the women.
- The women in the study often had sixty-hour workweeks and 24/7 responsibility.
- When becoming mothers, about half wanted to cut back work hours and/or increase their schedule flexibility—with inflexibility being a major decision factor to quit.
- Those who chose to work part-time or in shared jobs found themselves "mommy tracked," a career derailment that played a role in their decision to quit.
  - Promotions cease.
  - They were given uninteresting jobs.
- When companies reorganize, merge, or go through rapid expansion, working mothers felt the company's culture became less supportive of women.

They also saw increased pressures and hours, which further added to their decision to quit.
  - They saw their lives transformed by dictates of new bosses.
  - Old bosses had often been mentors—they missed that support.

Child-Related Factors

Seventy-two percent of the women studied spoke of the pull of children as a decision factor to leave the workforce.
- Child care was not a good substitute for mothering.
- Women wanted the time and pleasure of being with their children
- Older, school-aged children as well as infants and toddlers exerted a pull.

Husband-Related Factors

Roughly two-thirds of the women discussed their husbands as one of the key influences in their decision to leave the labor force.
- Husbands often were not able to assist in child care due to their job demands.
- Women did not see their husband as having a responsibility to cut back or leave his career—they saw their careers as more dispensable.
- About one-quarter of husbands expressed the desire for the wife to stay home.

Future Work

Women were asked about their plans to return to work in the future.
- Two-thirds had a desire to reenter the workforce.
- Most wanted to return on a part-time basis.
- They would want workplace flexibility in any future job.

Study Concusions

Although women cite personal choice, the study shows women are not freely choosing family over work. The study shows the following:
- A choice based not on traditional gender roles but rather on their experience of gendered realities at work.
  - Workplaces that assume the male model of work.
  - Lack of flexible hours for mothers.
- Women face great pressure to be successful at work and at the same time to be good mothers.
- They have a weaker position in the labor market than their husbands and see their jobs as secondary—true even among women with higher-powered jobs.

Policy Implications

The study suggests several recommendations that would presumably enhance the labor force attachment and improve the work and family lives of those who remain at work.
- The creation of meaningful part-time opportunities without penalties to workers who choose them.
- The creation of a professionalized child care workforce to give mothers a higher degree of comfort with using child care.
- The implementation of work-family policies as gender neutral.

NOTE: Employers must move beyond existing programmatic, human resources–based approaches to reduce the hours of work and enhance flexibility through work redesign.

SECTION TWO: WITHIN THE PROFESSIONS

Marriage and Baby Blues:
Redefining Gender Equity in the Academy

Mary Ann Mason and Marc Goulden,
University of California, Berkeley

Background

The results of the study discussed in this article indicate that gender equity in terms of familial gains is as elusive as gender equity in terms of professional employment, raising the issue of what gender equity means in a university setting or in any fast-track employment setting.

- Programs and policies designed to promote gender equity in academia must take into account family outcomes as a measure of gender equity.
- Although women have progressed in the area of educational achievement, a discouraging picture emerges in the employment rates of men and women at the professor level.
  - In 1999, women were just 29 percent of tenured faculty.

Workplace Structure Rigidity

One proposed explanation for why women fail to progress in the upper ranks of academia is the rigid structure of the American workplace.

- The structure is configured for the typical male of the nineteenth century who was the sole breadwinner in the household.
- Such rigidity forces women to choose between work and family.
- Rather than blatant discrimination against women, it is long work hours and required travel that force child-rearing women to leave fast-track professions.
- There is a direct conflict between the resources needed to meet professional responsibilities and those for home duties.
- Female professors spend much more time on domestic chores than male counterparts.

Tenure for Women

Male tenure is much higher in the sciences and social sciences compared to women with children younger than six years of age.

- Women with young children were pushed into, or chose, second-tier, nontenured jobs in academia because of their family situation.
- Even women who had babies later in their career had less tenure than men with early career babies.

Effects of Gender and Family

There is a clear understanding of the effects of gender and family on the pipeline to tenure for women and men in academics.

- Women with children younger than age six were the least likely of all groups to secure a ladder-rank faculty position.
- Married men with children younger than six were the most likely of all groups to secure a tenure-track position.
- Single women without children younger than six were a little more likely than single men without children younger than six to enter ladder ranks.
- Women faculty worry about the impact of family formation, particularly children, on their careers, and they may forgo or delay childbirth or have babies in the summer to avoid negative career consequences—men and women in academia have very different family formation patterns.

NOTE: Gender-family interactions are associated with the greater likelihood of women leaking out at the Ph.D. receipt to tenure-track entry stage. It was concluded that babies and marriage account for why women Ph.Ds disproportionately leak out of the pipeline.

Family Formation Patterns

Analyses confirm that ladder-rank faculty women are different than ladder-rank men and second-tier women in their post-Ph.D. family formation patterns.
* Women appointed as ladder-rank faculty within three years of receiving their Ph.D.s have a 50 percent lower probability of being married than do men and a 52 percent lower probability than women appointed to second-tier positions.
* These same ladder-rank faculty women also have a 61 percent lower probability of having a child younger than age six than do ladder-rank men and a 65 percent lower probability than second-tier women.
* Ladder-rank women have a 144 percent greater probability of being divorced than the men and a 75 percent greater probability than second-tier women.

NOTE: The data show that women Ph.D.s in professional, nonfaculty positions also experience lower rates of marriage and fertility and higher rates of divorce than do ladder-rank men, men in other jobs, and second-tier women.

Timing and Rate of Births

University of California (UC) faculty women may have made a conscious decision to delay childbirth until their mid- to late thirties for career reasons.
* The consequences are that ladder-rank women are less likely than men to have children within twelve years of hire.
* UC faculty women are also more likely than men to indicate that they had fewer children than they wanted to have.

Work-Family Conflict

Faculty mothers face a time bind.
* Among UC faculty aged thirty to fifty, women with children report an average total of 101 hours per week engaged in family and work duties.
* Men report an average of eighty-eight hours.
* Women report more tension and stress than men and experience greater conflict in balancing professional and parenting demands.

Family Formation Differences

Women who successfully pursue ladder-rank faculty careers are quite different in family formation patterns from men and also from women who drop out of the pipeline to tenure.
* They are less likely to marry and have children and more likely to divorce.
* They make conscious decisions to forgo or delay family formation to better their careers.
* They may drop out of the pipeline to marry, have children, or avoid divorce.
* Women who are dissatisfied with their rates of academic progress may be more likely to marry, have children, or stay married.

Conclusion

The life-course approach suggests that gender equity in terms of familial gains and losses is as unbalanced as gender equity is in terms of professional gains, raising the issue of what gender equity means in a male-dominated profession.
* Equality is more an aspiration than a reality.
* The gap between family outcomes of men and women, as measured by marriage, children, and divorce, is as wide as the gap in employment.

Overworked Faculty: Job Stresses and Family Demands

Jerry A. Jacobs and Sarah E. Winslow,
University of Pennsylvania

Background

Analyzing a 1998 survey, the authors examined the teaching and publishing workweek in relation to professors dissatisfied with their workload.
• Dissatisfaction increases among those with the longest hours.
• However, very long hours contribute to research productivity and an increase in published articles.
NOTE: The conclusion is that there is a need for a set of expectations for academic employment that are compatible with responsible parenting in dual-career couples.

Women in Professions

In recent years, the progress many women have made in entering the professions has begun to stall.
• The gender gap in earnings is not closing—most apparent at the highest levels of corporations.
• There is concern about the ability of working mothers to balance job and family due to
   ⸰ demands of work;
   ⸰ demands of home; and
   ⸰ cultural expectations—the ideals of successful parenting and successful careers.
• The levels of work-family conflict have been increasing for parents.
   ⸰ Exacerbating the increased expectations on the job are increased expectations at home.
NOTE: The goal should be to have family-friendly institutional arrangements in our society that also promote equal opportunities for men and women. How can we maintain and enhance women's access to the best jobs while making it possible for successful workers to be responsible and caring parents?

Work-Family in Academia

The authors look at the work demands of faculty in colleges and universities.
• The average workweek exceeds fifty hours for all levels of faculty.
• The timing of tenure decisions collides with that of family formation for many assistant professors in their late thirties and forties—thus, waiting for tenure before having a family is not a good option.
• Dual-earner careers are prevalent among academic families.
• Professors may self-impose their heavy workloads to feel they perform at an acceptable level and because they are dedicated to their profession.
• On the other hand, professors are caught in a set of expectations for tenure and success.
   ⸰ They face research demands and publishing demands.
   ⸰ They must juggle many time-consuming meetings and reviews.

There are four main sources of growing time pressures on faculty:
- a greater emphasis on teaching time by the general public;
- rising expectations for research productivity;
- technological changes that increase productivity, but at the cost of time; and
- the rise of part-time employment that increases the pressures on full-time faculty because part-time teachers work for much lower salaries.

An analysis of the available data was done to look at workload's effect on job satisfaction.
- In general, professors are quite satisfied with their jobs.
- One common area of dissatisfaction is workload.
  - Although professors choose to work more hours, the more time they spend on the job, the more dissatisfied they become.
  - Interestingly, parents report lower dissatisfaction levels than childless professors—probably because married mothers and fathers work four hours less per week than others.
- Those with the highest level of degrees feel more workload dissatisfaction than those with fewer credentials—expectations for these professors may be higher.
- Assistant professors do not have the highest dissatisfaction levels—associate professors have the most complaints.
- Department chairs report the highest levels of workload dissatisfaction.
NOTE: The more satisfying the work, the fewer complaints about the workload.

Work and family are compatible when expectations of work are not excessive.
- The demands of academic life are becoming excessive and are making it difficult for individuals to succeed at work while having time to be caring and responsible parents.
- Efforts to promote a better balance between work and family should go beyond parental leave policies and try to establish limits on the apparently limitless demands of academic jobs.

The Mommy Track and Partnership: Temporary Delay or Dead End?

Mary C. Noonan, University of Iowa;
and Mary E. Corcoran, University of Michigan

The study described in this article shows that men are less likely than women to leave private law practice and more likely to become partners.
- Among partners, men earn significantly more than women.
- Lawyers who take time out of the labor force for family responsibilities are less likely to be partners and earn less if they do become a partner.
- Women are disproportionately selected out and discouraged at each step on the way to partnership.
- Women are far less likely than men to become partners.
- Women often do not remain in the firm long enough to be considered for partner—attrition perpetuates the "glass ceiling" as fewer women are avail-

able for promotion and, as a result, more men are making the partnership decisions.

- Previous studies have reported that both men and women identify sex discrimination as one of the main reasons for women leaving firms.
- The primary personal factor constraining women's partnership chances is their cutback of hours, family leave, and balancing the demands of motherhood and practicing law.

Reasons
Women Leave
the Law Field

Common reasons women report for leaving the field of law are the lack of flexibility offered by firms, long hours, child care commitments, and the stressful nature of the work.

- A woman associate may opt to work part-time and thus reduce her chances of making partner.
  - Choosing to work part-time ("mommy tracking") can stigmatize women as not serious.
  - The stigma may fall over to childless women as well—sex matters.
- The choice may be all the firm offers.
- The choice itself may be strongly conditioned by the expectations of others—family, colleagues, the larger culture—things that do not constrain men.

Sex

Sex affects promotion rates for lawyers who remain for at least four years.

- Women, regardless of having children, are less likely to be promoted to partner.
- Marriage, however, is a positive for partnership compared to remaining single.
- Part-time work significantly decreases the chance for partnership for women, but not for men.
- Having a lawyer as a spouse increases women's chances, but not men's, of becoming a partner.
- Men are less likely to leave or work part-time for family reasons and more likely to make partner, at a rate twice that of women.
- Lawyers with a high grade point average (GPA), a mentor, and more work experience are more likely to become a partner.
- Men partners' average earnings are 32 percent higher than those of women.
- Women partners are less likely to be married and more likely to be childless compared to their male counterparts.
- Women partners, on average, have worked part-time for one year and spent 1.7 months out of the labor force.

NOTE: Previous studies have posited that direct discrimination and sexual harassment, as well as a wide array of institutional practices, marginalize women in law firms.

Women's
Disadvantages

Women experience several disadvantages in law firms.

- Although firms offer part-time work, it may not count for partnership time, and it may preclude returning to the partnership path.
- Part-timers get assigned less important cases.
- Part-timers are labeled as less motivated after having worked part-time.
- Previous studies have claimed that high rainmaking demands (generating new clients), a lack of mentoring, sex discrimination, disproportionate shares of pro bono work, and mixed messages about personal style may all reduce women's chances at making partner.

*Changes
Needed*

Some changes could make law firms more family-friendly.
- Reducing billable hours requirements and using factors other than hours as performance criteria.
- Officially counting part-time work toward partnership.
- Developing a work climate in which part-time work and family leave do not stigmatize.
- Part-time partnerships.
- Employer-assisted emergency day care.
- Mixed compensation composed of a combination of time off and money.

Mobility

Some things can change institutional barriers to women's mobility.
- Pursuit of legal avenues on sexual discrimination and harassment.
- Programs to improve the mentoring for women.
- Broadened criteria for partnership.
- Reduced extent that women's personal styles are viewed as less effective in a legal setting.
NOTE: These changes require shifts in law firm culture.

*General
Changes*

Women cannot reach true equality within firms since large numbers of women are considered atypical because they fail to conform to the male-based definition of the ideal worker.
- Firms need to see that the benefits of changing culture are great; high billable hours and constant availability are inefficient.
- High hour demands for all lawyers need to be addressed as a health issue and reduced so lawyers can have time for community service, pro bono work, scholarship, and education for professional development.
- Expectations of performance need to be less rigid to reduce attrition for men and women.
NOTE: Programs that change law firms' cultures to be open to a wider range of work and personal styles have the potential to reduce disaffection, raise morale, enhance professional development, increase efficiency, and improve productivity—powerful change incentives.

Mothers in Finance:
Surviving and Thriving

Mary Blair-Loy, University of California, San Diego; and
Amy S. Wharton, Washington State University

Background

Work-family balance is a salient issue for professionals and managers in financial services.
- Managers and professionals in financial services organizations have seen work hours increased, and they are expected to demonstrate commitment by making work the central focus of their lives.
- They work in a fast-changing and demanding environment.
- The increase in working mothers and the rise in dual-earner couples adds to the time squeeze for families.

Q R S

Well-Being   The article analyzes two aspects of well-being: salary and work-family conflict.
- Studies suggest that these two aspects of well-being are somewhat incompatible because employees pursuing work-family balance are penalized with slower career advancement and lower salaries.
- Some employees perceive the use of corporate work-family policies to have career penalties attached.
- In a previous analysis, mothers who took advantage of work-family policies were penalized with reduced earnings.
NOTE: This article also analyzes those factors that reduce or enhance the well-being of professional women who are mothers.

Earnings   Research shows that marriage and children are associated with higher incomes for men and lower incomes for women.
- Women with children younger than age sixteen do not suffer an earnings penalty *compared to other women*.
- Mothers with children younger than six and mothers who have sole or shared responsibility for child care earn more than other women in the study.
- Fathers of school-aged children earn more than other men.
- Men with a homemaking wife enjoy a marginal wage premium.
- Parents who use corporate policies for family care earn less.
NOTE: The preferred elite worker is unencumbered by family responsibilities, while men manifesting too much devotion to family may be penalized.

Gender Gap   The difference between men's and women's average earnings is $31,614.
- About one-fourth of the gender earnings gap can be attributed to human capital and job status variables.
- There is also evidence of an earnings penalty for caregiving—men without a homemaking wife have lower incomes.
- Mothers did not suffer a wage penalty compared to nonmothers.
- Mothers of young children and those most involved in child rearing seem to enjoy a wage premium relative to other females.
- Overall, about one-third of the earnings gap is due to gender differences in family status variables.

Work-Family   Employed women generally take on more responsibility for family caregiving
Conflict   and domestic work than men.
- One thing that helps ease the conflict is flexible work hours.
- The company in this study provides a generous array of helpful policies, but employees avoid using them for fear of penalties that they believe are placed on employees who use these benefits.
  - Higher-earning fathers and mothers are less likely to use these policies, but mothers do use flexible hours policies without negatively affecting their income.
  - Managers and professionals are extremely unlikely to use policies such as dependent care leave that may be very visible to others, more intrusive to work flow, and thereby more risky to their careers.
- Women who maintain full-time careers after bearing children are likely to be highly successful and dedicated to their work and at the same time take on much of the responsibility for child rearing.

Job
Characteristics

Several job characteristics are related to work-family conflict.
• On average, parents who work longer hours are more likely to say they experience work-family conflict.
• Parents who use scheduling flexibility tend to have less work-family conflict .
• Married parents report higher levels of work-family conflict than unmarrieds.
• Mothers count similar amounts of time away from family and children as more troubling than fathers.
NOTE: Reducing one's work hours for family care reduces work-family conflict but can also reduce earnings. Moreover, compared to fathers, mothers earn lower incomes and endure greater levels of work-family conflict.

Mothers and
Career

The research shows that mothers maintaining full-time careers as finance professionals are corporate treasures.
• They work long hours and show high levels of achievement despite responsibilities at home.
• Finance firms would do well to support the careers of these women.
• Flexibility can help these women without affecting productivity.
• Financial services firms need to address the earnings gender gap.
• These firms should address the importance of some of their family-friendly policies.
• They should also be concerned with the earnings penalty associated with involved caregiving by men—if firms penalize fathers, then career-oriented mothers will have to take on more responsibility at home and find it harder to stay on the fast track.

Q
R
S

The Evolution of Gender and Motherhood in Contemporary Medicine

Ann Boulis, University of Pennsylvania

Background

Successfully combining work and family for female physicians remains elusive, but compared with working women in general, it has been favorable.
• Women physicians are more likely to marry and less likely to divorce, and the gap in childbearing has narrowed.
• Among employed physicians, gender differences in earnings and work hours are narrowing slightly.
• However, there is a growing gap between female physicians with children and childless female physicians.
• A small but growing percentage of young physician mothers are not working.
NOTE: Reconciling work and family remains a major challenge, and young physician mothers still suffer significant professional sacrifice.

Gendery
Disparity

In spite of profound changes in the past few decades, significant gender disparities remain among physicians.
• Women are underrepresented in the upper echelons of medical academia and medical administration.
• Women are concentrated in the lower-paid and lower-prestige specialties—primary care positions.

Q
R
S

- Women are more likely to work as employees rather than partners in a medical practice and work fewer hours—given this, they have significantly lower earnings.
- Some studies suggest women doctors pursue lower-paying careers to enable them to have the time to assume the bulk of domestic and child-rearing responsibilities, and other studies emphasize discrimination is at play.
- There is a dramatic difference in marriage, divorce, and fertility for male and female physicians, such that women are less likely to marry, more likely to divorce, and less likely to have children.

Gender Research

Much of the research on gender differences in physicians' incomes highlights the role of marriage and family.
- Women reduce their total work time after marriage and children.
- Women may also be more interested in providing care than in income or status.
- Medicine is a clear case of an occupation being designed for a full-time male with a stay-at-home wife.
  - Women physicians rarely have stay-at-home husbands.
  - Women in medical academics note differences in the accessibility of key resources, such as mentorship.
  - Most feel gender discrimination.

U.S. Health Care System

The evolving structure of the U.S. health care system may be affecting the family formation, work, and gender differences among physicians.
- As medicine has become more corporate, opportunities for controlled work schedules may have increased in the lower-paid, primary care specialties so attractive to women.
- It is possible the changes have influenced the type of people who decide to pursue medical careers and seek balanced work schedules over income.

Analyses

The author's analyses look at how gender relates to family formation and earnings.
- Marriage rates:
  - Women physicians were less likely to be married than they were twenty years earlier, and males more likely than females in all the years studied.
  - However, the decline in marriage among women in the general population was sharper than for female physicians.
- Divorce rates:
  - More women physicians divorce than men.
  - Women physicians are now markedly less likely to be divorced than women in the general population.
- Children:
  - Women physicians are only slightly more likely to have children than before.
  - It is easier for men physicians to start families.
  - The fertility gap between women physicians and women in general has narrowed.

Gender and Earnings

Gender and the earnings of physicians:
- Between 1990 and 2000, female physicians experienced marked increases in real mean income.
- Males still have substantially higher earnings.
- The specialties women choose and their desire to work fewer hours have an effect on the lower income levels.

Gender and
Work-Family
Concerns

The gap between physician mothers and other female physicians is growing.
- For men, married physicians, especially fathers, tend to earn the most.
- The earnings gap in general is improving between all male and female physicians.
- The disadvantage suffered by female parent physicians relative to male parent physicians remains significantly larger than the corresponding disadvantages suffered by married and unmarried childless women.

Parenting and
Hours

The work effort of female physicians is coming to resemble the men who share their household composition.
- Youngest mothers show reduced hours—they have the youngest and most dependent children.
- Physician mothers show significantly lower average workweeks than childless females or males.
- There is increasing inequality in work effort between physician mothers and other female physicians.
- Part-time employment (thirty-five or fewer hours) remains very much the exception for physicians younger than age fifty, with women more likely to be part-time.
- Women physicians appear to be faced with a decision between parenting with reduced hours and earnings and childlessness with hours and earnings more closely aligned with males.
- Although the work effort of employed males and females is becoming equal, the trend is slowly drifting in the opposite direction.

Conclusions

This article suggests that the significant influx of women into medicine has been accompanied by a modest but notable decline in the gender gap among physicians in a variety of areas.
- However, an inequality is growing between top echelon physicians and those at the lowest earnings levels.
- Physician mothers trail their male counterparts by a large amount and increasingly are falling behind other women physicians.
  - The gender gap shows narrowing partly because young mothers may leave the workforce, and those working have opted to remain childless and work the same hours as males.
- The profession has taken few steps to better accommodate women.
  - Part-time employment remains limited.
  - The hours are not flexible enough for women with families.
- The large unexplained gaps for men and women in the same marital and parental status is consistent with discrimination.
- Women are not on equal terms either in terms of earnings prospects or the chances to become married and have a family.
  - They experience delayed marriage and childbearing, have small families, and face significant chances of divorce.

SECTION THREE: COMMENTS AND OTHER CONTEXTS

Mommies and Daddies on the Fast Track in Other Wealthy Nations

Gwen Moore, State University of New York at Albany

Background

Social and cultural contexts, as well as public policies, shape the experiences of women and men in demanding occupations.

- In wealthy nations, women's employment in influential positions in the public and private sectors varies from country to country.
- Most top business and political leaders face the dilemma of combining a demanding career and family life.
  - They rarely cut back on working time.
  - Few women and almost no men had worked part-time or interrupted their careers.
  - Most can pay for child care, yet often women did some of the care themselves, and this burden fell disproportionately on women.
- Marriage and, even more, parenthood impinge on women's careers to a far larger extent than on men's.
- Men more often have wives not in a demanding career and who are thus more available for child care, housework, and building his career.

Nordic Model

The Nordic countries stand out as models of women- and family-friendly societies.

- Gender equality norms are widespread.
- Government policies support women's equal participation in public life.
- Women's rates of paid employment are high.
- The Nordic countries have replaced the male breadwinner model with the dual-earner model.
- There are fewer gender differences in family status and duties than seen elsewhere.
- Public child care is widely available.
- Nordic men leaders were more involved in household labor.

NOTE: Despite men's greater participation in family care in the Nordic countries, women leaders do even more than the men.

Work-Family Conflicts

Career pathways and occupational settings also affect work-family conflicts.

- Careers in management and science require an early and steady commitment, often beginning in high school.
- Dropping in and out or beginning a career later in life is hardly an option in the above fields.
- Some careers are more flexible and more easily entered at an older age such as elected politicians—women can more easily enter politics after child rearing.

NOTE: Compared to the United States, the Nordic countries appear more successful in lessening work-family conflicts, even for men and women in top positions.

Elite Careers and Family Commitment: It's (Still) about Gender

Scott Coltrane, University of California, Riverside

Background
Men and women in high-status professional careers are likely to share breadwinning, but the sharing of family concerns is limited by nostalgic family ideals and gender stereotypes.
- The basic assumption that family caregiving is the responsibility of women remains.
- Women in professions face difficult choices and are more likely than men to delay or forgo marriage or childbirth.
- It is now easier to achieve work-family balance in middle- and working-class occupations than in the professions.
- The elite professions have been slow to change or to embrace fully the concept that family caregiving demands should allow a person to work part-time at various stages of the life course.
- The ideal professional worker is still a man with a stay-at-home wife who is expected to devote huge amounts of time and energy to his career.

Men's Advantages
The work-family juggling act is easier for men.
- When men become husbands and fathers, they are perceived as more serious and more deserving of career advancement than their single or childless counterparts.
- There is a career advancement double standard for men and women in the same profession.
  - Family men are seen as partner material and are assumed to possess the mature leadership qualities that qualify one to be a manager or CEO.
  - Conversely, when women marry, they are seen as moving from the fast track to the mommy track and become "less qualified" for advancement.
- Even recent federal efforts at welfare reform put the monetary onus on men and encourage women to marry.

Separate Spheres
Previous studies have shown how separate spheres ideology shapes personal and institutional expectations about women being more kind, caring, and nurturing.
- Women are expected to do "intensive mothering," but they find they must spend time and effort developing parenting skills.
- Men are expected to be the breadwinners.
- Men accept work and family obligations, but their breadwinning counts symbolically as a family contribution, whereas women continue to provide most of the homemaking and child care even if they also work.
- Wives schedule and manage family life, and husbands typically remain as helpers, which reinforces the separation of work and family life for the husband.
- The problem is continued acceptance of separate spheres ideology and the failure of our social institutions to accept gender equality in the home and workplace.
Changes in the division of family labor have been relatively slow, and few couples report equal sharing.

Division of
Family Labor

Q
R
S

- There is an increase in time fathers spend with children, but it is still not equally shared.
- Women still do about twice the routine housework.
- The allocation of household tasks is associated with variation in the employment hours of both men and women, their relative earnings, their beliefs about gender and family, and their living arrangements.
  - Family size, age, life stage, ethnicity, pressure, and contribution of children and a host of other factors also affect allocation of labor.
  - When men participate in nurturing, they are more likely to share in child and home maintenance activities.
- Employers still feel that women will specialize in family work and cut back work hours after marrying or having children.
- When women in elite professions hire working-class and immigrant women, they reduce their household hours but do little to challenge the privileged positions of husbands and often contribute to perpetuating race, class, and gender hierarchies in the larger labor market.

NOTE: To counter inequities, we should stop assuming that women should provide domestic services and emotional support and stop assuming that men are incapable of nurturing and housework.

STATEMENT OF OWNERSHIP, MANAGEMENT, AND CIRCULATION
P.S. Form 3526 Facsimile

1. TITLE: THE ANNALS OF THE AMERICAN ACADEMY OF POLITICAL AND SOCIAL SCIENCE
2. USPS PUB. #: 026-060

3. DATE OF FILING: October 1, 2004

4. FREQUENCY OF ISSUE: Bi-Monthly
5. NO. OF ISSUES ANNUALLY: 6
6. ANNUAL SUBSCRIPTION PRICE: Paper-Bound Institution $ 490; Cloth-Bound Institution $ 554; Paper-Bound Individual $ 75; Cloth-Bound Individual $ 113

7. PUBLISHER ADDRESS: 2455 Teller Road, Thousand Oaks, CA 91320
   CONTACT PERSON: Michael Rafter, Director of Circulation
   TELEPHONE: (805) 499-0721

8. HEADQUARTERS ADDRESS: 2455 Teller Road, Thousand Oaks, CA 91320

9. PUBLISHER: Sage Publications Inc., 2455 Teller Road, Thousand Oaks, CA 91320
   EDITORS: Dr. Robert W. Pearson, Univ., of Pennsylvania, Fels Center for Goverment
   3814 Walnut St., Philadelphia, PA 19104
   MANAGING EDITOR: Julie Odland

10. OWNER: The American Academy of Political and Social Science, 3814 Walnut St.
    Philadelphia, PA 19104-6197

11. KNOWN BONDHOLDERS, ETC.
    None

12. NONPROFIT PURPOSE, FUNCTION, STATUS:
    Has Not Changed During Preceding 12 Months

13. PUBLICATION NAME: THE ANNALS OF THE AMERICAN ACADEMY OF POLITICAL & SOCIAL SCIENCE

14. ISSUE FOR CIRCULATION DATA BELOW: JULY 2004

15. EXTENT & NATURE OF CIRCULATION:

		AVG. NO. COPIES EACH ISSUE DURING PRECEDING 12 MONTHS	ACT. NO. COPIES OF SINGLE ISSUE PUB. NEAREST TO FILING DATE
A.	TOTAL NO. COPIES	3358	3496
B.	PAID CIRCULATION		
	1. PAID/REQUESTED OUTSIDE-CO, ETC	1927	1923
	2. PAID IN-COUNTY SUBSCRIPTIONS	0	0
	3. SALES THROUGH DEALERS, ETC.	383	375
	4. OTHER CLASSES MAILED USPS	19	0
C.	TOTAL PAID CIRCULATION	2329	2298
D.	FREE DISTRIBUTION BY MAIL		
	1. OUTSIDE-COUNTY AS ON 3541	79	79
	2. IN-COUNTY AS STATED ON 3541	0	0
	3. OTHER CLASSES MAILED USPS	0	0
E.	FREE DISTRIBUTION OTHER	0	0
F.	TOTAL FREE DISTRIBUTION	79	79
G.	TOTAL DISTRIBUTION	2408	2377
H.	COPIES NOT DISTRIBUTED		
	1. OFFICE USE, ETC.	950	1119
	2. RETURN FROM NEWS AGENTS	0	0
I.	TOTAL	3358	3496
	PERCENT PAID CIRCULATION	97%	97%

16. NOT REQUIRED TO PUBLISH.

17. I CERTIFY THAT ALL INFORMATION FURNISHED ON THIS FORM IS TRUE AND COMPLETE.
    I UNDERSTAND THAT ANYONE WHO FURNISHES FALSE OR MISLEADING INFORMATION ON
    THIS FORM OR WHO OMITS MATERIAL OR INFORMATION REQUESTED ON THE FORM MAY
    BE SUBJECT TO CRIMINAL SANCTIONS (INCLUDING FINES AND IMPRISONMENT) AND/OR
    CIVIL SANCTIONS (INCLUDING MULTIPLE DAMAGES AND CIVIL PENALTIES).

8/30/2004
Date

Michael Rafter
Director of Circulation
Sage Publications, Inc.

East European Politics & Societies

Editor: Ilya Prizel, University of Pittsburgh

East European Politics and Societies covers issues in Eastern Europe from social, political, and economic perspectives. The journal focuses on expanding readers' understanding of past events and current developments in countries from Greece to the Baltics.

East European Politics and Societies maintains a tradition of imaginative and erudite vision, uniting the cutting-edge social research and political analysis of leading area specialists, historians, economists, political scientists and anthropologists from around the world.

Visit the **East European Politics and Societies** homepage at: www.sagepub.com/journal.aspx?pid=9186

Frequency: Quarterly
ISSN: 0888-3254
Current Volume: 18

Published in association with the
American Council of Learned Societies

⑤SAGE Publications
THE ACADEMIC AND PROFESSIONAL PUBLISHER OF CHOICE
2455 Teller Road, Thousand Oaks, CA 91320 U.S.A
Phone 800-818-7243 (U.S) • 805-499-9774 (Outside U.S.)
Fax 800-583-2665 (U.S) • 805-499-0871 (Outside U.S.)
Email order@sagepub.com • Website www.sagepub.com

1043031

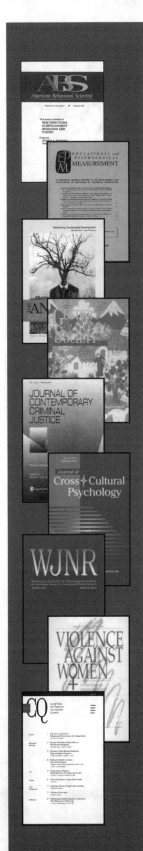

4 ways to order and share the best scholarship in your field

■ Back Issues

Make sure you don't miss any important articles that you need for your own practice, research, or classroom. To order, call Journals Customer Service at (805) 499-9774 or e-mail: journals@sagepub.com.

■ Reprints

Customize your instructional materials to fit your classroom and symposia needs with powerful new ideas from leading scholars in the field. Reprints make cost-effective additions to your course materials and conference packets. They are convenient and easy to obtain. To order multiple copies of a recent article, call Sage Reprint Services at (805) 499-0721, ext. 7594 or e-mail: reprint@sagepub.com.

■ Special Issues

Occasionally an entire issue is devoted to a single relevant topic, viewing it at length and depth. The pertinent information in these Special Issues is something you will refer to again and again. Sage offers discounts of up to 25% on multiple copies for classroom adoption. For more information on multiple-copy prices, call Journals Customer Service at (805) 499-9774 or e-mail: journals@sagepub.com.

Sample Issue Copies can be viewed @ www.sagepub.com

SAGE Publications
2455 Teller Road, Thousand Oaks, CA 91320
Tel: (800) 818-7243 (toll free) or (805) 499-9774
Fax: (800) 583-2665 (toll free) or (805) 499-0871
Visit us at www.sagepub.com

A new and more powerful way to access SAGE Journals.

The content you want, the convenience you need.

SAGE Journals Online will offer a new and more powerful way to access SAGE journal content. The new online delivery platform will host SAGE journals and will represent one of the largest collections in the social sciences as well as an extensive STM list.

Powered by HighWire Press, the new SAGE platform will enable users to access content more easily and powerfully through

- Flexible browsing and searching capabilities
- Social science specific taxonomy
- User personalization (eTOCs, My Favorite Journals)
- Toll-free inter-journal reference linking
- External links (to/from ISI, CrossRef, MEDLINE)
- PDA downloading capabilities
- Pay per view options

Library friendly features:

- Familiar subscription and adminstration tools
- COUNTER compliant reports
- User-friendly usage statistics
- Subscription expiration notification services
- Enhanced subscription options – available in 2005. For more information visit http://www.sagepublications.com/ 2005subscriptioninfo.htm

SAGE Journals Online will be available in September 2004!

Bookmark **www.sagepublications.com/sageonline** for the latest details

⑤SAGE Publications www.sagepublications.com